NEW PROCLAMATION

Year C, 2000–2001

Advent through Holy Week

Edited by Marshall D. Johnson

ADVENT/CHRISTMAS
Richard S. Ascough

EPIPHANY
Renita J. Weems

LENT
John Stendahl

HOLY WEEK
Samuel E. Balentine

FORTRESS PRESS
Minneapolis

NEW PROCLAMATION
Year C, 2000–2001
Advent through Holy Week

Cover and book design: Joseph Bonyata
Illustrations: Tanja Butler, *Graphics for Worship,* copyright © 1996 Augsburg Fortress.

Library of Congress Cataloging-in-Publication Data

New proclamation year C, 2000–2001 : Advent through Holy Week

p. cm.

Includes bibliographical references.

Contents: Advent/Christmas / Richard S. Ascough—Epiphany / Renita J. Weems—Lent / John Stendahl—Holy Week / Samuel E. Balentine.

ISBN 0-8006-4243-0

1. Bible—Homiletical use. 2. Lectionaries. 3. Church year. I. Ascough, Richard S.

BS534.5.N49 2000
251'.6—dc21

00–035467
CIP

The paper used in this publication meets the minimum requirements of American National Standard for Information Sciences—Permanence of Paper for Printed Library Materials, ANSI Z329.48-1984. ∞ ™

AF 1-4243

Manufactured in the U.S.A.

05 04 03 02 01 00 1 2 3 4 5 6 7 8 9 10

Contents

The Season of Epiphany
Renita J. Weems

The Season of Lent
John Stendahl

Holy Week
Samuel E. Balentine

FOREWORD

New Proclamation continues the thirty-year Fortress Press tradition of offering a lectionary preaching resource that provides the best in biblical exegetical aids for a variety of lectionary traditions.

Thoroughly ecumenical and built around the three-year lectionary cycle, *New Proclamation* is focused on the biblical text, based on the conviction that those who are well equipped to understand a pericope in both its historical and liturgical contexts will be well equipped also to preach engaging and compelling sermons. For this reason, *New Proclamation*—like its predecessor, *Proclamation*—invites the most capable North American biblical scholars and homileticians to contribute to the series.

New Proclamation retains the best of the hallmarks that made *Proclamation* so widely used and appreciated while introducing changes that make it more user-friendly.

- *New Proclamation* is published in two volumes per year, designed for convenience. The volume you are holding covers the lections for approximately the first half of the church year, Advent through Holy Week, which culminates in the Great Vigil of Easter.
- This two-volume format offers a larger, workbook-style page with a lay-flat binding and space for making notes.
- Each season of the church year is prefaced by an introduction that offers insight into the background and spiritual significance of the period.
- There is greater emphasis on how the preacher can apply biblical texts to contemporary situations. Exegetical work ("Interpreting the Text") is more concise, and thoughts on how the text addresses today's world and

our personal situations ("Responding to the Text") have a more prominent role.

- Although they are not usually used as preaching texts, brief comments on each assigned psalm ("Responsive Reading") are included so that the preacher can incorporate reflections also on these readings in the sermon.
- Boxed quotations in the margins help signal important themes in the texts for the day.
- The material for Series C is here dated specifically for the years 2000–2001, for easier coordination with other dated lectionary materials.
- These materials can be adapted for uses other than for corporate worship on the day indicated. For example, the volume can function as a resource for informal lectionary study by adult groups. And Samuel Balentine's treatment of the "Servant Songs" would be an effective basis for a series of Lenten midweek services.
- A calendar for December 2000–April 2001 is included at the end for quick reference and notes.

We are grateful to our contributors, Richard S. Ascough, Renita J. Weems, John Stendahl, and Samuel E. Balentine, for their insights and for their commitment to effective Christian preaching. We hope that you find in this volume ideas, stimulation, and encouragement in your ministry of proclamation.

Marshall D. Johnson

THE SEASON OF ADVENT

RICHARD S. ASCOUGH

THREE ASPECTS OF CHRIST'S COMING into the world are properly celebrated during this season. First, we rejoice at the past coming of God in Jesus. Second, we celebrate our present experience of God coming to us and renewing us in our present lives. Third, we look forward to a future, unknown time when Christ will come again and God will break into human history (the parousia). Thus, the focus of Advent is the triple coming of Christ: in history, in grace, and at the end of time. The name of the season itself is derived from two Latin words, *ad* ("to") and *venire* ("to come"); thus: "to come to" (*adventus,* "coming").

All three aspects of Advent emphasize preparedness: the preparation of the prophets and of John the Baptist for the coming of Jesus, our own preparedness in the present through repentance, and our preparedness for the return of Christ through our prayers, our patience, and our proclamation. For this reason, Advent is a solemn time, a time for reflection and to consider one's own sins. As such, it is a penitential season, much like Lent (in fact, it is sometimes known as the "Winter Lent"). But it is also a time of hope, a time of anticipation of the fulfillment of God's promises to us through Christ. Each year, Advent begins on the Sunday closest to November 30. The liturgical color for Advent is purple or blue, a symbol of royalty and repentance.

One of the biggest challenges of preaching in Advent in our time is the competition of the season with Christmas preparations and celebrations. For those in the United States, the end of Thanksgiving marks the beginning of Christmas preparations, and many begin the frantic rush of food preparation, party attendance, purchasing of presents, coordinating of family schedules and travel plans, and, for some, family altercations and increased loneliness and depression. In the church the season is filled with carol sings, special meals, decorations, and parties. In the midst of all of this the preacher, who can also be overwhelmed with business at this time, needs to help the congregation prepare spiritually for Christmas through reflection, repentance, hope, and joy. At the same time, Advent is the season in which Christians are summoned to prepare the way of the Lord throughout the entire year and to live in a way that reflects not only Christ's presence in their midst but also Christ's imminent second coming.

The three aspects of the past, present, and future coming of Christ are reflected in the Advent readings. The readings from the Hebrew Bible focus upon God's preparation of the world for the coming of the Messiah through the words of the prophets and the psalmists. The Gospel readings tend to focus our attention on the words of John the Baptist as a call to repentance. At the same time they point to the coming of Christ, both in John's time and in the future. The readings from the epistles tend to point to the future coming of Christ and the hope and joy that its anticipation brings to Christians, although the reading from Hebrews points to the salvation Christ brought to us in his incarnation in history.

THE FOCUS OF ADVENT IS THE TRIPLE COMING OF CHRIST.

For further reading, see the suggestions at the end of "The Season of Christmas," below.

FIRST SUNDAY IN ADVENT

DECEMBER 3, 2000

REVISED COMMON	EPISCOPAL (BCP)	ROMAN CATHOLIC
Jer. 33:14-16	Zech. 14:4-9	Jer. 33:14-16
Ps. 25:1-10 (14)	Psalm 50 or 50:1-6	Ps. 25:4-5, 8-9, 10, 14
1 Thess. 3:9-13	1 Thess. 3:9-13	1 Thess. 3:12—4:2
Luke 21:25-36	Luke 21:25-31	Luke 21:25-28, 34-36

TODAY'S READINGS HELP US TO FOCUS on the Advent themes of expectation and personal reflection. They are full of prophetic and apocalyptic language heralding the final intervention of God in human history, which will bring about the conclusion of that history and establish a new creation. Christians expect that Jesus Christ will return to mark this final culmination of time. The passages read today all point in some way to this time. Rather than get caught up in details, however, we can use these texts to reflect on what it means that God will again intervene in human history and what difference this might make in our lives.

FIRST READING

JEREMIAH 33:14-16 (RCL/RC)

Interpreting the Text

Jeremiah lived during the time of Judah's exile in Babylon and the destruction of Jerusalem (587 B.C.E.). This event marked the end of the royal throne in Jerusalem and the Temple as the dwelling place of the God of the Israelites. The effect on the morale and spiritual life of the people must have been devastating (as it was intended to be). In antiquity, temples were thought of as the dwelling place of the gods and symbolized a god's presence with a people. Thus, the destruction of a temple indicated a god's abandonment of a people. Such was the case for Israel, for whom the destruction of the Temple could only mean their abandonment by God and the cessation of the covenant. Jeremiah explained these events as God's punishment for Israel's disobedience.

The context of our passage is Jeremiah's announcement of a more hopeful future for the people, a new covenant between God and the people that would never be broken (Jer. 31:31-37). Jeremiah brings a new message to the people:

God does not dwell in buildings but is with God's people. In chapter 33, Jeremiah predicts the rebuilding of the walls of Jerusalem (Jer. 33:1-13) and the coming of a righteous king from the line of David, a symbol of the future hopes of Judah (Jer. 33:14-26). The promises of Jeremiah 33:14-16 proclaim that God has not abandoned the people.

Responding to the Text

In the history of Israel, the Babylonian exile and the ultimate return to the land was a time of transition and new vision. A new understanding of covenant with God was forged from the experience and a new relationship developed. For Christians, this has happened once again through the person and work of Jesus Christ. It is Jesus who has fulfilled Jeremiah's expectation of "a righteous Branch" from the line of David. This in turn has brought about a new understanding of the covenantal relationship.

ZECHARIAH 14:4-9 (BCP)

In the coming Day of the Lord, a divine warrior will fight on the side of God and Israel. Using his power over creation, he will create a rift in the Mount of Olives to allow the Lord to enter into the city of Jerusalem (v. 4). This action will culminate in God becoming king over all the earth (v. 9). Verses 6-8 describe a new creation, one in which the ills of cold, frost, darkness, and drought are abolished and in which light and the waters of life are constant.

Zechariah looks toward the culmination of history. The second advent of Jesus will establish the kingdom of God on earth. While the picture is fearsome, we are meant to focus upon the new age, which the disruptions in the natural world inaugurate. It is this new age of light and life, when God rules over all the earth, that brings us hope in a desperate hour.

Responsive Reading

PSALM 25:1-10 (RCL); 25:4-5, 8-9, 10, 14 (RC)

This individual lament calling for deliverance from enemies is an acrostic poem. Following the invocation to God (vv. 1-2a) the psalmist cries out for help (vv. 2b-3), asking that he not be shamed and that his enemies not be given power over him. The psalmist continues to petition God, but now desires a closer relationship (vv. 4-5). A reminder of the already existing relationship is followed (vv. 6-7) by an expression of trust in God's essential character (vv. 8-10, 14). The psalmist highlights God's "steadfast love," a concept encompassing God's love, compassion, mercy, and protection within the bonds of the covenantal relationship. This psalm brings to consciousness both our sin and our experience of the forgiveness of God's grace.

PSALM 50 (BCP)

This psalm, composed as trial proceedings, proclaims the coming judgment of God on all who do not live within the covenant, namely, those who sacrifice to God while living in wickedness (vv. 7-11, 16-22). Even worse, these people have considered God to be a mortal, just like themselves (v. 21). Yet there is hope for those who are faithful and truly keep the covenant through the sacrifice of thanksgiving and prayer (vv. 14-15). God will deliver such ones from judgment (vv. 4-6, 15, 23). The covenant must be lived in both personal conduct and worship.

SECOND READING

1 THESSALONIANS 3:9-13 (RCL/BCP); 3:12—4:2 (RC)

Interpreting the Text

Paul's primary purpose in writing the Thessalonians was to encourage them to persevere and progress in their Christian lives. Today's reading concludes a lengthy section in which Paul narrates his connection with the Thessalonians in the past, present, and future (2:1—3:13). Paul is pleased to hear from Timothy that the Thessalonians' faith is growing stronger (3:5-6) and is grateful that they have provided much encouragement for him and his companions during their times of distress. In our passage Paul opens with an expression of the magnitude of his gratitude to God for the Thessalonians and the great joy that they bring him (v. 9). He then tells them that he prays "night and day" that he might see them again (v. 10). In 3:11-13 he offers an example of what such a prayer might sound like, emphasizing his desire for a face-to-face meeting with the Thessalonians (v. 11), an increase in the Thessalonians' interrelationships with one another (v. 12), and their relationship with God (v. 13a). All of this, it seems, is preparatory for "the coming of our Lord Jesus with all his saints" (v. 13). The Greek word *parousia*, a term often used for the visit of a king or emperor or of the appearance of a god, is used in 3:13 for the "coming" of Jesus. Paul's overwhelmingly positive assessment of the Thessalonians is affirmed in 4:1-2 when he urges them to continue to live out their Christian life as they learned it from Paul and his companions.

Responding to the Text

Advent is a time to wonder at the first coming of Jesus and, in today's readings, to ponder his return. This particular passage makes some suggestions as to what type of preparations we might undertake, notably community-building and personal holiness. The entire passage is saturated with the language of personal relationship—Paul's relationship to the Thessalonians and the Thessalonians' relationships with one another. At the beginning of this season of secular greed and consumption, it is worthwhile to reflect on what it is that brings us joy. For Paul it was relationships, whether in person or at a distance. People mattered to Paul, so much so that he prayed constantly to be with them. What are we praying for this Christmas? Is it material goods, toys and trinkets to make us happy? Or do we rather pray for the festivities and the safe arrival of family and friends? Surely presence is better than presents by anyone's standards. But as we begin Advent we must also reflect on our longing for connection with God. Is our relationship with God one that brings us not external happiness but deep-seated joy? Paul's relationship with God is manifested in three aspects of his prayer life that come to the fore in these verses: thanksgiving to God, rejoicing before God (3:9), and petitioning to God (3:10). Perhaps this could be our focus during Advent.

The Gospel

LUKE 21:25-36 (RCL); 21:25-31 (BCP); 21:25-28, 34-36 (RC)

Interpreting the Text

The first Gospel text of Advent begins with a look at the future advent—the second coming, or "parousia," of Jesus. This apocalyptic, "revelatory" passage is full of the language and imagery of the Hebrew Bible. In Luke's account Jesus delivers his entire eschatological discourse (21:5-38) not on the Mount of Olives to four chosen disciples, as in Mark, but in public at the Temple (cf. Luke 20:45). The people of Jerusalem are being warned about the fate of the city (vv. 20-24) but are also given hope for redemption (v. 28). The reading itself is divided into three sections: an apocalyptic warning (vv. 25-28), a parable (vv. 29-33), and an ethical exhortation (vv. 34-36).

The passage opens with a warning about the coming cosmic signs and unnatural phenomena and the reactions of humans to these (vv. 25-26). It follows two earlier signs, persecution (21:12-19) and the destruction of Jerusalem (21:20-24). All three signs are given in outline in 21:7-11. The events of 21:25-27 look beyond the destruction of Jerusalem (specified in 21:20-24) to a period that will mark the end of human history.

Jesus' declaration that the powers of the heavens are shaken is a reference to the cosmic agents who, upon being shaken, cause regular patterns of nature to be disrupted. This disruption is seen in two ways: astrological signs and human distress in the face of unnatural patterns in the ebb and flow of bodies of water. Such descriptions have antecedents in Old Testament passages such as Isaiah 13:10, 34:4; Ezekiel 32:7-8; Joel 2:10, 30-31; and Haggai 2:6, 21. The "shaking of the powers of the heavens" might allude to Isaiah 34:4, a depiction of the destruction of God's enemies. The unnatural phenomena in the heavens and on the waters, as well as the collapse of the heavenly hierarchy, might suggest a reversal of the created order—in which heaven and earth, land and water, were separated—and a return to primeval chaos.

Yet all these are only pointers to the real event, the coming of the Son of Man in a cloud (v. 27), an image taken from Daniel 7:13-14. The vision of Daniel of the descent of one like a "son of man" dates from the time of Jewish persecution by Antiochus IV Epiphanes (167–164 B.C.E.). This figure of heavenly origin is presented as coming to the "Ancient of Days" to receive "dominion, glory, and kingship" over all nations and then to bring about Israel's supremacy over all the nations for all time. In the Gospels this image of one like a Son of Man is applied to Jesus. In our passage, it is the risen, exalted Jesus who returns with kingly prerogatives ("power and glory"), although there is an underlying sense of judgment with it (v. 36). Through Jesus, the kingdom of God will be brought to earth (cf. 21:31). The promise is one of redemption, perhaps also rendered "deliverance" or "release." The rich images of this text are all pointers that our redemption is approaching—not that it has arrived (v. 28). Christians are told to "stand erect and hold your heads up high." Although the images are dark and foreboding, they are meant to create a sense of hope and expectation. These events represent "good news."

> ADVENT IS A TIME OF WARNING AND ENCOURAGEMENT, FEAR AND HOPE, PERSONAL REFLECTION AND COSMIC CHANGE

The parable of the fig tree works on the level of an analogy or simile. It is not difficult to determine the present season by looking at a tree. Most people look forward to the bursting forth of the trees in the spring. Winter supplies get low and the coming of spring signals a new growing season. For Jesus, the signs referred to in v. 25 serve a similar function—pointing to the beginning of a new season.

The announcement that "this generation" would not pass away until the fulfillment of these things is fraught with difficulty (v. 32, omitted in the Episcopal and Roman Catholic readings). On one level it certainly reflects the belief that at least some first-generation Christians would live to see the return of Jesus.

Since the average life span in antiquity seems to have been about forty years, however, very few of Jesus' own generation would have still been alive by the time Luke wrote. Thus, whatever the original intention of the statement, by the second generation (and certainly two thousand years later) a different understanding of this text is required. Some have suggested that "generation" here might mean "descendants" (either Jewish or humanity generally), but there is no obvious reason why this should be the case. A better (although not ideal) explanation is that the generation referred to is the generation of the end-signs—those who experience firsthand the things described in these verses. Whatever the exegetical problems with "this generation," the following affirmation is meant to allow the promise of redemption to stand for all time. Jesus proclaims, "My words will not pass away," even if the entire cosmos collapses.

The force of the imperative "be on guard" in v. 34 is one of constant vigil to our situation lest we be depressed (perhaps a more appropriate term than "weighed down") with hangover ("dissipation"), drunkenness, and the worries of this life (or "daily apprehension"). Life in antiquity was hard, with many or most families barely making enough to survive for the day. Most wage earners brought home enough bread to feed their family one day at a time. Poor nutrition, inadequate sanitation, and ill health were part and parcel of everyday life, with little hope for improvement. Many people sought temporary refuge through membership in social clubs, the primary purpose of which was conviviality and drunkenness. The cares of daily life were temporarily lost in the blur of cheap alcohol, singing, and debate (and perhaps a few dancing girls). Such people would be surprised when God's judgment falls upon the entire earth. In contrast, Christians are to "be alert" (v. 36), a call to constant vigil, as was the imperative to "be on guard" (v. 34). Such vigilance is marked by prayer, which results in strength.

Responding to the Text

The reading of an apocalyptic passage might seem somewhat awkward at the beginning of a season celebrating the coming of the baby Jesus. To remember the return of Christ within the context of his "advent" or coming, however, is not improper. Certainly vv. 34-36 and the warnings against "this-worldly" practices fit a season of prayer and fasting, as Advent is for some. Being "alert" or "watchful" (v. 36) has a twofold impact in our day and age. On the one hand, the increased threat of violence and crime in our society cause us to remind ourselves and our loved ones to "take care" whenever we go out. On the other hand, much of our time is spent passively observing the lives of others as presented through our television screens; some of us are not even patient enough to endure more than a few minutes at a time, as we continually surf from channel to channel. In our spiritual lives we are to be vigilant in watching for the return of Jesus, not swayed by the temporary distractions of life.

The biblical genre of apocalyptic also needs to be considered carefully. The apocalyptic genre originated within Israel around the time of Ezekiel and is embedded in some of the writings of Israel's prophets (Ezek. 38-39; Isa. 24-27, 56-66; Zech. 9-14; Joel 2). The clearest example is found in Daniel 7-12. The trajectory leads through some of the deuterocanonical and pseudepigraphal writings (1 and 2 Enoch; 1 and 2 Esd.; 2 Bar.) to early Christian literature (1 Thess. 4-5; Mark 13; Rev.). These visionary writings purport to reveal the mystery of the end of the world and the glory of the age to come. In fact, they express the hopes and visions of minority groups who stand outside of the mainstream. The hope is maintained that life will become better through the breaking in of a divine agent—in the case of early Christianity, the return of Jesus. Although often presented in dualistic terms as a battle between good and evil, with attendant ethical imperatives for those who would be found righteous, the purpose of apocalyptic was to bring hope to an oppressed group.

Although life is much improved for many persons today, particularly in the so-called first world with the burgeoning middle class, many still seem beset with financial and personal anxieties. The huge market for entertainment (music, movies, computer games) and the growing use and abuse of intoxicating substances suggests that at their core many still feel the dissatisfaction with life that those in antiquity felt. Thus, the hope held out in this passage can still resonate today. Those who are truly "alert" and praying at all times are those who carry out their daily tasks with the constant awareness that a larger scheme is at work and that at any time God can break into our lives, individually or collectively, in powerful ways. The ultimate hope is based on the return of Jesus as the Son of Man in power and glory. It is this hope that sets Christians apart from the ethos of despair that surrounds them.

As we anticipate the celebration of the incarnation, today's texts bring into focus the second coming of Christ. We are reminded that even our own generation may not pass away before all things have taken place. Perhaps as the end of this year approaches there is less apprehension than there was at this time last year, on the eve of the new millennium. Nevertheless, we need to always be watchful and act as if the return is imminent. No matter how bad our personal, political, and natural contexts become, God's hand is firmly upon the events.

There is a wonderful short story by Leo Tolstoy that often appears on television in animated form during the holiday season. "Where Love Is, God Is" (1885) tells the story of a cobbler, Martin Avdéiteh, who wishes to see God and hears a voice in a dream tell him, "Look out into the street tomorrow, for I shall come." As the next day draws to a close Martin is disappointed that Christ did not appear. Then a vision reveals to him that Christ was with him in the old man to whom he gave tea, the poor woman and her baby to whom he gave food and warmth, and the old women to whom he taught forgiveness. During this season, as we recall the past event of Jesus' coming and look forward to his coming again let us not also miss opportunities to meet God in our midst here and now through our relationships with others.

SECOND SUNDAY IN ADVENT

DECEMBER 10, 2000

REVISED COMMON	EPISCOPAL (BCP)	ROMAN CATHOLIC
Mal. 3:1-4 or Bar. 5:1-9	Bar. 5:1-9	Bar. 5:1-9
Luke 1:68-79	Ps. 126	Ps. 126:1-6
Phil. 1:3-11	Phil. 1:1-11	Phil. 1:4-6, 8-11
Luke 3:1-6	Luke 3:1-6	Luke 3:1-6

TODAY'S LECTIONS HAVE A TWOFOLD THRUST. On the one hand, they highlight the role of John the Baptist as God's messenger preparing the way for the coming of the Lord in the person of Jesus (Luke 1:68-79; 3:1-6). On the other hand, they point beyond the first advent to a future "day of the Lord" in which God will break in again in judgment (Mal. 3:1-4; Phil.1:3-11). Neither aspect should be lost as we work through these passages. In both cases, and in all of our passages, it is clear that the proper response is repentance from sins, aiming toward purity and righteousness, and a joyful expectation that God will indeed visit God's people once again.

FIRST READING
MALACHI 3:1-4 (RCL)

Interpreting the Text

Little is known of the prophet Malachi. His name simply means "my messenger," and his prophecies are undated, although they belong somewhere between the rebuilding of the Temple (516 B.C.E.) and the end of the Persian period (330 B.C.E.), probably around the time of Ezra. Malachi speaks to a nation that is no longer following the ways of its God and to people who doubt that God even cares for them (2:17). To their surprise, God will come personally to visit them. Preceded by a messenger (or "angel"), God will appear suddenly in the Temple. Yet this is no friendly visitation. Rather, God will exact judgment upon the people. Two metaphors are used: that of a refiner's fire, which purifies metal through intense heat, and that of a fuller's soap, which cleanses wool through abrasive chemical action. Although there is no destruction of persons indicated in the text, the metaphors illustrate that surely no one can endure and stand before God on that day of the Lord. This appearance of God will bring about a reversal in the way the people approach God in worship.

Responding to the Text

It is easy to slip comfortably into "churchianity" by having a complacent attitude about our spiritual lives. Although paying lip service to God, in our hearts we long for the service to be over so that we can return to our weekend chores. The church itself, even on the local parish level, becomes little more than a collection of individuals. There may be no true community and no true worship. This is perhaps more acute a situation during Advent and Christmas, when church attendance swells with those who have ignored the worship of God throughout the year (with the possible exception of Easter).

The reading from Malachi warns against such situations. In recalling this passage the early Christians thought of John the Baptist and saw him as the forerunner of God's breaking into our world in Jesus (see Mark 1:2; Matt. 11:10; Luke 7:27). As was the case in the time of Israel, the response called for by John was repentance. This is no less the proper response today as we hear these words of the prophet.

BARUCH 5:1-9 (RCL alt., BCP, RC)

The book of Baruch was written to encourage and console a nation that was discouraged or persecuted. Although set in the period of the Babylonian exile, it actually dates to the later Hellenistic period. Our passage concludes a series of prophetic oracles aimed at bringing hope to those in exile and advocating trust in the Lord. Despite the harshness of the current situation they are to look toward the future when they will learn that God indeed has been in control of their situation all along and will now lead them out of exile.

Baruch appropriates one set of circumstances to bring hope to those living in another set of circumstances. The prophecies look forward to God leading the people back to Jerusalem after the exile. And, indeed, the people did return. When the people would be faced with difficult situations again some three hundred and fifty years or so later, they could look back on God's actions and know that God was still in control. In Advent we can have that same assurance. God did break into human history in the past and, based on God's past actions, we can have assurance that God will break into history again in the future.

Responsive Reading

LUKE 1:68-79 (RCL)

Zechariah, the father of John the Baptist, opens this prophetic hymn, known as the *Benedictus*, with praise to God (v. 68). The text refers to the visitation of God upon God's people and the resulting political redemption that they have experienced in the past. The most obvious example of this is the Exodus, the paradigm for the hope of liberation throughout Israel's history. Zechariah sees in John the inauguration of hope for a new act of redemption by God, liberating the people once again (the Greek word translated "visited" in v. 68 is repeated as a future in v. 78). Although the people of Judea are living under the occupation of the Roman forces, the emphasis here is upon spiritual salvation—the forgiveness of sins (v. 77). God's mercy is highlighted as the means by which peace will be attained (v. 79). The hymn shows how the events of the life of Jesus are connected to a larger plan of salvation that goes back to God's promises to Jewish ancestors.

Despite the highly personal aspect of the *Benedictus*, we should not overlook its important political implications (cf. v. 74). Society can be transformed through the forgiveness of sins and by walking in the way of peace. Although in our own day we in North America are not subject to occupying forces, we still need to hear the offer of forgiveness and peace that comes through the "horn of salvation" raised up for us (v. 69).

PSALM 126 (BCP); 126:1-6 (RC)

This communal lament opens by recalling the joy when God acted on behalf of the people in the past (vv. 1-3). Confronted with the debris that lies where Jerusalem and the Temple once stood, the people call upon God to act once again to turn the people's mourning to joy (vv. 4-6).

In Advent we recall the first coming of Christ but also look forward to his return, we anticipate God acting once again as God has in the past to bring joy and liberation. We recognize that the tears of repentance come before the joy of our experience of salvation. Often we must lament together before God can move us forward. In our personal times of distress we can call upon God, remembering previous times when God has carried us through and expressing our trust that God will do so once again.

SECOND READING

PHILIPPIANS 1:3-11 (RCL); 1:1-11 (BCP); 1:4-6, 8-11 (RC)

Interpreting the Text

Paul wrote his letter to the Philippian church in circumstances of some hardship. He was in prison awaiting trial (he does not say where, but many scholars suggest Ephesus), and some mean-spirited persons in the city of his captivity were preaching about Christ with the sole purpose of increasing Paul's suffering during his incarceration (1:17). Nevertheless, he wrote this letter to express his joy over the Philippians' progress in the faith and to encourage them to greater endurance and unity in the face of opposition and dissension.

In the opening of the letter Paul greets "all" the saints at Philippi, along with some of the leaders. The "bishops" and "deacons" (Greek: *episkopoi* and *diakonoi*) should not be thought of along the lines of the later church hierarchy; here they simply represent the local leadership of the Christian community. Paul greets the congregation first, before the leaders, highlighting the inclusivity that the community should be evidencing. What follows is a typical Pauline greeting, emphasizing "grace" (rather than "greeting") and the Hebrew concept of "peace" (*shalom*).

Paul then adds a thanksgiving section, as is his practice in all his letters except Galatians. This constitutes the remainder of our reading. He notes that he expresses his thanks to God and then explains to the Philippians what this entails. First, it is constant: every time Paul thinks of the Philippians he expresses his thanksgiving to God. Second, he not only thanks God but also constantly petitions God for their specific needs. Third, he does this in a state of joy. Fourth, he thanks God because of the Philippians' partnership (*koinonia*) in the gospel. This odd expression probably indicates that the Philippians have not only supported Paul financially but also have cooperated with Paul and one another in living out the gospel both in their own Christian community and in the larger social context. Paul's thanksgiving also rests in his confidence that God is at work in the community life of the Philippians and will ensure that their spiritual lives together will be completed (v. 6).

Paul continues in vv. 7-11 to express how close he feels to the Philippians. He begins by noting their part in the relationship (v. 7)—they hold him in their (collective) heart and they are fellow sharers (again using a cognate of *koinonia*) in both Paul's work and Paul's suffering. Paul then notes his own part in the relationship (vv. 8-11)—a deep longing to be present with the Philippians and a prayer, probably an example of the prayers he mentioned earlier, that their love "may overflow more and more with knowledge and full insight" and that they might be fully prepared for the day of Jesus' return.

Responding to the Text

Although this passage is often read personally, Paul wrote it to a community, not individuals, and it is best understood as an expression of corporate life. As such, it speaks to the season of Advent and Christmas as a reminder of how Christians should be responding to those around them. By the second Sunday in Advent people's minds are likely to be on the preparations necessary to fulfill social and family obligations: gifts have to be purchased, food stockpiled, cards written, and parcels mailed. For many it is an exciting, although often frustrating time. For others it is a very lonely time, when feelings of isolation and separation from family and friends become acute.

In today's reading Paul celebrates community—living with one another in "partnership" or "fellowship." In some congregations simply using the untranslated Greek word *koinonia* is sufficient to indicate this communal notion. Paul gives us a glimpse of a *koinonia* that works together for the upbuilding of the community, the spread of the gospel message to others, and the supporting of all levels of leadership. While it is not easy, it is within community that we can attain the purity and blamelessness so many of us would like to attain on our own. But it is also in community that these very ideals get challenged. This season of Advent may be an appropriate time for some community self-reflection. If Paul were writing to your Christian community for what would he give thanks, how often, and why? Such expressions of thanksgiving can serve not only to build up a community, but also challenge its members to strive for their ideals "more and more" (cf. 1:6). In this way, we can be fully prepared for "the day of Christ" that Advent anticipates.

The Gospel
LUKE 3:1-6

Interpreting the Text

Luke dates the beginning of the ministry of John the Baptist and Jesus with precision as the fifteenth year of Tiberius Caesar (29 C.E.) and names the people who ruled the administrative divisions of Palestine. Pontius Pilate was governor in Judea from 26 or 27 C.E. (some suggest 19 C.E.) until he was removed from office by the emperor sometime around 37 C.E. His governorship is mentioned in a number of sources, including Josephus, Philo, and Tacitus. Archaeological evidence for his reign comes from coins and also from an inscription found in 1961 at Caesarea Maritima which reads "Tiberius Pontius Pilate, Prefect of Judea." As governor, Pilate was responsible for the Roman administration of Judea, including the collection of tributes and taxes, the distribution of funds, and the overseeing of the judicial system. His tenure was marked by disruption and dissatisfaction among the Jews and Samaritans of the land, although seemingly not much more so than with any other Roman ruler. It was a particularly violent incident in which Pilate suppressed an armed demonstration of Samaritans that led to his removal from office.

The Herod mentioned here is Herod Antipas, who inherited from his father, Herod the Great, control of the areas of Galilee and Perea, and was granted the title "tetrarch" by Augustus. His brother Philip received the area to the north east of the Sea of Galilee and the title "tetrarch" while another brother, Archelaus, received Judea and the title "ethnarch." In the case of the latter, his ineptitude led to his eventual replacement by a Roman governor (6 C.E.).

The mention of Lysanius, tetrarch of Abilene (Syria; modern Jordan), is odd. This ruler does seem to have existed and is mentioned by Josephus, although he is not one of the tetrarchs of Herod's kingdom and does not play a part in the history of Jesus or of the early church. The naming of "the high priesthood of Annas and Caiaphas" is also odd at first glance. The two men named seem to share the post, although it should be occupied by only one man. Annas was the officially appointed high priest at the time; Caiaphas was his father-in-law. Caiaphas served as high priest from 6 C.E. until he was deposed in 15 C.E. Despite his removal from office, however, he continued to assert his influence over the high priests who followed, to the point where it was as if he held the official position (cf. John 11:49; 18:13, 19, 24).

RECALLING THE EVENTS OF THE PAST CAN BRING US JOY, HOPE, AND PURPOSE AS WE LOOK FORWARD TO GOD BREAKING INTO HUMAN HISTORY ONCE AGAIN.

All this is preamble for introducing John. Although Luke uses the designation "John the Baptist" elsewhere (7:20, [28], 33; 9:19) he does not do so here, preferring to refer to John as "the son of Zechariah." In this way Luke provides a link between this narrative and the infancy story of Jesus. In particular, there is a link to the last passage in which Zechariah was mentioned—the *Benedictus* (1:68-79; see above). John's activity is carried out throughout the region of Jordan, probably on both sides of the river. As anticipated in the song of Zechariah (1:77), John's message is one of the "forgiveness of sins." The word of God "came" to John: John received a call from God.

It is interesting to note that Luke does not include a description of John, as do Mark and Matthew. This probably reflects his sensitivity to his audience, who seem to be largely gentile. Whereas in a Jewish context the description of John would immediately bring to mind the prophets of old, particularly Elijah, for a gentile, unfamiliar with the prophetic tradition in the Hebrew Bible, it would seem rather odd.

The passage concludes with a lengthy quotation from Isaiah 40:3–5. In its original context the passage speaks to the comfort promised to the people in exile in Babylon. The imagery of the wilderness recalls the Exodus experience. A voice cries out from the heavenly assembly to announce that God will lead a new exodus through the desert. In witnessing this great event all nations will recognize the glory of God. Mark's Gospel was the first to appropriate this quotation and apply it to John the Baptist, although he quotes only Isaiah 40:3. Certainly it fits John's role as the herald of Jesus' arrival. Matthew uses this verse in a similar vein. Luke is the only one to extend the quote to include Isaiah 40:4–5. Doing so fits into Luke's particular concern to show the universality of the salvation that will come through Jesus—"all flesh shall see the salvation of God."

Responding to the Text

Two themes highlighted in today's Gospel reading are specificity and universality. Luke begins the passage with very specific historical notations, giving as precise a time as possible for the beginning of John's ministry. But this is quickly broadened to suggest that the message he heralds will be known to the whole world. This is the core message of the incarnation. In this season of Advent we anticipate the event in which God became human. But God became human in a very specific time and place. This involved God's self-limitation to acting within the bounds not only of humanity but also of the sociocultural world of Palestine under Roman occupation. Why that time and place, we can only speculate. Would not another time or place have been more strategically effective? We might ask, as does the character of Judas in the musical *Jesus Christ, Superstar,* "Now why'd you choose such a backward time and such a strange land? If you'd come today you would have reached a whole nation; Israel in 4 B.C. had no mass communication."

These questions are unanswerable. The earliest Christian witness simply asserts that God chose this time and place to become human. Luke notes this fact but wants to draw the reader beyond it to see that, despite the specificity, the message that the incarnate God brings will have an impact on the entire world. Indeed, it has. For better or for worse, there is hardly a place in the world today that has not felt the impact of Christianity to some degree. We truly live in a time when the way is not only "prepared" but many have trod on that way to proclaim the salvation of God. That being said, one wonders whether Christians have truly fulfilled this vision that "all flesh shall see the salvation of God." The great abuses people have suffered throughout the centuries at the hands of Christians need not be recounted here. The fact remains that for many, this is all that is known of Christianity. During this time of Advent we might reflect on how we can re-prepare (or "repair") the way of the Lord so that truly all peoples will see what is so central to the Christian proclamation—the love and salvation of God.

THIRD SUNDAY IN ADVENT

DECEMBER 17, 2000

REVISED COMMON	EPISCOPAL (BCP)	ROMAN CATHOLIC
Zeph. 3:14-20	Zeph. 3:14-20	Zeph. 3:14-18a
Isa. 12:2-6	Ps. 85 or 85:7-13 or Canticle 9	Isa. 12:2-6
Phil. 4:4-7	Phil. 4:4-7, (8-9)	Phil. 4:4-7
Luke 3:7-18	Luke 3:7-18	Luke 3:10-18

THE THEME FOR TODAY IS REJOICING. In the first reading there is a call for great rejoicing over the presence of God in the midst of the people. This is reinforced in the responsive reading from Isaiah in which we are called to praise God for mighty deeds of the past. In the second reading we rejoice that Jesus' return draws ever nearer. The Gospel announces the good news of Christ's coming, for which we can rejoice. Yet this is tempered with a reminder that the coming of the Lord is paved not only with rejoicing but also with repentance and righteous living, a message embedded in the alternative responsive reading, Psalm 85.

FIRST READING

ZEPHANIAH 3:14-20 (RCL/BCP); 3:14-18a (RC)

Interpreting the Text

Although Zephaniah the prophet seems to have been active around the time of Josiah (640–609 B.C.E.) many scholars consider the final verses of the book (3:9-20) to come from a later time, probably the postexilic period. Certainly our passage is filled with a message of hope that resonates with the emphases of postexilic eschatology. It is a clear shift from the message of doom and destruction that dominates the first two chapters of Zephaniah. For those who are in exile in Babylon, this text brings a fourfold message. First, God has taken away the punishment that was meted out upon them for their turning away from God. Even in exile God has not abandoned them. Normally in antiquity the destruction of the temple of a deity and the exile of the followers of that deity would indicate to the people that their god had abandoned them. During their period of exile, however, the people of Israel came to understand that God had not abandoned them but was chastising them. Despite their punishment, God was still in control and still looking after them. Verse 15 announces that the punishment has ended, and with it the enemies of the people have been turned away.

The second message is that the people in exile will return to Jerusalem. There is a shift in tense at the end of v. 15 from what God has done to what God will do. First and foremost, the people will rejoice in their salvation in Jerusalem (3:16; cf. 3:20). The third message is that their reputation will become known throughout the earth ("I will make you renowned and praised"; 3:19, 20). In so doing, God will fulfill the promise made to Abraham long ago that God would make of him "a great nation" (Gen. 12:2-3). The fourth, and perhaps most shocking message is that "the Lord is in your midst," a repeated phrase (3:15, 17). God is not far off, powerfully controlling the destiny of the people yet standing aloof from their struggles and their triumphs. Rather, God stands with them, as a warrior giving victory (3:17) and protection from their enemies (3:15, 19). Yet despite the military metaphors God also stands with the people in love and compassion and celebration. The entire message is put into the framework of praise by the opening call to exult in 3:14.

Responding to the Text

The shift in v. 15 from present status (the enemy has been turned away) to future events of triumph in Jerusalem reflect the status of Christians, one that is worth highlighting during the season of Advent. In relationship with God we now experience salvation through Jesus Christ. But it is only in the future that our current status will be fully realized. We can celebrate the incarnation as the point at which we came to understand the full extent of the salvation offered by God. We must look to the future, however, to the return of Christ, to experience fully the extent of that salvation. In the meantime, like the prophet, our proper response is one of praise (sing, shout, rejoice, exult; 3:14) and continued work for the kingdom of God ("do not let your hands grow weak"; 3:16).

The salvation that will come to the "lame and the outcast" most likely refers to Israel as an exiled nation, but it anticipates Jesus' ministry among such people, as announced in Luke 4:16-21. In Jesus, both in the first century and in the present, God is not standing on the sidelines or hiding in some corner of heaven. God is in our midst, at the center of who we are, individually as Christians and corporately as a body of worshipers. Jesus is our "Emmanuel," God with us.

Responsive Reading

ISAIAH 12:2-6 (RCL AND RC = BCP CANTICLE 9)

This hymn begins with a commemoration of God's turning from anger (12:1). The writer then celebrates the salvation of God and looks outward to proclaim that salvation among all peoples. All the inhabitants of Jerusalem are to celebrate the presence of God in the Temple, and thus in their midst (v. 6). So also do we seek to praise God as we recall God's presence among us in the past through Jesus, God's indwelling presence among us now through the Spirit, and God's coming among us once again in the future.

PSALM 85 or 85:7-13 (BCP)

This hymn of communal lament opens with praise for God and remembrance of God's blessings in the past (vv. 1-3). It then turns to the present crisis and appeals to God once again to turn away from anger and restore a relationship with the people (vv. 4-7). In vv. 8-9 an individual proposes to hear the message from God, proclaiming that "surely God's salvation is at hand," a proclamation the Christian church echoes at Advent. The psalmist concludes with a description of that salvation, which will include love, faithfulness, righteousness, peace, and prosperity for the land. But it will not come about unless the way is paved though human righteousness, much as John the Baptist calls for repentance before the coming of the Lord in today's Gospel.

Second Reading

PHILIPPIANS 4:4-7 (RCL/RC); 4:4-7 (8-9) (BCP)

Interpreting the Text

In the last chapter of Philippians, Paul gives personal exhortations and greetings. Having reaffirmed the need for unity (4:1), Paul briefly addresses a situation of disunity in the community (4:2-3). He then extends some general exhortations outlining the types of actions involved in standing firm: prayer (4:4-7) and meditation on that which is good (4:8-9), both of them given with the reminder that Paul is the one to be imitated in such things (4:9b). The reading is framed by the opening imperative calling for rejoicing, which is immediately repeated. The rejoicing called for is not a one-time celebration but a continuous and habitual action that pervades one's life. A second imperative indicates that one is to let one's attitude of gentleness be known to all people. The "gentleness" advocated here is not simply meekness, but an ability to submit to injustice and dishonor without seeking retribution.

Paul then affirms the "nearness" of Jesus, although in somewhat ambiguous terms. It could mean that Jesus is near spatially—"God is in our midst"—or, more likely, that the time of Jesus' return is near. However, both the spatial and temporal aspects could be affirmed. Anxiety serves to undermine the stability of the Christian life, so Paul urges the elimination of all anxiety through general prayer, specific requests, and thanksgiving to God for past dealings. To illustrate the results of such a course of action, Paul draws on a military metaphor in which we are to imagine soldiers standing guard at the gate of the city, ensuring the safety of those inside. For the Christian, that which is guarded is the heart, the center of emotions and will, and the mind, the center of the thinking faculty. Together the heart and mind represent the entire inner life of a person.

The Episcopal lection includes as an option vv. 8-9, which introduce two more imperatives, both of which indicate continual or habitual action. Verse 8 concludes with the exhortation continually to take into account or reflect on the virtues just listed. In Greek, v. 9a is structured similarly, placing the imperative call to practice after listing the things to be practiced. The conclusion is a promise: the result of following Paul in these things is that God will be in their midst.

Responding to the Text

How many worries do you have in a day? Just think about today. What are you anxious about (apart from the preparation of the sermon for this Sunday)? Every day we face worries about time, money, family, and illnesses. Media advertising plays on this, emphasizing our deficiencies in order to urge us to purchase a particular product: Does my hair measure up, am I using the right deodorant, are my investments secure? News media are little better, often presenting sensationalistic situations in ways that intensify our insecurities and feelings of helplessness. Large-scale natural and human disasters, particularly grizzly crimes and seemingly random illnesses and deaths are thrust forward with dire warnings about the times in which we live.

Even magazines we read can add to our anxiety. I subscribed to a health magazine, with the thought that an active interest in my physical well-being was overdue. Although it had helpful suggestions, as I looked at the firmly toned models and read about all the healthy things I should be doing (but could not possibly fit into thirty hours a day, never mind twenty-four) I felt my blood pressure rise! And I worry—am I ever "really" going to be healthy?

You and I are not alone in our anxiety. All persons to whom you preach have their own set of anxieties. Even as you preach, their minds will be doing calculations, making plans, inventing excuses, all the while processing your sermon material.

It is said that we live in an age of an accelerated culture, and that changes are happening so fast that they bring higher levels of anxiety. Yet, however high our anxiety is, I don't think that it is much different from what it was in antiquity. We are no more anxious about things than were the Philippians—perhaps only about different things. The Philippians had to face a number of troubles. Since the majority of persons in antiquity lived at subsistence level, earning only enough in a day for that day's expenses, money must have been an anxiety. It is said that the only sure things in life are death and taxes and, to be sure, the Philippians faced both. Even Paul himself, when he penned these words, faced the possibility of death while sitting in a dark, dank, and miserable prison. But from there comes his message: rejoice, and don't worry about anything.

Paul's advocation of prayer and petition and thanksgiving to God is not a magic formula for peace, as is sometimes presented. The peace of God comes about as we present general and specific requests to God balanced by thanksgiving for what God has already done. Recognition that God has acted in the past then allows us to understand that God will act again in the future in the situations about which we pray. While the details of our requests are not guaranteed, we can rest assured that God is in our midst and will take care of us. And not only now but in the near future we will be joined again with Jesus, either through his coming again or through our own passing on to the next world. According to Paul, even this latter situation is a good thing, not a cause for anxiety (Phil. 1:21-24). Hence, we rejoice! It is a joy not based on external circumstances but on the inner quality of recognizing God in our midst here and now.

The Gospel
LUKE 3:7-18 (RCL/BCP); 3:10-18 (RC)

Interpreting the Text

Today's Gospel opens with John the Baptist addressing the crowds who have come out to be baptized. The name-calling of v. 7 (literally "offspring of snakes" or "snake bastards") is interesting, because it is aimed not at the Jewish leadership, as is the case in Matthew (3:7), but at the common people, those that are generally favorable to Jesus throughout his ministry. Although it is clear that the audience includes commoners, tax collectors who are probably wealthy, and Roman soldiers who have authority (3:10-14), John groups them all together. He wants them to understand that there is no basis for righteousness in their birth. They cannot claim the heritage of Abraham as a means to obtain God's favor (3:8). Rather, true righteousness comes from right moral action, which, John announces, begins with repentance.

On the basis of the closeness of the Day of the Lord, John urges those in the crowd not to imagine that the ritual of baptism alone will suffice without repentance, not to think that belonging to the children of Abraham will protect them, and not to waste the little time that is left. John not only warns these groups but also makes some charges against them.

John's exhortations have a positive effect on the crowds. The threat of imminent judgment causes them to ask John, "What then shall we do?" (3:10, 12, 14). This response and John's answer are unique to Luke and reflect some concerns of Jesus' ministry that Luke will highlight throughout his Gospel. Three groups are addressed in turn: the crowd, tax collectors, and soldiers. In each case they are exhorted to maintain social practices that would benefit society at large. The members of the crowd are told to share food and clothing (3:10-11). The "coat" mentioned is the garment worn next to the skin, not extra outerwear. Thus, from the very beginning of Luke's narrative, even before Jesus' ministry, crowds are told to share the essentials of life—warmth and food. Such social action is imperative in a time when the authorities did little to provide some sort of welfare system to take care of the disadvantaged. This social practice is taken up by the early Christians in Acts 1–5, where the followers of Jesus are presented as living an ideal communal existence in which their needs are met through the sharing of resources (Acts 2:43-47; 4:32-37; 6:1-6).

REJOICING, REPENTANCE, AND RIGHTEOUSNESS HERALD THE COMING OF GOD INTO OUR MIDST.

Due to their status in society, the next two groups, the tax collectors and the soldiers, stand apart from the crowd. Although they occupy positions of privilege and power, they were perceived by the common person as oppressive, abusive, and the cause of many social ills. When the tax collectors approach John they are advised to collect what is necessary, but no more (3:13). These words are later illustrated through the figure of Zacchaeus in Luke 19:1-10, when he announces that he already practices charity and just taxation, and Jesus pronounces salvation upon his household. The soldiers are told not to abuse people by robbery, violence, or false accusation, and to be content with their wages (3:14), which were low and often supplemented through extortion. This is exemplified in Luke through the lives of the centurion whose slave is healed (Luke 7:1-10) and the centurion Cornelius whom Peter converts (Acts 10). Both are said to have treated the Jewish people well.

As a result of John's preaching the people begin questioning "in their hearts concerning John, whether he might be the Messiah" (3:15). John answers them with the announcement of the coming of one mightier than himself who will baptize with the Holy Spirit and fire. As a person, Jesus is mightier than John; likewise, Jesus' baptism is more powerful than John's. The image of the axe (3:9) is a symbol of divine punishment, which will cut off the people from God, the source of their being. We saw above that Zephaniah interpreted the exile in Babylon as God's punishment on an unrighteous and unrepentant people. Here the stakes are higher. No longer is exile the punishment, but chopping down and burning up is the punishment. Yet embedded in John's message of the coming of God to bring judgment is a message of baptism by the Holy Spirit and fire. The imagery is ambiguous. Fire is presented in the passage as destructive and the source of punishment. In this case, the separation of the wheat and the chaff results in two very different baptisms, one with water for repentance and one with the fire of judgment. However, the fire might also be of a different sort, since Luke's description of Pentecost involves the Holy Spirit coming upon the gathered Christians with the appearance of tongues of fire (Acts 2:1-4).

Responding to the Text

Imagine that you have just been elected president of the United States. One of the first tasks before you is the choosing of a PR person—someone to talk to the press, make contact with the people, and generally smooth the way for your public life in office. As the curriculum vitae roll over your desk, you come across one for a person by the name of Jonathan Baptista. Upon opening it you find that rather than giving his academic credentials and work-related experience he has simply included a portfolio of PR work he has done in the past. The first example—today's Gospel! As president of the United States, would you hire this person for the job?

It is difficult to image John the Baptist as a PR person. Despite the fact that Luke has omitted the description of his peculiar clothing and wilderness food, John remains a somewhat unattractive PR person. He hurls insults on his audience and threatens them with horrifying judgment. John nonetheless is able to draw an audience—not just the curious gawkers who enjoy a good performance and those who trust only in their own ancestry and achievements but also the spiritually curious, who see in John a messenger from God.

What might a contemporary John the Baptist be like? What sort of things would he say to your congregation in this season of Advent? Part of the challenge of preaching this text is the difficulty of imitating John in our own proclamation. Should we harangue the congregation, hoping to prompt the response, "What should we do?" Should we identify particular groups that need to be exhorted to just action? Or does our desire for acceptance compel us to preach only messages of encouragement?

A few years ago I was walking along the street in downtown Toronto when I was accosted by a bedraggled, foul-smelling person. He appeared before me from an alley and began to harangue me, telling me that the end of the world was coming and that I had to change my ways. Although I had never met him before, his generalized condemnation of my life rang too true for comfort. So I crossed to the other side of the street!

If you are like me, you are uncomfortable with the extraordinary. Being accosted about my lifestyle by a complete stranger is not my recreation of choice. However, there is an element in our society that thrives on such abuse. Television evangelists who hurl abuse and condemnation upon their listeners continue to draw large followings. The practitioners of various sectarian movements often break people down through abuse in order to build them back up. Certainly this is the way the military is portrayed in contemporary cinema, where a person becomes worthy of military service only after having suffered the abuses of boot camp.

How we decide to preach this message depends very much on our personality and style. Nevertheless, however we emphasize repentance and justice we should also keep in mind the other readings of today, which have proclaimed the joy associated with the coming of God into the midst of humans. Ultimately, this is what John's message of repentance and righteous and justice is all about—it is the "good news" (3:17) of the coming Messiah that John proclaims to the people. Over such good news we rejoice and celebrate, conscious that such rejoicing carries with it a responsibility to live in a way that recognizes that God truly is in our midst.

Today's theme is rejoicing. What sorts of things bring you joy? They might be subtle or simple things—discovering a lost ring, a telephone call from a friend, a gentle pat on the back from a parishioner. What difference in intensity should we experience in the joy that comes from knowing that God has broken into human history in the past, that God is present in our lives, and that God will break in once again? Zephaniah calls us to sing aloud and shout in our rejoicing. What form of rejoicing are you comfortable with? What form does rejoicing take in your congregation? How will you lead them in rejoicing in having God present in their midst today? Along with repentance and the need for righteous living, joy is an essential part of our relationship with God—so the Jerusalem Talmud: "God's Holy Spirit infuses only hearts that are joyous" (*Sukkah* 5:1).

FOURTH SUNDAY IN ADVENT

DECEMBER 24, 2000

REVISED COMMON	EPISCOPAL (BCP)	ROMAN CATHOLIC
Micah 5:2-5a	Micah 5:2-4	Micah 5:1-4a
Luke 1:47-55 or Ps. 80:1-7	Ps. 80 or 80:1-7	Ps. 80:2-3, 15-16, 18-19
Heb. 10:5-10	Heb. 10:5-10	Heb. 10:5-10
Luke 1:39-45 (46-55)	Luke 1:39-49 (50-56)	Luke 1:39-45

On this last Sunday of Advent our focus is most clearly upon the preparation for the incarnation of Christ in antiquity. We begin with a reading from the prophet Micah that speaks of the coming shepherd-king of Israel whose birthplace is Bethlehem. Psalm 80 appeals to the Shepherd of Israel with a thrice-repeated plea for restoration and salvation (vv. 3, 7, 19). The messianic program of salvation is given in more detail in the reading from Hebrews. Finally, the person through whom the Messiah comes, Mary, and her psalm of descriptive praise are elucidated in the Gospel. Although salvation is an important theme to be aware of as we read these lessons, we must be conscious that their focus is not simply spiritual salvation but also a new sociopolitical reality in which the poor and oppressed are brought liberation.

FIRST READING

MICAH 5:2-5 (RCL/BCP); 5:1-4a (RC)

Interpreting the Text

Micah lived in the late eighth century B.C.E., about the same time as Isaiah. Unlike Isaiah, however, Micah was not a court prophet and was not of noble birth. Micah was from Moresheth-gath, a small village southwest of Jerusalem. His prophetic words reflect no interest in the affairs of state, Jerusalem, or the Temple, but rather focus on the agricultural year and the weather. Micah was active at a time when the northern kingdom, Israel, was taken by the Assyrians, and Judah in the south was under constant threat. Micah saw this as God's judgment upon the people and the leaders, who had allowed injustices and evil to flourish in the land. But there was a bright light on the horizon. God would restore the fortunes of Israel through a king like David. But Micah points out that the king would not be born in Jerusalem, among the elite. Rather, like David himself, the king would be born in the town of Bethlehem, among the insignificant clans of Judah. God will send forth a ruler whose origin is "from old." This probably is indicative of Davidic lineage rather than preexistence (cf. John 7:42).

Whether this text was written down at the time of Micah or, as some believe, added to Micah's prophecy during the time of the Babylonian exile of Judah, it is clearly a text of great promise and hope. The years of oppression and darkness are to be lifted through the coming of a leader, a shepherd-king who, like David, will establish peace, prosperity, and the worship of God in the land.

Responding to the Text

Have you ever been to a sporting event in your city or town in which the crowd chants in unison, "We're number one"? Whether or not we are predisposed to chant at sporting events, many of us do feel a certain civic pride about our community. This is reflected in keeping our streets clean and safe, promoting our city as a not-to-be-missed tourist stop, volunteering in community events, and the like. But civic pride can have a dark side—it can imply that other cities are not as good. And sometimes, their supposed inferiority is translated into a smug, self-congratulatory feeling of superiority. This subtly shifts from the civic context to the lives of private citizens with thoughts such as, "If their city is inferior, so must be the people from that city."

This sense of civic pride is nothing new. It can be traced back through history, almost to the very beginning of human collective living. Such pride is often reflected in biblical texts, as one nation goes to battle against another, or one city challenges another. Within Israel, pride of place fell upon Jerusalem. Chosen as the capital by David, it was the political, cultural, and religious center of the nation. Yet, as Micah recognizes, when God chose a place in which to reveal the one chosen to bring salvation to the nation, it was not to be the great capital city. Rather, it was the inconsequential village of Bethlehem. Jesus was born in Bethlehem, and when his family moved to Nazareth his civic status did not change much. A typical assumption about Nazareth is reflected in the words of the disciple Nathanael, "Can anything good come out of Nazareth?" (John 1:46).

All of this is illustrative of God's dealings with human beings. God cares nothing for one's place of residence. All human beings are equal in God's sight, whether from Jerusalem or Bethlehem, New York City or Moose Jaw. In fact, God favors the outsiders, the outcasts, and the despised and often chooses as leaders those who, by the world's standards, would not qualify. This suggests that we should not expect God only to work through those who possess the dominant pedigree in our culture. God will surprise us by raising up leaders from "nowhere."

RESPONSIVE READING
LUKE 1:47-55 (RCL)

This text is treated below under the Gospel for today.

PSALM 80 (BCP); 80:1-7 (RCL/BCP alt.); 80:2-3, 15-16, 18-19 (RC)

This community lament reflects the Assyrian threat to the northern kingdom of Israel. As shepherd, God is expected to lead, protect, and provide for his charges. The lament is predicated upon God removing God's leadership and protection from the people. Mourning and humiliation are their present lot, and their prayers amount to nothing (4-6).The remainder of the psalm develops the image of the nation as a vine, tended by God in the past but now neglected. These images of despair are interspersed with cries for deliverance through God turning again to lead the people (vv. 3, 7, 14, 17-19). It is in the coming of the shepherd-king that we as Christians find the answer to these prayers.

SECOND READING
HEBREWS 10:5-10

Interpreting the Text

In Hebrews, an anonymous Jewish-Christian work, the writer adapts Platonic philosophy in his understanding of the message of salvation. Everything in the material world is imperfect and changing, and will eventually pass out of existence. These are, however, but pale reflections of the heavenly world (10:1). Thus, although the Torah prescribes sacrifices as atonement for sin, they were just a foreshadowing of what was to come through Christ. For the writer of Hebrews, Christians have access to the heavenly world through Christ, unmediated through the regular sacrificial system. Although framed with a distinctly Christocentric thrust, this passage does not stand in direct contrast to the religious experience of ancient Israel. In fact, much of this passage is a direct quotation of Psalm 40:6-8. The emphasis on God not desiring sacrifices and offerings without the full commitment of the whole person is found throughout the Hebrew Bible. Ritual sacrifice made without an accompanying commitment to justice reflects a transgression against God's will.

According to the writer, God became enfleshed in Christ, taking on a human body (10:5), a body that was to be sacrificed in a once-for-all action to satisfy the requirements of Torah. The consequences of this action are not simply the attainment of God's forgiveness but also the abolishment of the necessity of regular sacrifice and the freeing of God's people to do God's will (10:9). It is a demonstration of God's love for humanity. No longer is it necessary to sacrifice with a pure heart; we are freed from the ritual in order to enact righteousness and justice.

Responding to the Text

In the seasons of Advent and Christmas we quite rightly celebrate the incarnation. Many, however, have a sentimental approach to the little babe in a manger, and feel nostalgia or the longing for parenthood. The reading from Hebrews is a stark reminder that the babe in a manger came with a horrifying mission—to give his own body in death as a once-for-all sin offering to God to open the way for the sanctification of humankind. The writer's use of Platonic philosophy presents an image by which we can again see that there is no divide between God and God's people, there is no longer any mediation necessary. God has come into our midst, and through Christ we can enter into God's midst directly. Yet with this opportunity comes the responsibility to consider the plight of others.

While today's reading from Micah carries with it a message of the humble origins of God's servant, Hebrews speaks of the great work this person did when he did come into the world. The movie *Simon Birch* (1998; loosely based on John Irving's novel *A Prayer for Owen Meany*) is a wonderful illustration of someone who grew up in anonymity and was scorned by many, yet, knowing his calling from God, was willing to put his own life at risk to save the lives of others. Born unusually small of stature, Simon Birch grew up on the margins of society in his rural town. He was neglected by his parents and shunned by most of his schoolmates, with the exception of his friend Joe. As a young boy Simon believed that God had a special plan for him, and part of that plan included his below-average size. Simon came to face his destiny one day as a busload of young children plunged into an icy lake. Because of his size, Simon was able to gain the confidence of the children and lead them out of the bus safely. His size also allowed him to squeeze back into the sinking bus to rescue a trapped boy. This proved to be the final undoing of his weak body, but for Simon this one act was the reason God had created him so small. Scorned by many, he stuck to his calling to become God's instrument. Through Simon Birch, God's love and compassion was evidenced.

THE GOSPEL

LUKE 1:39-45 (46-55) (RCL); 1:39-49 (50-56) (BCP); 1:39-45 (RC)

Interpreting the Text

Our Gospel has two related parts. The first provides a description of the events surrounding Mary's visit to Elizabeth. The second is a beautiful hymn celebrating the work that the Messiah will accomplish. Upon receipt of a visitation from an angel and the announcement that she will bear the child of God (1:26-38), Mary hurriedly sets off to visit her relative Elizabeth. Elizabeth's response to Mary is fourfold. First, she is filled with the Holy Spirit. The Holy Spirit is quite active in Luke's infancy narrative, having been promised to John (1:15) and Mary (1:35) and causing a number of characters to praise God: Elizabeth (1:41), Zechariah (1:67), and Simeon (2:25-27). The Spirit is also quite active in Jesus' baptism (3:16, 22), temptation (4:1), and inaugural mission in Galilee (4:14, 18). All of this suggests that the Spirit should be seen as an integral part of God's preparation for the full manifestation of Jesus. In the particular case of Elizabeth, the Spirit inspires the second part of her response, the proclamation of a christological confession, "the mother of my Lord." This is the first such confession in Luke and the only one made by a woman in this Gospel. Her third response to Mary is to testify to the joy she felt expressed in her own womb when Mary entered into her presence. Finally, she pronounced a blessing upon Mary for her faith in the message given to her by God. Overall, Elizabeth's response to Mary gives the entire scenario the feel of spirit-filled joy bursting out at the prospect of God visiting God's people—and thus we proclaim joy to the world!

> THE COMING OF CHRIST BRINGS US FREEDOM TO WORK FOR JUSTICE.

The *Magnificat* (which "magnifies" or "exalts" the greatness of God) proclaims that present salvation is rooted in God acting to save Israel in the past. Salvation in the present, however, is to be found in Jesus, the fulfillment of God's promises to God's people. It opens with a general statement of introductory praise (vv. 46b-47). This is followed by an individual hymn of praise (vv. 48-50) that recounts Mary's experience. Then follows a community hymn of praise (vv. 51-53) that universalizes Mary's experience. The concluding verses recapitulate God's dealings with Israel (vv. 54-55).

In v. 48 Mary includes herself among the "lowly" or "those of afflicted state." There are many theories as to the composition of this group of "lowly," including: the poor in an economic sense; the spiritually poor who have no recourse except to YHWH; the humble; Israel, who is referred to as "lowly" in the psalms.

Each of these suggestions has something to recommend it. Most scholars favor the first suggestion, although few would discount the others entirely.

In vv. 51-53 there is a series of verbs in the past tense (*aorist*) describing God's actions. God has shown strength, scattered the proud, put down the mighty, exalted the lowly, filled the hungry, and sent away empty the rich. However, these things have not already happened, even in Luke's narrative world. Commentators have sought to explain what these mean. Some suggest a "prophetic aorist," that Mary is predicting what will come through Jesus, while others suggest "gnomic aorists" used to show God's regular, recurring action. Still others suggest that it is a Hebrew proleptic perfect, which speaks of future events as if they had come to pass. One of the most compelling arguments suggests that the *Magnificat* speaks of a past event from Luke's perspective and indicates that the coming of Jesus Christ also has consequences that reach into the future. So decisive is the event that one can speak as if the age to come has already arrived (aorist). Thus it speaks of a past event with future (eternal) consequences and creates a tension between the fulfilled and the unfulfilled. The *Magnificat* declares that God has acted decisively for Israel in the death and resurrection of Jesus. This present salvation is a fulfillment of God's past promises to God's people (vv. 54-55).

Responding to the Text

In first-century Palestine, the "rich" constituted less than ten percent of the total population. The remaining ninety percent or so were poor. There was no middle class. The elite not only had political and economic power but also social power in the form of ascribed honor. That is, by virtue of their riches they were to be deferred to and given preference by the poor majority most of the time. Most of the elite lived in Jerusalem but owned the farmland throughout Palestine, which the peasants worked as tenant farmers.

In the postindustrial revolution world many of us in the West find ourselves in a position of relative comfort and security. Although perhaps not as wealthy as we would like to be, we have food and shelter, toys and vacations, and modest savings towards retirement. We are middle class. However, many others, both in the West and beyond, do not enjoy the level of prosperity of the middle class. I recently traveled to a youth rally with a group of teenagers from a small city in Ontario. Along the way we spent a night at a church in Toronto. In the park outside the church window, a homeless family had spread out some sleeping bags and was attempting to find enough comfort from the October chill to sleep through the night. The young teenagers I was traveling with could not resist the urge to stare, and kept slipping back to the window to see how the family was doing. Once the leaders realized this, we called the teens together and had a discussion about homelessness and the respect and dignity all people deserve, no matter what their circumstances. Upon reflection, two particular aspects of that discussion disturbed me. First, I was disturbed that these teens from a small city were so sheltered that they had never seen homeless persons. Second, I was disturbed that, having lived in major cities in Canada, the United States, and England, I was so used to seeing homeless persons that they no longer registered on my conscience. Opposite ends of exposure to this problem resulted in the same reaction—complacency.

I wonder whether we would dare to sing the *Magnificat* today. What would it mean? Mary preaches as the prophet of the poor; as their representative she encapsulates the person who has suffered and been vindicated. And as a representative, God touched her personally. Having presented her with a challenge, to carry to term the incarnation of God, she has accepted her task with joy. Thus, Mary's is the ideal response to the word of God: obedient trust and sacrifice.

The pattern of promise-fulfillment-praise found in today's readings can serve as a paradigm of our response to God in this season of Advent. To be sure, we celebrate the promise of a Messiah and its fulfillment in Jesus during the Christmas season. Based on God's track record of fulfilling God's promises, however, the appropriate response to the coming of Jesus into our own lives and the coming of Jesus into the world in the future is one of praise. Like the prophets of old, and like Mary, we can be sure that God will bring to fruition the promises made—and thus we celebrate.

Yet in claiming this assurance, we need to be sure that we are serious in seeing the gospel as bringing justice to the oppressed, the downtrodden, the sick, the poor, the powerless. Certainly that was a big part of Jesus' ministry and also that of the apostles. The liberation about which Mary sings is tied to service and sacrifice. We as disciples of Christ are called forth from the joy of celebrating Christmas to serve all humankind in love and justice.

Jane Schaberg states that "the Magnificat is the great New Testament song of liberation—personal and social, moral and economic—a revolutionary document of intense conflict and victory. . . . Mary's song is precious to women and other oppressed people for its vision of their concrete freedom from systemic injustice."[1] As we move from Advent and the anticipation of Christ's coming into Christmas and the celebration of Christ's coming we need to be reminded that as joyous an occasion as Christmas is, for God's people it brings not only salvation but responsibility to do justice.

THE SEASON OF CHRISTMAS

RICHARD S. ASCOUGH

For many people Christmas is primarily a commemoration of the birth of Jesus as an historical event. But we should not lose sight of Christmas as a celebration of salvation wrought through the coming of God in the flesh. Too many people in our secularized society get caught up in the sentimentality of the babe in the manger and are unable or unwilling to move beyond the manger to the cross. The coming of God into the midst of humanity in the past gives true life to our present and secures our future.

The name of this celebration, "Christmas," comes from the Old English phrase *Christes Maesse* or *Cristes-messe*, meaning "Mass of Christ." It was first celebrated as the Feast of the Nativity around 336 C.E. It is unclear why the particular dates of the Christmas season were picked. The actual year of Jesus' birth is not known. Luke 1–2 includes some historical information, but not enough to determine the year in which the events took place. Despite ours being the first year of the "third" millennium according to the current calendar, the most likely time of Jesus' birth is somewhere between 8 and 4 B.C.E. The actual day of the year is even less easy to determine.

CHRISTMAS IS A CELEBRATION OF SALVATION WROUGHT THROUGH THE COMING OF GOD IN THE FLESH.

There are two predominant theories as to the origins of Christmas. The first suggests that Christmas began as a Christian adaptation of existing public holidays in honor of other deities. The winter solstice usually occurred around December 25 on the ancient Julian calendar and led to a number of "pagan" festivals, including Saturnalia, honoring Saturn, the ancient god of agriculture, and Mithra, the ancient Persian mystery deity, whose adherents celebrated the birthday of the invincible sun (*dies natalis solis invicti*) on December 25. On that day in 274 C.E. the emperor Aurelian proclaimed the sun god to be the principal deity of Rome and the empire. As a challenge to the widespread worship of Mithra, as early as the third century we find church writers referring to Christ as the "Sun of Righteousness." Once the empire was Christianized, one deity simply replaced another while keeping the day of the festival the same.

The second predominant theory of the origin of Christmas revolves around the determination of the date of the death of Jesus as March 25. Ancient thinkers would have assumed that Jesus lived a complete number of years. His conception therefore must have also taken place on March 25, and he would thus have been born nine months later, on December 25. This was confirmed by the computation of the birth of John the Baptist six months earlier (cf. Luke 1:36), on the day of the summer solstice.

As early as Augustine, Christmas was a commemorative event that celebrated the historical event of Jesus' birth. However, in opposition to the Arians, who denied Jesus' full divinity, it began to take on the form of a mystery feast with liturgical celebrations of the mystery of the incarnation. As Christianity increased throughout Europe and Egypt, the Christmas festival continued to be diffused and expanded through the development of new traditions and the Christianization of old, non-Christian traditions and rituals. The commemoration took on different forms in the Eastern and Western parts of the Roman Empire. Even today the Eastern churches continue their historic practice of celebrating Christmas on January 6.

Because the Bible offers no guidelines on how Christmas is to be celebrated, the festivals and liturgies were often adopted and adapted from the rituals and popular traditions of the cultures that celebrated it. This included such things as the crèche, the decorating of trees, mistletoe, exchange of gifts, and mythical figures who deliver presents (Saint Nicholas, Santa Claus, Father Christmas). The current trend in North America to emphasize family gatherings and gift exchanges stems from the industrial revolution and the growth of the middle class. Although churchgoing is still practiced by some, the Christmas season has become primarily a domestic holiday. Merchants, many of whom rely on the Christmas season for their annual profitability, actively stimulate the exchange of gifts and the consumption of food and drink.

Although Christians traditionally exchange gifts as a reminder of God's gift of a Savior, today many lament the commercial overtones of Christmas and long for a return to a more simple time. The challenge for preachers during the Christmas season is to present the joyful proclamation that God is born among us in a way that is not drowned out by the commercial din. Properly done, the liturgies of Christmas can go beyond the commercialism, tackiness, and controversies that plague this season.

For Further Reading

Brown, Raymond E. *The Birth of the Messiah: A Commentary on the Infancy Narratives in the Gospels of Matthew and Luke.* Updated edition. New York: Doubleday, 1993.

Farris, Stephen. *The Hymns of Luke's Infancy Narrative: Their Origin, Meaning and Significance.* JSNTSup 9. Sheffield: JSOT Press, 1985.

Fitzmyer, Joseph A. *The Gospel According to Luke.* AB 28. New York: Doubleday, 1981.

Hagner, Donald A. *Hebrews.* NIBC 14. Peabody: Hendrickson, 1983.

Horsley, Richard A. *The Liberation of Christmas: The Infancy Narratives in Social Context.* New York: Crossroad, 1989.

Mays, James Luther. *Psalms.* Interpretation. Louisville: Westminster John Knox, 1994.

Tannehill, Robert C. *Luke.* ANTC. Nashville: Abingdon, 1996.

Witherington, Ben. *John's Wisdom: A Commentary on the Fourth Gospel.* Louisville: Westminster John Knox, 1995.

Note: Footnotes for both Advent and Christmas may be found on page 67.

NATIVITY OF OUR LORD CHRISTMAS EVE

DECEMBER 24, 2000

REVISED COMMON	EPISCOPAL (BCP)	ROMAN CATHOLIC
Isa. 9:2-7	Isa. 9:2-4, 6-7	Isa. 9:1-6
Ps. 96	Ps. 96 or 96:1-4, 11-12	Ps. 96:1-3, 11-13
Titus 2:11-14	Titus 2:11-14	Titus 2:11-14
Luke 2:1-14 (15-20)	Luke 2:1-14 (15-20)	Luke 2:1-14

THE READINGS TODAY HELP CHRISTIANS TO FOCUS on the actual event for which many of us have spent the last month preparing—the coming of God into our midst. The emphasis is on rejoicing, but in each of today's lessons the rejoicing is predicated on a perceived need. People oppressed by external forces rejoice at the coming of a benevolent ruler (Isa. 9:2-7). People fighting an internal struggle for self-control and self-worth rejoice in the strength given through Jesus (Titus 2:11-14). People on the margins of society rejoice as they are brought into the center of God's love for humanity (Luke 2:1-20). The psalmist universalizes such experiences by proclaiming God's praise and God's promises among all nations.

FIRST READING

ISAIAH 9:2-7 (RCL); 9:2-4, 6-7 (BCP); 9:1-6 (RC)

Interpreting the Text

The prophet Isaiah proclaims God's message to Judah and Jerusalem during the time when the Assyrian Empire overshadowed the entire land, first annexing and then exiling the northern kingdom, Israel (721 B.C.E.; cf. 2 Kings 17). In today's reading Isaiah shifts from the Assyrian threat to the hope that he sees in the coming of a messianic king. The first verse sets the tone by noting that the gloom and anguish of the land of Galilee will be replaced by a time in which they are held in high esteem. Hope is first held out through the contrast of darkness with light (9:2). Darkness is the situation of those living under the oppression of Assyria. God, however, has broken in with a light—a child has been born (9:6).

This child bears the titles and authority that will usher in a new living situation marked not only by peace and justice but also loving care, the type given by a parent to a child ("everlasting Father," v. 6b).

In its original setting the child referred to here was probably Hezekiah, who was king in Jerusalem during Isaiah's time. Hezekiah held out great promise through a series of religious and political reforms throughout the country. Eventually, however, he acquiesced to Assyria by paying tribute. When he did not meet the expectations Isaiah made of him, this and other oracles became projected onto a future messianic king (cf. Isa. 11:1-9).

Responding to the Text

People who walk in darkness often cast about aimlessly with no point of reference on which to focus, or they stumble and trip with no light to reveal objects in their way. Many people may feel this way by the time Christmas Eve arrives. The people in the pew are often tired. Deadlines at work, deadlines at home, deadlines for shopping have all been intermingled with parties at work, parties at school, and parties in the home. Some may feel that their capacity for rejoicing has itself been exhausted. The Christmas Eve service is yet one more thing to "do" before the arrival of the day that has been so much in focus. Yet it is within that exhaustion, that preoccupation, that we are called to reflect on the implications of the coming of Jesus and the promises of God made through the babe in the manger.

What is causing darkness in our midst? For most of us in the West it is not political oppression. Yet there is an underlying malaise in our culture. In not-too-distant memory, if one passed by a colleague or neighbor and asked, "How are you doing?" one would receive a polite but vague, "Fine, thanks." A more common response today seems to be an equally impersonal but reflective, "I'm tired and stressed." Some even bear this as a badge of honor—the more tired and stressed I am, the more important I must be in my various social worlds.

God through Jesus has already given the light needed for such situations. Although the Isaiah text speaks of a new sociopolitical reality ushered in through the Messiah, it also has implications for the individual. The titles given to the messianic child reflect a personal intimacy with God's people—advisor, parent, peacemaker. In the face of our own personal darkness, Christmas provides an opportunity for us to allow the light of Jesus to shine forth with hope that this darkness will pass and we shall be brought into a time of experiencing the peace of God.

Responsive Reading

PSALM 96 (RCL/BCP); 96:1-4, 11-12 (BCP alt.); 96:1-3, 11-13 (RC)

This enthronement psalm begins with a summons to Israel to praise God among all nations, based on what God has done for the people (vv. 1-3). This is followed by the reason for such praise—God has created everything, while the other deities are mere idols (vv. 4-6). The summons to praise is then elaborated and extended to the peoples of all nations themselves (vv. 7-10). The nations are to turn from their gods and worship God alone. The promise of equality and justice are held out to those who will thus praise God (v. 10b). The psalmist then invites all of creation to join in praising God—the heavens, the earth, the sea, the fields, the trees (vv. 11-12). The psalm climaxes with the promise in v. 13 that God is coming to judge the world with righteousness and truth.

Christians also can look both backward to the past deeds of God and forward to the future fulfillment of the promises of God. In doing so the nativity of Jesus stands at the center, as the point at which God first came into our midst in a fully human form.

Second Reading

TITUS 2:11-14

Interpreting the Text

In his letter to Titus, Paul (or one of his later followers) includes a lengthy section encouraging Titus in the giving of practical advice to members of the Christian community that he pastors (2:1—3:11). Today's reading, included in this section serves as a brief, albeit very important aside on the source of the Christian's ability to live up to the admonitions being put forward.

It begins with the statement that "the grace of God has appeared, bringing salvation to all" (v. 11). Paul imagines that God's grace extends beyond national boundaries to all human beings. But there is also a close connection with the previous section through the conjunction "for" or "since." It is important to note that the previous section concerned the ethical imperatives that a slave must follow. In antiquity slaves were not considered true human beings. Under Roman law they were "talking things," possessions of their masters. As such they had no rights and often suffered terribly at the hands of cruel masters. At the same time, little was expected of them and one would not expect them to be able to live up to any ethical imperatives. Slaves who were questioned by civic authorities were assumed to be lying unless their evidence was produced through torture. In contrast to such attitudes, Paul here extends salvation to all people, including in that category of "people" those who are slaves. Perhaps by today's standards Paul does not go far enough in arguing for abolishment of slavery, but he does recognize the human worth of each individual. Alongside this, he also recognizes that slaves who are Christians have the capacity and responsibility to live out their Christian lives.

Paul goes on to point out that the grace given by God through Jesus has become our educator and guide in Christian living. The training provided through grace enables us to refuse the inclination to deny God and pursue that which is only available in the material world. On the positive side, through grace we are able to live with self-control, righteousness, and godliness (v. 12). Our training is provided by looking both to the future and the past. We look to the future time in which Jesus will once again break into human history and be with God's people—this is our "happy hope" (v.13). We also look to the past, to that time when Jesus first broke into human history and gave himself to provide the means for both redemption and purification. Redemption, or ransom, is particularly significant in the context of slavery in that it was one of the means through which slaves could be set free. As grace is offered to all people, even slaves, so also were we all once slaves to lawlessness until set free by Christ. Through Jesus' actions in the past the way is set for God's people to become "zealous for good deeds" (2:14).

Responding to the Text

A psychiatrist friend of mine tells me that one of the more frequent problems he encounters with his patients is the inability to grant forgiveness to oneself for past actions. This is as true for Christians as for non-Christians. As one reflects back on one's life various actions can stand out for which a person can find no justification and will not allow any forgiveness. Along with this comes a lack of self-worth. In the Christian context this can be become manifest as "worm theology." Like the psalmist, the Christian's inner voice proclaims, "I am but a worm" (Ps. 22:6). Such feelings are only exacerbated by the Christian's seeming inability to act differently here and now. Constant failures in moral battles, however small, cause feelings of self-loathing to grow.

Such crippling self-loathing is surely not what Christianity is all about. Paul boldly declares that the grace of God has touched all humans, even the lowest ranking in society—slaves—who had no status as human beings under Roman law. Old and young, masters and slaves, all have been given the grace of God through Jesus. On this eve of the day that celebrates the inauguration of Christ's actions, we can rejoice, knowing that God has already erased from memory those things upon which so many of us continue to dwell. Yet the only event of the past that we should recall is the "manifestation of the glory of our great God and Savior, Jesus Christ" (v. 13). Although this is accomplished by the "grace of God" (v. 11), it has an effect that continues into the present. God's grace continues to be our teacher, helping us to know what is right, correcting us when we are wrong.

The Gospel

LUKE 2:1-14 (15-20) (RCL/BCP); 2:1-14 (RC)

Interpreting the Text

Luke begins this section with reference to the historical period involved (2:1-2). This is the second of three historical contextualizations that Luke includes in his preface to Jesus' ministry (1:5; 2:1-2; 3:1-2). There is some problem with the inclusion of Quirinius, since the Syrian governor by that name conducted his census around 6 C.E., some eight to ten years after the probable date of Jesus' birth. Whatever the historical details (and numerous explanations have been offered), Luke is attempting to give a reasonable explanation of how Jesus came to be born in Bethlehem even though his home town was Nazareth. Matthew addresses the same problem by suggesting that Mary and Joseph were residents of Bethlehem and ended up in Nazareth only when they returned from Egypt. In either case, the two Gospel writers agree on Jesus' birth taking place in Bethlehem of Judea while his upbringing occurred in Nazareth of the Galilee.

According to Luke, Joseph and Mary travel from Nazareth in the Galilee to Bethlehem in Judea. Although each place is labelled as a "city," neither was much more than a hamlet of perhaps a hundred persons or so. The "inn" in which Jesus was born was likely a large furnished room attached to a peasant house, often used for kinship guests. That Joseph and Mary's expected place of stay was occupied suggests that there was someone who socially outranked them there already. In rural houses there was often an adjacent room occupied by domestic animals (particularly goats). It served as protection for the animals and warmth for the humans (even today in Middle Eastern villages animals are kept beside or below a dwelling). In such a room Jesus might have been born, as this is where one would find a manger.

> THE BABY'S BIRTH BRINGS A HAPPY HOPE TO ALL PEOPLE.

Outside in the adjacent fields an angel announces to some shepherds, "I bring you good news of great joy which will come to all the people" (2:10). This announcement evidences four of the five elements typically found in an announcement story in the Hebrew Bible: (a) the appearance of an angel or the Lord (2:9); (b) fear on the part of the person confronted (2:9); (c) the heavenly message (2:10–12); (d) an objection expressed by the person confronted (missing here); (e) the giving of some sign of reassurance (2:13–14). The missing element is the expression of an objection by the one(s) who receive the message: the shepherds do not question the message they receive but act on it immediately.

In the Hebrew Bible shepherds were seen as honorable and their lives were often romanticized. For example, David was a shepherd boy who grew up to be king of the whole nation. By the first century C.E., however, shepherd were despised and dishonored. Being a shepherd was among the most disdained of professions. It was considered dishonorable because a shepherd was away every night and thus could not protect his household—his wife and children. He was also considered a thief, because he grazed animals on other people's property. That Luke has shepherds come to worship the infant Jesus is suggestive of his concern for the outcasts of society being brought into God's care through Jesus. It is also interesting to note that Luke does not include a story about the Magi, who would have been among the elite, coming to Jesus.

In the announcement of a messianic Savior "for all the people," the referent of "the people" is most obviously "Israel" (v. 10). Yet "Savior" is a Lukan title for Jesus that not only has a background in the Hebrew Bible but also a non-Jewish background. As a title, "Savior" is frequently used in contemporary Greco-Roman literature, often applied to gods, philosophers, physicians, statesmen, kings, and emperors (e.g., the birth of Augustus). Thus, the reference here to "people" probably has the expanded sense of the whole world. This is a foretaste of the universal nature of the peace of God that will be outlined in the development of Luke's two-part story (Luke and Acts). Thus, through the shepherds the care of God for the outcast and despised is announced, and to the shepherds the extension of salvation to the gentiles is announced. It is for this reason that the shepherds return to their sheep "glorifying and praising God" (v. 20; on vv. 15-20 see further the comments on the Gospel reading for January 1, 2001, "The Name of Jesus").

Responding to the Text

While in our mid-twenties, my wife and I had the privilege of spending a few months in Israel. It was one of the most profitable educational experiences we have ever had. There we were exposed to the geography and archaeology of the biblical world. At the same time, we were able to visit many sites sacred to Christians, Jews, and Muslims. While in Jerusalem we crossed paths with an American Jewish rabbi who offered to take us in his car on a tour of the surrounding area, including Qumran and Herod the Great's fortress Herodium. We had much planned for a single day and set off early. Along the way, however, the rabbi made a detour to Bethlehem. We must, he insisted, see the Church of the Nativity. Despite our protests that we did not want to spend time in "yet another church," this rabbi was insistent, and we ended up there for an hour-long tour. It was profitable but disorienting. The grandeur of the edifice and the complexity of the ceremonies therein are a far cry from the humble beginnings of the birth of Jesus among the animals and his adoration by shepherds.

I think back to that experience each Christmas Eve. Although himself not a Christian, our rabbi guide thought that this church reflected the core of what Christianity was about. He was horrified that we would even consider missing it. Now, while I'm all for honoring God through beautiful structures, the reading of this passage from Luke gives me cause to ponder. It is almost commonplace, even among non-Christians, to lament the "materialism" of Christmas. Yet even through our own churches we Christians reflect materially our expression of thankfulness for God's grace. Rather than simply decry "materialism," perhaps the challenge of preaching on the infancy narratives within our ecclesial edifices is to focus on the values behind these expressions. We give gifts because we love another person, not because we are constrained to (one hopes). In the same way, God gave God's Son because of love. We build our buildings not to keep people out but to invite people in, all people, much like the shepherds were invited in to see the infant Jesus.

In many ways our rabbi guide was correct. The Church of the Nativity stands for what we as Christians see as central to our faith—not, as he seemed to think, in ceremony and iconography but as a memorial to God's grace in loving us and living among us so that all people may be included in the kingdom of God. And in that message we too "glorify and praise God."

What needs do you perceive in yourself this Christmas Eve? What needs do you perceive in your congregation? How can the birth of Jesus address these needs and bring hope and rejoicing to you and those to whom you minister?

NATIVITY OF OUR LORD CHRISTMAS DAY

DECEMBER 25, 2000

REVISED COMMON	EPISCOPAL (BCP)	ROMAN CATHOLIC
Isa. 52:7-10	Isa. 52:7-10	Isa. 52:7-10
Ps. 98	Ps. 98 or 98:1-6	Ps. 98:1-6
Heb. 1:1-4 (5-12)	Heb. 1:1-12	Heb. 1:1-6
John 1:1-14	John 1:1-14	John 1:1-18 or 1:1-5, 9-14

On this day of central importance in the Christian calendar the readings help us focus on two equally pivotal aspects of the Christian life—purposeful proclamation and christological confession. The reading from Isaiah 52 praises those who announce the reign of God. The psalmist likewise calls for all people of the world to lift up their voices in praise to God for God's salvation. The reading from Hebrews focuses on Jesus as "the exact imprint of God's very being," while in John it is clear that Jesus is the Logos who "was with God and was God." On this day we proclaim Christ as God.

FIRST READING

ISAIAH 52:7-10

Interpreting the Text

These verses are usually attributed to "Second Isaiah" and should be read within the context of the exiles in Babylon. There is to be a new exodus of the people back to the land of Israel. The return is seen from the perspective of ruined Jerusalem as the prophet describes poetically the return of God to the city. The passage opens with the image of a messenger coming over the mountains that surround Jerusalem. Although such messengers usually bear news from the battlefield, in this case the news is the reenthronement of God in Jerusalem. There are three implications of this announcement (v. 7). First, there will be a cessation of hostilities between nations. Second, it is good news, implying that it comes with the blessing of God. Third, it brings with it salvation, not only from captivity in Babylon but also from the wrath of God that threatens humankind. The announcement of God's reign inaugurates a new age in human history.

The sentinels who stand watch over the ruined walls of Jerusalem have a clear, unobstructed view of God on the horizon, leading the people back to the city. They sing for joy, repeating the proclamation of good news brought by the messenger (v. 8). The "return of God" does not indicate that God had left or that God no longer reigned during the exile. Rather, it suggests that from this point on God is taking up rule in an active way. The summons to praise in v. 9 pictures the desolate, crumbling ruins of Jerusalem erupting in song to God. God has fulfilled God's promises to bring comfort to the people and restoration to the city. This is no mere local manifestation of God. Using the military image of a bare arm, unobstructed for use in battle, the prophet underlines God's readiness to bring salvation to all people on earth.

Responding to the Text

These days we are inundated with "news" from all fronts. Radio newscasts occur almost hourly. Newspapers continue to flourish and newsmagazines are widely read in print and through the Internet. Television broadcasts news on many channels, sometimes twenty-four hours a day. But how much of our news is really good? Most newscasts tell of war and woe, often with an underlying message that we need to fear. "Investigative reporting" often "uncovers" some new scare that plagues our daily life—hardly good news!

But today is Christmas Day. Today is the day for Good News. As Christians we declare boldly and loudly, "Our God reigns!" The joy of this day should cause us to sing in such a way that the very structures of the buildings we are in seem to break forth in joyous song. Despite many newscasts on the "true" meaning of Christmas, very few actually proclaim the good news of peace and salvation that Jesus has brought into our world. For this reason, it is incumbent upon us as Christians to be the broadcasters of this good news. This is why Paul appropriates our passage from Isaiah to underline his point that people can only believe if they hear, and they can only hear if the ones who are sent proclaim it: "As it is written, 'How beautiful are the feet of those who bring good news'" (Rom. 10:15).

Responsive Reading

PSALM 98 (RCL/BCP); 98:1-6 (RC/BCP, alt.)

This is a hymn of praise proclaiming the establishment of God's kingdom on earth in the context of the return from exile. The psalm is divided into three separate parts. The first part begins with a summons to Israel to worship (v. 1), followed by the reasons for worship (vv. 2-3). God's love and faithfulness have caused God to bring victory to Israel (literally, "salvation"; vv. 1, 2, 3). As a result of seeing this victory all nations are invited to the celebration (vv. 4-6). Doing so entails an admission that the Lord God is King over all peoples. Finally, the summons to praise is extended to the physical universe, anthropomorphized to join in the celebrations (vv. 7-9a). The psalm climaxes with the proclamation of the coming of God into our midst to judge the world with righteousness. Thus, upon this Christmas day we loudly proclaim,

> Joy to the world, the Lord is come!
> Let earth receive her King;
> Let every heart prepare Him room
> And heaven and nature sing.
> (Isaac Watts, "Joy to the World," 1719,
> based on Psalm 98)

Second Reading

HEBREWS 1:1-4 (5-12) (RCL); 1:1-12 (BCP); 1:1-6 (RC)

Interpreting the Text

The book of Hebrews was written to Jewish-Christians who had been tempted to abandon their faith in Christ. The author warns against such action and affirms the absolute superiority of Christ as the one who reveals and mediates God's grace. The author begins with the acknowledgment of a shift in God's vehicle of communication, which quickly becomes an affirmation of the fulfillment of God's promises through Christ. In times past God spoke variously through the prophets, but in "these last days" he speaks through his Son. The phrase "these last days" probably carries the expectation of Christ's imminent return. Although we live almost two millennia later, we still live on the edge of the end.

The vehicle for God's revelation is God's Son. The author then elaborates on this identity with seven phrases. The first two phrases address the issue of the identity of the Son. He is the one who will inherit from God all that is in God's possession, including the earth. Beyond that, the Son also acted as God's agent in the creation of all that exists. The next two phrases address the issue of how this filial relationship exists. As the sun radiates light so the Son radiates God's glory—and, like the sun and light, the two are inseparable. The Son is also an exact replication or reproduction of God—"clone" might be a more modern analogy. The next two phrases explicate what the Son does. In the present the Son's word (using the Greek word *hrema* rather than *logos*) sustains all things as the rational, underlying principle of the universe. In the past the Son has made a once-for-all cleansing for wrongdoing (cf. Heb. 7:27; 9:12, 26, 28; 10:10). Finally, the Son is now in the presence of God, not standing before God but seated beside God, indicating that his work is completed and God's purposes are fulfilled.

Verse 4 begins another contrast between Christ and Judaism. Drawing on the Hebrew Bible, the writer argues that Jesus is superior to angels because he is God's Son (1:5), because he will reign forever (1:8), and because he sits at God's right hand (1:13). One must keep in mind the setting within which the argument is set—Jewish-Christians are renouncing their faith and returning to Judaism. The author wants to sway them back to Jesus. The underlying message is not anti-Jewish so much as pro-Christ.

Responding to the Text

In "telephone line," a particularly popular game among youth groups, the players sit in a circle and the leader whispers a long message to one person. That person then whispers the message to the next person. The rules state that the message cannot be repeated or explained upon each whispering. By the time the message makes it around the circle it usually only bears cursory resemblance to the original message and can end up being quite hilarious. Although this exercise is usually used to illustrate the destructive effects of gossip, we might also see it as an analogy for Hebrews 1:1. In the past God spoke "in many and various ways by the prophets." God's communication was not compromised by this, but in each instance the prophets presented God's message variously, stamping it with their own personalities and sometimes only able to communicate part of the overall plan of God. It is as if each person in the telephone game called out her or his version of the message. Somewhere in the mix one could piece together the original communication, but it would take some effort (this is probably about as far as we should push the analogy, as it starts to break down!).

In contrast to this multifarious messaging system, the writer of Hebrews suggests that in Jesus we have a direct and unmediated communication from God. The identifications made—Son, heir, reflection, exact imprint—are there to underline Jesus' connection with God. There can be no clearer means whereby a message can be conveyed. In this, Christ is a superior revelation to anything in the past. To play with our analogy a bit, we might suggest that in Christ we have a divine equivalent of the cellular telephone—a clear and direct link between God and us.

JOHN 1:1-14 (RCL/BCP); 1:1-18 or 1:1-5, 9-14 (RC)

Interpreting the Text

John 1:1-18 functions as a prologue to the Fourth Gospel. As such, it raises some of the important themes, which will be pursued in more detail in the ensuing narrative, especially in christological statements, and the motifs of acceptance and rejection. The most profound statement in the prologue is the opening verse where the author introduces his "Logos theology." Although the Greek word *logos* (usually translated "Word") is used throughout the Gospel, the only reference to it in the distinct sense of a preexistent divine being is here in the prologue. There is no clear way in which to translate "logos" in this text, because it can stand for any one of a number of English concepts, including "word," "saying," "speech," "reason," or "plan." In fact, the large edition of the Greek lexicon by Liddell, Scott, and Jones lists fifty-three different possibilities. In some ways, it is perhaps better left untranslated.

The use of *logos* has its background in Jewish and Hellenistic culture, but it also carries a unique sense in the prologue. It plays on what the reader already knows while at the same time moving their thoughts into new areas. The Jewish reader would have been reminded by the opening words, "in the beginning," of the first chapter of Genesis. The parallel continues into the next verses where the themes of creation and light and darkness are recalled from Genesis. *Logos* would then have been connected with a personified, preexistent wisdom that was present at the creation of the world (Wis. 6–9). However, such readers would be amazed that wisdom could have personal attributes and, especially, incarnation in the flesh (v. 14). The Greek readers of the prologue would have been amazed that the rational principle of the universe (*logos*) became personalized and incarnate.

In the first verse "was" is used three times with three different connotations: existence, relationship, and predication. First, in terms of existence there is no indication how the Logos came to be; the Logos simply was. Second, in terms of relationship, the Logos was with God and as such provides the link, the only link, between God and the created order to which the reader belongs. Third, the Logos is predicated as God. "The Logos was God" is akin to the I-am sayings of Jesus in this Gospel, which climax in 8:58, "before Abraham was, I am." Divine claims are here being made for Jesus.

Many scholars argue that vv. 6-8, along with v. 15, are interpolations into the hymnic structure of the prologue and reflect a conflict between the Johannine community and the disciples of the Baptist. Other early Christian sources attest to such a conflict going on until the close of the first century. While not denying the Baptist's role as a messenger sent from God, these verses make a clear distinction between John and Jesus, with the emphasis being placed on the fact that the Baptist himself made that distinction. The affirmation in v. 15 again points to Jesus' preexistence.

John's Gospel is full of dualistic contrasts, such as light and darkness, spirit and flesh. We also find throughout the Gospel the contrast between those who accept Jesus and those who reject Jesus (an emphasis in the prologue). Those who reject Jesus are sweepingly characterized as "the world" and here are said to have "known him not" (v. 11). The pathos in this is emphasized in the notation that this nonrecognition came despite the fact that the world was made by the Logos/Jesus and has become his own home. Those who reject the Logos are thus characterized as "darkness" (v. 5). In contrast, those who have received him are characterized as "light." Light not only makes it possible for one to see but is also used in the Greco-Roman world of the sphere of ethical good and wisdom, whereas misdeeds are said to take place in darkness. In the Hebrew Bible, light is the first thing created—is supreme over all other elements.

ON CHRISTMAS DAY WE JOYOUSLY PROCLAIM TOGETHER THAT CHRIST OUR GOD IS IN OUR MIDST.

Verse 13 includes a contrast of birthing processes. To be born "of blood" is to be conceived in a human womb through the diversion of menstrual flow. To be born "of the desire of the flesh" is to be conceived as a result of sexual intercourse. To be born "of the desire of man" is to be conceived as the result of social convention, that is, a householder's desire for children to confirm his status in the world. All of this is to participate in the original creation and be one of "those who are his own" but who rejected him. In contrast, to know the Logos requires something more, namely, to be born "of God" in a new sense that will become apparent only as the Gospel unfolds (cf. John 3:1-10).

The climax of the entire prologue occurs in v. 14 with the shocking revelation that the Logos actually became human and "pitched his tent among us." In doing so, the divine presence is now localized in a single human presence living among other human beings. The author goes on to note that we have beheld his glory, not so much in his physical presence, but in the commitment of God in loving loyalty (grace) and faithfulness (truth) to the covenant God made with humans. The glory is manifest not only in the presence of the incarnate Logos but in the death and resurrection of Jesus that we know to be his purpose on earth (cf. 12:23-27).

It is Christmas Day, a day of family warmth, of giving and receiving, of celebration. In all these things we are reminded of the event upon which this day is founded. It is a day of family insofar as God the Father sent the child Jesus to bring light to human beings in the world and turn many of them into children of God to make them part of the family of God. It is a day of giving and receiving insofar as God gave the child Jesus to the world and those in the world either received him or do not. But in receiving the gift from God one enters into the new familial relationship with God. Finally, it is a day of celebration when we lift up our voices in praise and adoration of the child whose presence among us reveals that God is in our midst. "This is Christmas Day, the anniversary of the world's greatest event. To the one day all the early world looked forward; to the same day the latter world looks back. That day holds time together."[2]

One of the more controversial questions of the new millennium is the question concerning Jesus' identity. Jesus once asked his disciples, "Who do people say that I am?" Their varied responses are multiplied when that question is posed today. Despite the fact that in North America church attendance is generally on the decline, contemporary interest in the figure of Jesus has not waned, and there are still many for whom Jesus is important. During the Christmas season (and again at Easter) Jesus' "picture" frequently appears on the cover of widely read newsmagazines. Despite this interest, not everyone holds to a similar understanding of Jesus' identity. Among those sitting in the pew this morning, various—and often competing—Christologies will be operative.

The writer of the Fourth Gospel makes no apologies for his view. The ending of John's Gospel indicates that it was written to promote and sustain belief in Jesus as the "Christ, the Son of God" (20:30-31). Through such a belief one gains "eternal life"; faith is the condition of such salvation. Throughout the Fourth Gospel it is clear that Jesus makes divine claims for himself: "Before Abraham was, I am" (8:58). Much of this is predicated on the opening claim, "In the beginning . . . the Logos was God" (1:1). Dare we preach this challenging view today?

Henry Nouwen, in his diary of his experience at Genesee Abbey, writes of the crèche scene under the altar. The crèche consisted of three small, featureless, wooden figures representing the holy family. Although smaller than a human hand, a bright light shining upon them projected their large shadows upon the wall of the sanctuary. "Without the radiant beam of light shining into the darkness there is little to be seen. I might just pass by these three simple people and continue to walk in darkness. But everything changes with the light."[3]

FIRST SUNDAY AFTER CHRISTMAS

HOLY FAMILY

December 31, 2000

Revised Common	Episcopal (BCP)	Roman Catholic
1 Sam. 2:18-20, 26	Isa. 61:10—62:3	1 Sam. 1:20-22, 24-28
Ps. 148	Ps. 147 or 147:13-21	Ps. 84:2-3, 5-6, 9-10
Col. 3:12-17	Gal. 3:23-25, 4:4-7	1 John 3:1-2, 21-24
Luke 2:41-52	John 1:1-18	Luke 2:41-52

The occurrence of this first Sunday after Christmas on New Year's Eve means that many people will again be in a celebratory mood as they anticipate more time spent with family and friends. The readings for Holy Family Sunday allow us to focus on three aspects of family life: relationships within families, relationships within the family of God, and the relationship between families and God. It is an opportunity to look forward to how we will situate ourselves toward each of these aspects of family life in the coming year.

First Reading

1 SAMUEL 2:18-20, 26 (RCL); 1:20-22, 24-28 (RC)

Interpreting the Text

This short reading contrasts young Samuel with the sons of Eli, scoundrels who had no regard for the Lord (2:12) and whose sin was great (2:17). While "they treated the offerings of the Lord with contempt" (2:17), Samuel ministered before the Lord wearing a linen ephod, an indication of priesthood. The little robe brought each year for the growing boy by his mother served as a sign of her love and care. While Hannah and her husband attend to their annual sacrifice they also received a blessing from Eli (v. 20), resulting in the birth of five more children (v. 21)—an indication of the importance to God of Samuel's presence in the Temple. The final verse (26) again contrasts Samuel with the evil of the sons of Eli of whom the people speak ill and whom God desires to kill (vv. 22-25).

Despite her barrenness, Hannah prays to God and is answered with the birth of Samuel, which means, "name of God," indicating the close affinity that he will have with God throughout his life. Hannah fulfills her earlier vow by dedicating Samuel to God as a nazirite (cf. 1 Sam. 1:11). Samuel was taken to the house of God when he was weaned, probably around three years old.

Children are gifts from God. While rarely do we recognize these precious gifts through the radical sort of votive made by Hannah, we do bear responsibility to raise up our children in the presence and knowledge of God.

Responding to the Text

There is a threefold aspect to Samuel's ministry. First, Samuel served God (v. 18). Second, Samuel served his parents by being a source of pride and blessing (vv. 19-20). Third, Samuel served the people (v. 26). Yet all of this is based upon the willingness of Hannah to "lend" Samuel to God for the duration of Samuel's life (cf. 1 Sam. 1:28). How difficult it must have been to give up her firstborn child, particularly when she did not know whether she would bear another. Yet all parents must one day set their children free to pursue their calling in life. As we struggle through years of upbringing there is a strong desire to hang on, to hold back, to delay the inevitable. For some, this can be quite destructive. In letting go of our children, however, we can watch as they soar, serving God and others. In that, they too can bring to us pride and blessing.

ISAIAH 61:10—62:3 (BCP)

The prophet speaks from the perspective of Jerusalem of the salvation and restoration God will bring to the city after the exile (61:10a). It is like a set of clothing, the adornments of a bride and groom (v. 10b). The metaphor of the garden (v. 11a) underscores the point that the adornment is to be seen by others (v. 11b). Returning to the voice of God, the prophet declares in further detail how God will not rest until Jerusalem is restored and recognized among the nations (62:1-3).

Like the inhabitants of restored Jerusalem, as the recipients of salvation through the events of Christmas and Easter we collectively join in praise to God as a witness to all the world.

Responsive Reading

PSALM 148 (RCL)

This psalm is a progressive call to praise to the entire created universe. Those who inhabit the heavenly cosmos are first called to praise (vv. 1-3), then the earth and everything in it (vv. 7-12): ocean creatures and the weather, mountains, vegetation, animals, birds, and insects. Finally, human beings are called to worship God, beginning with those in positions of authority and concluding with all men and women. Let the whole universe praise God.

PSALM 147 or 147:13-21 (BCP)

The psalm begins with praise for God who cares for the oppressed (vv. 1-6). The second section sings the praises of the God of nature (vv. 7-11). The psalm concludes with praise for God's care for God's chosen people. The psalmist throughout brings together a sense of God's vast power over creation and God's loving care for particular groups of people.

PSALM 84:2-3, 5-6, 9-10 (RC)

Psalm 84 is set in the context of a pilgrimage to and from the Temple in Jerusalem. Verses 2-3 express a longing to dwell in the Temple. Verses 5-6 reflect the journey on the way to Jerusalem, and vv. 9-10 are part of the meditation at the Temple itself, in which the psalmist recognizes that a humble position before God is preferable to luxury among the wicked. Being in the presence of God brings great joy, and we rejoice in the presence of God among us in this Christmas season.

Second Reading

COLOSSIANS 3:12-17 (RCL)

Interpreting the Text

The new, continually renewed self with which Christians are clothed (3:10) carries with it community responsibilities as a people chosen, holy, and dearly loved by God (v. 12a). These responsibilities are given in four imperatives (in Greek). In the first imperative, "clothe yourself," the writer advocates ancient virtues of friendship: compassion, kindness, humility, meekness, and patience. These are illustrated with two cases: enduring one another and forgiving one another. One other virtue, however, he reserves to the end in order to highlight its significance—love (v. 14). The NRSV's "clothe yourself" is not present in the Greek, but the phrase clearly goes back to the original imperative. As in 1 Corinthians 13, love stands over and above all other actions that are lived out in community and in fact holds all other community actions together.

The second imperative, "let rule," plays on an athletic metaphor in making the peace of Christ the umpire or decision-maker in one's heart (v. 15). The reason given is the call of God to live at peace with one another in the one body of the Christian community. The third imperative declares simply, "be thankful," with no elaboration at all. The final imperative exhorts the indwelling of the word of Christ. This is worked out communally in three ways: teaching one another, admonishing and correcting one another, and singing together songs in praise of God (v. 16). Finally, Paul reminds the Colossians that whatever they do and say must be motivated by thanksgiving for what Jesus has done for them (v. 17).

Responding to the Text

For some years now a certain running-shoe manufacturer has run a fairly widespread and successful campaign advertising its shoes under the banner "Just Do It!" Appealing to our culture's heightened sense of individualism, magazine advertisements and television commercials show a lone runner pushing herself or himself to the limits of endurance. Of course, to be able to do this, one must put on a pair of their shoes!

In today's reading we have a Christian version of "Just Do It!" Love, compassion, kindness, humility, meekness, patience, tolerance, forgiveness, peace, thankfulness, admonishment, teaching, and singing—all are characteristics of the Christian life. As with the running shoes, we must clothe ourselves with these virtues. It is a precondition for optimum performance. However, unlike the running shoe commercials, living the Christian life is not individualistic and competitive. In fact, it is anything but that. All of these characteristics of the Christian life can be lived out only in community and mutuality. They require others to participate with us—it is a team sport, so to speak. Together we are God's chosen ones and together we must live as the family of God.

GALATIANS 3:23-25; 4:4-7 (BCP)

In this complex passage Paul uses a number of metaphors, many taken from the realm of family life, to explain the human situation before and after the coming of Christ. The context is a larger argument over the role of the Jewish law in the Christian life. Paul notes three distinct periods—before Christ, Christ's coming, and after Christ. Before Christ the law functioned as a protective guard, akin to a garrison watching over a town to keep out intruders, although it also functioned to keep those inside from leaving (3:23). It also had a supervisory role, akin to a teacher who looked after the raising of a child from ages six to sixteen in Greco-Roman households (3:24). In this capacity the law made us no better than slaves, as we had no freedom, no power of attorney (4:1-3, 7). After Christ's coming, the human-divine relationship has changed radically. We no longer need a supervisory guardian; we are grown up (3:25; 4:7). Under the law we were slaves/minors but in Christ we have become children/heirs. (See further the comments on the second reading for January 1, 2001, The Name of Jesus.)

1 JOHN 3:1-2, 21-24 (RC)

God's love for us is evidenced in the relationship God has established through the gift of giving us the status of God's children (3:1). According to John, however, as children we are not in our final state of maturity (3:2). Although unclear on the details ("it is not yet revealed"), John points out that we will be like God, when God is revealed. Having just moved back to the city of my upbringing, I frequently hear comments from friends and colleagues of my parents that I look more and more like my father. This growing resemblance to one or the other or both of one's parents is common enough. It is this same process that we experience as Christians. As part of that process we are able boldly to approach God (3:21) and receive good things from God (3:22). This, however, is predicated on our doing God's will, which the writer defines as believing in Jesus and loving one another (3:23-24).

The Gospel
LUKE 2:41-52 (RCL/RC)

Interpreting the Text

After Jesus is dedicated in the Temple (2:22-38), he returns with Mary and Joseph to Nazareth (2:39). Luke then briefly summarizes twelve years of Jesus' upbringing in one verse (2:40) and then tells the only story of Jesus' childhood found in the New Testament. The story opens with Jesus' parents making their annual pilgrimage to Jerusalem. While not out of the ordinary, this is the first of many parallels we find between this story and the story of Hannah and Samuel in 1 Samuel 1–3. In both stories there is a presentation of a child of the Lord (1 Sam. 1:22; Luke 2:22). Hannah sings praises of thanksgiving for Samuel (1 Sam. 2:1-10), and the prophet Anna praises God and gives thanks for Jesus (Luke 2:36-38; Anna is the Greek form of the name Hannah); Eli blesses Samuel's parents (1 Sam. 2:20) and Simeon blesses Jesus' parents (Luke 2:34). Both stories include a refrain about the growth of the child (1 Sam. 2:26; Luke 2:40). In both accounts the child appears in the Temple without his parents—in the case of Samuel, ministering under the guidance of Eli the prophet (1 Sam. 3:1-18), in the case of Jesus, having a discussion with the religious teachers (Luke 2:41-51). And both childhood accounts end with a second refrain (1 Sam. 3:19; Luke 2:52). There are too many parallels for this to be sheer coincidence. It is meant to draw attention to a role Jesus will play in his ministry in inaugurating a new era in salvation history. As Samuel the prophet was the key player in the shift of Israel from a federation of twelve tribes to a nation under a single king (the kingdom of Israel), Jesus now moves the people into a new epoch—the kingdom of God.

This story about Jesus' boyhood also functions in a number of other ways within Luke's narrative. Jesus' participation in discussion with the religious teachers of the Temple shows his intellectual abilities, his keenness for religious activity, and his honor among his elders. It also anticipates what is to come in the following chapters of Luke, when Jesus will frequently engage the religious leaders, especially during the Temple narrative of chapters 21 and 22.

The story also places Jesus within a larger tradition of wise persons beginning an early career. The Jewish historian Josephus tells us that "Samuel had now completed his twelfth year when he began to act as a prophet" (*Antiquities* 5.348). The Greco-Roman biographer Diogenes Laertius tells us that the philosopher Epicurus "began to study philosophy when he was twelve years old, and started his own school at thirty-two" (*Epicurus* 10.14). Thus, Jesus fits within the tradition of other great persons of antiquity.

THROUGH THE CHILD WE HAVE BECOME THE FAMILY OF GOD.

The story also hints at coming conflict between Jesus' mission and his family's expectations. Although "obey your parents" is one of the Ten Commandments in Judaism and a cardinal rule in the Greco-Roman world, often a higher rule of obedience to God (or the gods) could prevail. For Jesus, doing God's will ultimately will override familial obligations (cf. Luke 8:19-21). For this moment, however, he acquiesces to his mother's wishes and returns to Nazareth with his parents.

The story also shows Jesus' awareness that he has a special role to play. There is a twofold thrust to Jesus' response to his mother in v. 39. The Greek sentence quite literally reads, "Did you not know that I must be in my Father's?" The sentence is incomplete. It is a Greek expression used to indicate someone's house, hence "my father's house." However, as the NRSV note points out, it can also mean someone's business interests or affairs. Thus, Jesus is not only physically in God's house but is also going about God's business. This confuses his parents, not least of which because of the play on "father," by which Jesus means God rather than Joseph, as his mother means in v. 48.

Responding to the Text

I remember as a child an idyllic day at the beach being shattered when my parents realized that my six-year-old brother had wandered away when backs were turned. Seized with panic they enlisted family, friends, strangers, and park staff in an earnest search. A few hours passed before we found him. The magnitude of their panic never really impacted me until a few years ago when my own three-year-old daughter "disappeared" from the church basement. Within five minutes I had located her with the teens from the youth group. That was five minutes, only five minutes, of sheer panic!

Jesus was gone for an entire day before his parents began to look for him. Imagine the horror, the panic, when they realized that he was not with them. Group travel was customary along this road because there was safety in numbers, both from animal attacks and from bandits. It was not until three days later that they found him back at the Temple. Mary's subdued question in v. 48 hardly does justice to the emotion that was felt.

In both of my illustrations, my brother and my daughter, as in the case of Jesus, it is the seekers, not the lost, who are upset. Jesus is presented as doing what seems only natural, almost taken aback that his parents should expect to find him elsewhere. Where *do* we expect to find Jesus? Some would immediately suggest that we would find Jesus in church, just as his parents found him in the Temple. But this is hardly the point of the story. As we saw above, the story functions on a number of different levels in Luke's narrative. In each case it is not the "Where?" of finding Jesus that is important. Rather, the focus is on the "What?" of finding Jesus—"What was it that Jesus was doing?"

Jesus was bringing about God's kingdom upon earth. Each one of his actions, as a child and as an adult, whether debating, healing, teaching, or dying, was part of this larger program. In seeking for Jesus, then, perhaps we should not concern ourselves with "Where?" Perhaps we should ourselves be involved in the "What?" aspects of Jesus' ministry. As we engage in doing the will of God, we will find Jesus; or maybe it is better put that he will find us. In the film *Jesus of Montreal* (1989), an actor, Daniel, is asked to perform in a passion play. In doing research on his subject a librarian brings him a number of books about Jesus. She then whispers furtively to him, "Looking for Jesus?" When he nods, she cryptically responds, "It is he that will find you." Sure enough, as the story progresses, Daniel's investigation of Jesus leads him to become more and more like Jesus in his day-to-day life. As we seek for Jesus this year, perhaps it is Jesus who will find—and use—us.

JOHN 1:1-18 (BCP)

For comments on this text please refer to the previous chapter, The Nativity of Our Lord (Christmas Day), December 25, 2000.

There is an old Chinese story in which a teacher asks his students to identify the most satisfying thing in life. After many answers, such as "a happy marriage," "good health," and "close friends," the sage said that they had failed to arrive at the right answer. He said, "The most satisfying thing in life is to see a child confidently walk down the road on his own after you have shown him the way to go."[4] Samuel and Jesus struck out on their own at a young age. As ministers we need to nurture the children of God so that they too may walk down the road confidently serving God.

THE NAME OF JESUS (HOLY NAME)

NEW YEARS DAY

January 1, 2001

Revised Common	Episcopal (BCP)	Roman Catholic
Num. 6:22-27	Exod. 34:1-8	Num. 6:22-27
Ps. 8	Ps. 8	Ps. 67:2-3, 5-6, 8
Gal. 4:4-7 or Phil. 2:5-11	Rom. 1:1-7	Gal. 4:4-7
Luke 2:15-21	Luke 2:15-21	Luke 2:16-21

This final feast day of the Christmas season focuses on the name of God, particularly in the Gospel reading, which concludes with the naming of the infant Jesus at his circumcision (Luke 2:21). In Numbers 6:22-27 God's name is placed upon Israel. In the alternative reading from Exodus 34:1-8 the name of God is expanded through God's self-disclosure. Psalm 8 declares the majesty of God's name throughout all the earth, while Psalm 67 invokes the priestly blessing of Numbers 6:24-26. Each of the second readings also raises up the name of God, through the proclamation of "Abba" in Galatians 4:6, the "name above all names" in Philippians 2:9, and the mission for the sake of Jesus' name in Romans 1:5.

First Reading

NUMBERS 6:22-27 (RCL/RC)

Interpreting the Text

This blessing prescribes God's good gifts upon the people in three lines parallel in form and content, each with two clauses. The name of God (YHWH, "the Lord") is invoked in the first clause of each line as a means of emphasizing God as the one who bestows the blessing. Within each blessing the "you" is second-person singular and could be referring to the collective Israel or an individual within the people of God—probably both.

In the first line the word "bless" involves a full life, with such things as material prosperity, good health, and the presence of God. "Keep" is a term of protection from enemies, from misfortune and disaster, and from evil. The second line uses the anthropomorphism of God's face shining upon the people, a metaphor for benevolence and favor. That God would be "gracious to you" implies mercy in the face of some justified displeasure on the part of God. The third line calls for God to lift up God's countenance, an expression of turning to someone in friendship. The giving of peace is not only the absence of war and strife but includes prosperity, health, and the presence of God, the absolute well-being of the person. The concluding sentence delineates the role of the priests as mediators in placing the name of God upon the people of Israel.

Responding to the Text

The end of the Christmas season and the eve of a new year provides the appropriate setting within which to reflect upon the blessings that we have received over the last year and the promises that we can claim for the new year. The material blessings are often obvious at this time of year, when people may be wearing new clothes or jewelry, or young people may be playing the latest hand-held video game in the back pew! Yet these material things are simply a by-product of God's blessing upon us. God's real blessing is good health, peace, family and friends, and God's presence. Yet it is all too easy to forget such blessings in the face of rampant materialism. The priestly blessing from Numbers can create a time of corporate and individual self-reflection upon the true source of our blessings. In this we experience the presence of God in our midst.

EXODUS 34:1-8 (BCP)

God's self-revelation to Moses occurs in the context of the recutting and reinscribing of the tablets of the Commandments (vv. 1-4). A voice within a cloud on Mount Sinai proclaims the name of YHWH, the unutterable, indefinable name (v. 5). This self-disclosure is followed by a description of God's character (vv. 6-7). God's "steadfast love" was behind God's establishing the covenant with the people. God's "faithfulness" is God's truth and reliability in all things. However, there is a reminder that, despite God's mercy, grace, and slow anger, those who remain in their guilt, and their descendants, will bear the punishment of God (v. 7b).

Summit meetings are frequently used to bring together world dignitaries, politicians, and important business leaders for high-level negotiations and the brokering of important deals. One can imagine the level of posturing, grandstanding, and compromise that must take place for a summit to be successful. The "summit" meeting on the top of Mount Sinai is of a different sort. Moses enters into God's presence without pretense. In fact, the tone of the "summit" is set by the opening comments by God, in response to which Moses quickly bows and worships (v. 8). Although Moses goes on to broker a deal with God (Exod. 34:9-10), it is clear that the power lies with God.

RESPONSIVE READING

PSALM 8 (RCL/BCP)

This hymn of praise begins and ends with a refrain proclaiming that God's greatness is evident in all the earth (vv. 1, 9). It is the name, the identity of God that is manifest in the work of creation. God's character, however, is seen also in God's decision to establish and empower all human beings as stewards of God's creation (vv. 4-8). Unfortunately, we have not always been good stewards of the created order. The New Testament incorporates this psalm to proclaim that the work of Christ has begun the process of true subjection but not yet completed it (Heb. 2:6-10; 1 Cor. 15:20-28; cf. Matt. 21:15-16).

PSALM 67:2-3, 5-6, 8 (RC)

The reminder of God's promised blessing (v. 1) is invoked as a means whereby God may be known by all nations upon the earth (vv. 2-5). The specific context of this requested blessing is agricultural. The earth has yielded forth crops for which the people are thankful (v. 6). However, the people desire that this bounty continue (v. 7). Thus, the requested "salvation" of v. 2 is probably rain and good harvest.

SECOND READING

GALATIANS 4:4-7 (RCL/RC)

Interpreting the Text

Two primary actions of God are the focus of this passage. First, God sent God's son (vv. 4-5). Second, God sent the Spirit (vv. 6-7). For each statement a reason is given, the manner is expressed and the result is announced. First, God sent God's son because the time was appropriate for God to step into human history in a direct and unmediated way. To that end, Jesus came as any human being would, through the birthing process and "under law," that is, under the conditions of a fallen world, vulnerable to the temptation to sin. The result of Jesus' coming, predicated on the assumption of the cross and resurrection, was a new status for human persons. Rather than slaves, the potential to be God's children was opened up (v. 6). God then sent the Spirit for the reason that we are now

God's children. The Spirit is sent through the intimate, personal expression of familial connection ("Abba! Father!") with the result that we are not only children but heirs. We have full participation in the kingdom of God (for further comments on this reading see the alternative second reading in the previous chapter, pages 55–56).

Responding to the Text

Among the many songs of the Swedish rock band Abba was "Knowing Me, Knowing You." In the context of relationships they sing, "Knowing me, knowing you, it's the best I can do." Paul tells us that through Jesus we have a new relationship with God. God has reached down to us to change our status and empower us with the Spirit. We need to understand how this changed status has effected who we are—"knowing me." At the same time, it is now up to us to reach back to God from our side of the relationship. Calling God "Abba" is a privilege and an honor, but we must go beyond that to explore the full implications of God as loving parent—"knowing you." Although Abba did not put it into a religious context, when it comes to God, "knowing me, knowing you" truly is one of the best things that we can do.

PHILIPPIANS 2:5-11 (RCL alt.)

Interpreting the Text

Paul uses this hymn to address disharmony and competition for honor within the Philippian congregation (2:1-4) by suggesting that they adopt the same approach as Christ (v. 5). In the first half of the hymn Christ is presented as willingly undertaking a downward movement. First, he emptied himself of any status he had through association with the divine (v. 6). Second, he identified himself with the lowest rank of those in Greco-Roman society, the slave (v. 7), by his willingness to touch and be touched by the dregs of society. Third, he progressed even lower in undergoing a slave's death on the cross (v. 8).

There follows an upward movement wherein God is now the agent of the action. God "highly exalts" Jesus (v. 9a), lifting Jesus up to a place above everything else in creation, presumably through the resurrection. Unlike the first half of the hymn, there is no progression of movement here. God has simply raised Jesus to a position of supreme honor. With this comes the bestowal of the name "Lord," which becomes synonymous with the name Jesus (v. 9b, 11a). There is a clear connection here to the divine name of YHWH, rendered "Lord" in the Greek version of the Hebrew Bible. The response to the name "Jesus" is now expected to be the same as to "YHWH"—public honor, glory, and worship (vv. 10-11).

Name recognition is very important in North American society. Brand-name recognition is central to commercial marketing strategies, and a catchy name can be a key to business success. Name recognition is equally important in the entertainment industry, where some celebrities can command millions of dollars for walk-on appearances because their name will draw in large crowds and hefty profits. Even in Christian circles, big-name speakers are used to draw large crowds, sometimes for evangelism, sometimes for fund-raising. The Philippian hymn reverses all of this by tying together Christology and community. Jesus, who had "all-star" potential on earth chose to put it all aside to live a life of relative obscurity. For Christians, following Christ and living communally, in humility and service, will result in the further exaltation of Jesus as Lord among all the earth.

ROMANS 1:1-7 (BCP)

Between his introduction of himself (v. 1a) and his greeting of the Roman Christians (vv. 7-8) Paul has a lengthy excursus with a decidedly christological emphasis—what Martin Luther called Paul's "gospel in a nutshell." At the core of the "good news" is Jesus, about whom Paul gives three details. Jesus was a human being of the Jewish race (v. 3). He was known to be divine both through the Spirit and through his resurrection (v. 4). It was through Jesus that Paul was commissioned as an apostle (v. 5a) and the Romans were called to faith in Christ (v. 6). Paul then notes that his work is carried out not for his own glorification but to enhance Jesus' reputation among the nations (v. 5b).

In our society, one's identity is very much tied up in what one does. Introductions and handshakes are often followed with, "So, what do you do?" Paul's self-disclosure in our passage is also tied to what he does: he is a slave of Jesus and an apostle (or messenger) of God. Paul even presents Jesus not only in terms of who he is (God's son, descendant of David) but by what he does: Jesus brings grace and apostleship, and Jesus functions as our Lord. The passage presents an opportunity for us to reflect on how what we do reflects who we are.

THE GOSPEL

LUKE 2:15-21 (RCL/BCP); 2:16-21 (RC)

Interpreting the Text

In this reading we return to the story of the visit of the shepherds to the place of Jesus' birth. I have already made some observations about these shepherds in the comments on the Gospel for Christmas Eve, December 24, 2000, where the focus was on their social status. Here I want to highlight their three responses to the great events surrounding them. In the first instance, the shepherds respond to the appearance of the angel of the Lord and the heavenly host by going quickly to Bethlehem (vv. 15-16). In this case, they are probably motivated by curiosity and a need to verify what they have heard from the angel. When they arrive they respond to the sight of the babe in the manger by making known the heavenly message of a child born to be Savior and Messiah (v. 17; cf. 2:11). Finally, as they depart their response to the entire sequence of the events is to glorify and praise God (v. 20).

Alongside the shepherds' responses, two other responses are recorded in our text. Mary responds to the shepherds' message with thoughtful, intelligent reflection (v. 19). Although perhaps not yet fully comprehending everything that God plans (cf. 2:50), the process of coming to understanding is underway.

Another response occurs in v. 18, where we find a curious note in the text that is often glossed over quickly. Our usual depiction of the nativity includes Mary and Joseph, some animals, the shepherds, and some "wise men." However, in Luke's account there is no prior mention of the wise men. Nevertheless, Luke records that in response to the shepherds' message "all who heard it were amazed" (v. 18). To whom does the "all" refer? Surely not just Mary and Joseph, particularly because in the next verse Mary is distinguished from the "all" who were amazed. Some posit that it is all the residents of Bethlehem, suggesting that the shepherds have become the first evangelists. Yet the location of the event seems to be focused on the manger scene. In an earlier comment on Luke 2:7 (December 24, 2000) I suggested that Jesus was born not in a "barn" but in a room attached to Joseph's relative's dwelling in which the animals were kept. In such a scenario, Mary and Joseph would have been surrounded by friends and family, all of whom were amazed at the incredible story that the shepherds told.

When the name of God is revealed, we respond with worship and proclamation.

Although not a direct response to the words of the angels, Mary and Joseph participate in the general response of all Jewish parents to the covenant God established with Abraham and Israel—they take their baby boy to be circumcised on the eighth day in fulfillment of Jewish Torah (cf. Gen. 17:9-13; Lev. 12:3). At that time, the boy is named Jesus. The name itself is the Greek form of Joshua, and indicates salvation from God. Quite literally, it means "YHWH is salvation" or "YHWH is savior" and thus anticipates the role Jesus will play through his ministry and through his death and resurrection.

The assignment of this name to the baby was made by the angel at the annunciation to Mary (Luke 1:31). In the annunciation story (Luke 1:26-38) the angel Gabriel not only designates the name to be given to Mary's son but also expands it with two other names, or titles, that Mary's son will carry, along with the characteristics that these names imply. First, Jesus will be called "the Son of the

Most High" and will be given the throne of David to rule over Israel forever (1:32-33). Thus, Jesus is to be the kingly Messiah, fulfilling Israel's expectations of a righteous ruler. Second, Jesus will be called "Son of God"(1:35). The title used here is indicative of Jesus' divine origin and parallels the previous title in that "Most High" is a common title for God in the Hebrew Bible. In connection with the title "Son of God" the angel indicates that the child will be "holy" or perhaps "called holy," again emphasizing his divine origins. Thus, when Mary and Joseph give the boy the name "Jesus" as directed by the angel (2:21) they are giving him an identity that goes much beyond simple designation. They are proclaiming his true identity, Son of God, and his role, Savior.

Responding to the Text

My wife and I were just blessed with the birth of our second child, a son, and although he was born to great joy, he was almost born without a name. Each of us had names picked out for both a son or a daughter. However, agreement in our lists was almost impossible. While in the delivery room, we finally hit upon a name we both liked! This is not as bad (I hope) as another couple we know who deliberated over their son's name until nine months *after* his birth! In both cases, the deliberation over the naming of a child reflects a recognition that a person's name is very important; often a name can characterize a person. Biases for or against certain names are often grounded in experiences that we have had with other people that bear that name, or the names of characters in books, movies, and television shows. In the Bible, as in antiquity generally, names often carry with them meanings that express the character or emotions of the parents or child.

As today's reading shows, the name given to the child of Mary was not arbitrary or ill thought out. In very fact, the name given to the child was preordained before his birth through a messenger from God. That name, Jesus, so familiar to us, carries with it the destiny and the work of the child—"YHWH is savior." In itself it was a common enough name among Jewish males of the first century. However, it is imbued with new meaning through the death and resurrection of the one who bears that name.

Recognition of Jesus' name is not enough. One must also ask how we respond to God. And here the shepherds become a paradigm for us to follow, as the shepherds reflect the proper response to God. They glorify and praise God for all they have seen and heard and they make known their experiences to those around them. As Frederick Danker suggests, "What [the shepherds] found at Bethlehem is spelled out in detail in order to emphasize the nature of the response that follows. Depth of spiritual commitment is determined by the quality of one's fidelity after the majestic voice is no longer heard."[5] Once the Christmas season has passed and all the special services and Christmas carols have faded into the background, will we still hear and proclaim the wonderful message which was first proclaimed long ago in a small village in Judea through the naming of an infant?

In *Romeo and Juliet,* Shakespeare penned the words, "What's in a name? That which we call a rose, by any other name would smell as sweet" (Act 2, sc. 2.1.66). Although I would hardly attempt to contend with the great bard himself, there is indeed much in a name. Sometimes a name conveys the character of the one that bears it, and it is by a name that we recognize the person or object about which we speak. For Christians, it is the name of Jesus that we confess and proclaim as God.

NOTES

1. Jane Schaberg, "Luke," *The Woman's Bible Commentary*, ed. Carol A. Newsome and Sharon H. Ringe (Louisville: Westminster John Knox, 1992) 284.

2. Alexander Smith, quoted by Donna Green, *Christmas at our House* (New York: Smithmark, 1995) 46.

3. Robert Durback, ed., *Seeds of Hope: A Henry Nouwen Reader* (New York: Doubleday, 1989) 164.

4. Source unknown. Told by Paul J. Wharton, *Stories and Parables for Preachers and Teachers* (New York and Mahwah: Paulist Press, 1986) 35.

5. Frederick W. Danker, *Jesus and the New Age: A Commentary on St. Luke's Gospel*, 2nd ed. (Philadelphia: Fortress, 1988) 60.

THE SEASON OF EPIPHANY

RENITA J. WEEMS

EPIPHANY CELEBRATES THE MANIFESTATION of our Savior's glory in the ordinary here and now of human existence. "Epiphany," from the Greek word *epiphaneia,* means "to manifest, show forth, or make clear." Part of the expectation of Epiphany is that with our Lord's appearance come glorious displays of his saving power. Like the Bethlehem star that lit up the sky by throwing off thousands of tiny particles of light, each one more illuminating than the other, Epiphany allows us to journey into the new year beholding from different angles what it means that Christ was born in the world. Each time we glimpse him we understand more and better his mission to the world.

The word "epiphany" was not originally a religious term but first designated in the Greco-Roman world the official state visit of a king or emperor to a city in a province, especially those occasions on which he publicly displayed himself to the citizenry. The early church appropriated the term and came to apply it to Jesus' earliest manifestations to the world as Savior and divine, the chief of which took place at the time of his birth.

Not until the second half of the fourth century did both Eastern and Western churches accept feasts of the birth of Christ, with the Eastern Church reserving January 6 as the feast of the Epiphany, commemorating not only Christ's birth but also the arrival of the Magi from the East and the baptism of Jesus by John the Baptist in the Jordan. Eventually the nativity was detached from the feast of the Epiphany and was reserved for December 25, as was the custom with Western churches, leaving January 6 as the day celebrating his manifestation especially to the gentile world (hence the arrival of the Magi). Although the Magi's adoration of the Christ was always a main focus of the Epiphany feast, eventually the baptism of Christ and the miracle at Cana came to be associated with the feast, because also on those occasions, church authorities argued, Jesus manifested himself in a powerful way.

Drawn by the glory of the heavens at night, the Magi from the east embarked upon a journey that would take them away from home and far away from everything familiar and comfortable. They had to open themselves up to new experiences, new ways of knowing, and new revelations in order to behold the Christ child in his stall in Bethlehem. Their journey into new territory is not unlike the journey contemporary readers take each time they turn to the Bible for fresh revelations. To see him anew we must remain open to new perspectives. The lectionary during the Epiphany season presents a series of "epiphanies" that cast new light upon Jesus' mission. The message of Epiphany is that seeing Christ is the not the end but the beginning of the journey. Our journey through these epiphanies will take us into deeper knowledge of him as God's gift to the world.

SEEING CHRIST IS THE NOT THE END BUT THE BEGINNING OF THE JOURNEY.

Finally, basic to the Christian faith is a belief in a God who communicates, who acts, who reveals, who desires to be known. The Advent season teaches that the *mysterion* begins with God. God's initiative to be known and human yearning to know God come face to face during Epiphany. One of the collects for Epiphany in the Book of Common Prayer reads, "O Lord, we beseech thee mercifully to receive the prayers of thy people which call upon thee; and grant that they may both perceive and know what things they ought to do. . . ." Here and there, now and then, God breaks into the human realm, amidst all of its day-to-day ordinariness, leaving us forever transformed and transfixed. It is as if our eyelids open, curtains part, and for a brief moment, we receive a sudden glimpse into the total reality of a situation. Epiphany brings new learning, new insights, and new opportunities for us to know God's perfect will by sending Christ into the world. It also gives us the opportunity to glimpse once more what we may have forgotten since we last beheld him, and that is the depth, breadth, and height of God's love toward us. The lessons of Epiphany teach us that because he understands the frailty of our humanity, and out of his great love for us, Christ manifested himself not once, twice, but again and again—and desires to be manifested again and again to each generation.

THE EPIPHANY OF OUR LORD

JANUARY 6, 2001

REVISED COMMON	EPISCOPAL (BCP)	ROMAN CATHOLIC
Isa. 60:1-6	Isa. 60:1-6, 9	Isa. 60:1-6
Ps. 72:1-7, 10-14	Ps. 72 or 72:1-2, 10-17	Ps. 71:1-2, 7-8, 10-13
Eph. 3:1-12	Eph. 3:1-12	Eph. 3:2-3a, 5-6
Matt. 2:1-12	Matt. 2:1-12	Matt. 2:1-12

FIRST READING

ISAIAH 60:1-6 (RCL/RC); 60:1-6, 9 (BCP)

Interpreting the Text

At last the light has come! Arise, offspring of Zion, those who have languished in exile! The glory of Zion has risen over the people of God. Now every nation will discover what the righteous have always known, namely, that Yahweh, Savior, Redeemer, the Mighty One of Jacob, is neither impotent nor deaf (Isa. 59:1). When Yahweh saw justice turned back and righteousness standing at a distance (v. 14), Yahweh decided to come to Zion, robed as a Redeemer, on behalf of those in Jacob who turn from transgression (v. 20). The resurrection of Zion that is on the horizon will not be simply a historical event; but an eschatological event, rooted in eternity where Yahweh reveals to Israel and to the nations Yahweh's larger purpose and plan of salvation for the whole earth.

The prophet behind Isaiah 56–66 is an anonymous voice who focuses his prophecies on declaring what Yahweh expects a redeemed people to do as they take up their new life in the ruins of their old city. By fixing his attention solely on Zion and insisting in so many words that Yahweh's name is wrapped up in Zion's fortune, the prophet situates himself in a long line of preaching that stretches all the way back at least to the eighth century to Isaiah of Jerusalem (chaps. 1–39) who preached to Zion when the nation was still at the apex of its strength and glory (742–701 B.C.E.). Even back then Isaiah warned the inhabitants of the city against being haughty and overconfident and not trusting in Yahweh. But his words fell on deaf ears, and Zion would pay dearly two centuries later by being burned to the ground and having many of its citizens, if not killed during the invasion, then carted off into Babylonian captivity (597–538 B.C.E.). While still in captivity Second Isaiah would take up the thought of his predecessor by resurrecting Zion in the minds and hearts of those in Babylon through his lyrical preaching, claiming that Yahweh had not been defeated, as some supposed, but had punished Zion for her sins and was now prepared to pour his spirit on Zion and make a way in the wilderness for Zion's return (chaps. 40–55).The fate of Zion was never far from the minds of those who lived through its destruction in the sixth century nor of those who felt the aftershocks of its downfall for the decades that followed (Jeremiah, Ezekiel, cf. Lamentation and Pss. 126, 137). By the time Third Isaiah came on the scene, probably some time after 530 B.C.E., the former captives had begun to trickle back into Zion, and the sobering reality of what it would take to rebuild Zion from ruin was beginning to settle in, and doubts and discord were surfacing.

"Darkness" is a recurring metaphor used in Isaiah to suggest injustice, anarchy, and a lack of faithfulness on the part of the people of Israel (Isa. 5:20; 29:15; 42:7; 50:10). Third Isaiah uses "darkness" here to refer both to Zion's former splendor which has been overshadowed by ruin and devastation, and to the "cloud of unknowing" that covers the earth and prevents people from recognizing Yahweh as the Holy One of Israel. Third Isaiah's mission is to announce that darkness is about to end. The glory of Yahweh is about to burst forth and eclipse the darkness. Those whom the prophet refers to in the earlier chapter as groping about blindly, engulfed by the darkness of wickedness (59:10), who almost fainted from waiting for the light, will now have the opportunity to bask in the redeeming light of glory. "Light" and "salvation" are often used synonymously in the Old Testament, but the salvation Third Isaiah imagines Yahweh bringing is like a two-edged sword. It is a sign of piercing judgment against those guilty of misdeeds and at the same time a beacon of redemption for those languishing under injustice. Details are admittedly sketchy in Isaiah 56–66 giving rise to a wide range of speculation about the historical circumstances alluded to in the oracles. Nevertheless there is a clear sense in Third Isaiah that Yahweh is preparing to move on Zion's behalf, forgiving Zion for her wickedness, restoring her fortunes, and drawing people from the far parts of the world to take part in rebuilding her.

THE LIGHT OF THE GLORY OF YAHWEH IS AN IRRESISTIBLE FORCE.

The light of the glory of Yahweh is an irresistible force, according to the prophet, drawing all kinds of people to the light of Zion. Caravans of human beings sail and ride camels to make their way to the source of the light. Nations come bringing their wealth and spices. Distant offspring travel the distance home, even if it takes bringing the young who are still nursing at the breast. Even the inhabitants of Zion will find themselves radiating with joy and rejoicing upon beholding the one who comes to redeem the whole earth. But there is more.

Non-Hebrews, strangers, foreigners will have a place in the restored Zion. They will in fact play a threefold role in Zion's restored fortunes: they will see and behold Zion's vindication at the hands of Yahweh; they will contribute materially to Zion's rebuilding (61: 5); and, above all, they will become a part of the newly constituted Zion being invited to serve as priests, observe the Sabbath, and become a part of the newly constituted covenant people (56:3-8; 60:1-2).

Responding to the Text

Preaching as he was to an audience that had grown weary and listless by their humiliation as a nation during the sixth century, and feeling defeated by the slow and painful task of rebuilding, Third Isaiah used the image of a light shining through the darkness to rouse his listeners from their near slumber. He likens it here to the sun bursting through, announcing the dawn of a new day and making it difficult for those who are asleep to stay unconscious. "Arise! Wake Up! Get Up!" he shouts, "It's a new day!" Although the words "light" and "dark" are frequently used in scripture to characterize and contrast good and evil, modern interpreters would do well to shy away from relying too heavily upon the word "darkness" to characterize unrighteousness and wickedness lest they be guilty of being insensitive to the ways in which such poetic references have shaped our understanding of the universe and have played a part in demonizing and oppressing darker skinned peoples of the world. The time has come to think of new metaphors when old ones create more problems in our day than they solve.

While Epiphany celebrates God's revelation and manifestation, it also celebrates the vindication of the faithful. That vindication will be chiefly in the form of other nations acknowledging the authority of Yahweh as the one God. Behold the long awaited bright light shining above, cries the prophet. The pathway is clear. Strangers are coming. Family members are on their way. But even before the others come in their caravans, God's people must wake up, get up, behold the light for themselves, and make ready for this new thing that is being done on the earth. People—even strangers—are coming from far and near to see the light. What should be Zion's response to those coming? Resentment? No. There is no time for resentment. Radiance and rejoicing are the only appropriate response to the Redeemer's appearance.

RESPONSIVE READING

PSALM 72:1-7, 10-14 (RCL); 72 OR 72:1-2, 10-17 (BCP); 72:1-2, 7-8, 10-13 (RC)

This is a "royal psalm," so named because of its extravagant, courtly descriptions of the Davidic king as God's representative ruler on earth. Steeped in the mind-set of the ancient Near Eastern world, which believed that the gods carried out their purposes through earthly kings, royal psalms like Psalm 72 (cf. Pss. 2, 18, 21, 45) extol the king as the source of divine blessing in a nation.

Probably commissioned for a coronation ceremony for one of the Davidic kings, plenty of other occasions would come up during a king's reign when the flattering court language of Psalm 72 was called for. At a birthday celebration for the king, upon the birth of the king's heir, or on those rare occasions when the king made an official visit to one of his provinces with his royal brigade in tow, hymns like Psalm 72 were standard repertoire of courtiers and commoners who traveled from far and near to come out and see the king and praise him for his many beneficent acts and for his divinely appointed office.

SECOND READING

EPHESIANS 3:1-12 (RCL/BCP); 3:2-3a, 5-6 (RC)

Interpreting the Text

The language of Ephesians is so powerfully poetic and rhapsodic that some commentators have proposed that portions of the book are perhaps drawn from well-known Christian hymns and liturgies of the time. Widely regarded as a circular letter to gentile Christians, especially to those living in Asia, it was written to shore up the faith of gentile Christians, reminding them of their unique place in the mystery of what God did in Christ and urging them to aspire to unity of Spirit in the bond of peace (4:3).

Here we find many of the important themes of the previous two readings from the Old Testament reiterated and carried through to their next stage: (1) The idea that salvation is a result of God's initiative and authority (1:5) and that having been chosen for salvation we "might live for the praise of his glory" are reminiscent of some things in Isaiah. (2) The notion that the gentiles, who once were "aliens from the commonwealth of Israel, and strangers to the covenant of the promise" (2:12), and have now been brought near with the Jews and made to share equally in every spiritual blessing with them, is not only a gift of God. God's plan to include gentiles was not a twist in the original plan but was a part of the plan from the beginning (3:6). (3) The third theme is the notion of the gentiles as sharers in the promises of Christ as an event of cosmic significance. That cosmic import is evident in that God raised Christ from the dead and seated him at God's right hand, like the earthly king in royal psalms, far above all other earthly or heavenly rules and authorities (Eph.1:20, 21; 3:10).

Responding to the Text

Reading Ephesians reminds us during this season of celebrating the universality of Christ's manifestation how far the church has to go before it lives up to its earliest vision as a genuinely ecumenical body drawing people in its ranks from different races, nationalities, regions, and even confessions. The light of the world has once and for all come into the world through the manifestation of Christ, and now it is up to the church to witness to that heavenly realm and become the beacon of light that draws and unites people from all walks of life.

The Gospel
MATTHEW 2:1-12

Interpreting the Text

The church that the Gospel of Matthew addresses was in transition, trying to live out its climactic missionary charge in 28:19 ("Go, therefore and make disciples of all nations") and become the melting pot its founder Jesus envisioned. While written around 85–90 C.E. to a Jewish-Christian congregation that had begun to incorporate gentiles, this Gospel privileges neither Jew or gentile based on nationality, confession, or class. All are welcome in the new realm that Jesus inaugurates based on doing the will of heaven (7:21). A great deal of the material peculiar to the Gospel focuses upon Jewish Christians and the fulfillment of Old Testament prophecies in the ministry, death, and resurrection of Jesus—perhaps because of the sizable Jewish population that surrounded the community and the pressure on Jewish Christians to defend their beliefs. Even though the anonymous evangelist behind the Gospel may have been shy about revealing his own identity, he was anything but shy about his motives for writing. From the very beginning of the Gospel, which traces Jesus' genealogy through David back to the patriarch Abraham (1:1-17), the writer aims to show that Jesus is the legitimate heir to the royal house of David. The evangelist is not interested in obliterating Judaism but in showing how the ministry of Jesus fulfills both the laws and the greatest dreams of Judaism.

The Gospel, Matthew 2:1-12, is fraught with intrigue. Only someone completely naive about the political climate of the opening decades of first century Palestine could confuse the story of Jesus' birth in Bethlehem and his parents ferreting him off to Egypt as a simple birth narrative. This is an announcement story, one on par with Isaiah's prophetic announcement in Isaiah 60:1, intended to rouse the audience from their slumber and to disturb the status quo. It announces a new social and political order. Wake up! The evangelist banks on his audience's familiarity with Hebrew Scripture and their intimate knowledge of the signs that were to appear announcing the Messiah's birth. Members of the ruling priestly caste in Persia, those well versed in the astrological secrets of the heavens, come to Jerusalem bringing expensive gifts and exotic spices from the East because they saw the star shining through the pitch darkness of the night announcing his birth (Isa. 60:1-2). Bethlehem is the birthplace presaged in scripture (Micah 5:2; 2 Sam. 5:2). Jesus is not only son of David, son of Abraham, son of Joseph, and son of Mary, but God's own Son, just as the prophet Hosea had announced about the chosen one who would come out of Egypt (Hos. 2: 15).

The evangelist insists that no mere prophet or king has been born in Bethlehem. The anointed one is here (2:4)! He comes as the Son of the God who rules the whole earth showing his power to save not just the house of Israel but to draw also those "from the east and the west [who] will eat with Abraham and Isaac and Jacob in the kingdom of heaven" (8:11). Whether the king at the time of Jesus' birth was, as the Gospel suggests, Herod the Great (who died in 4 B.C.E.) or whether it was, more likely, his son Archelaus (4 B.C.E. to 6 C.E.), who was as cruel as his father, rulers of tiny vulnerable kingdoms can hardly afford to ignore rumors that a legitimate contender to the throne has risen up amidst them. Rumor that a male child has been born in the house of King David under presaging signs bears special checking out. That this one was born under a star so special that it attracted international attention, drawing learned men from the East, was enough to get him a death warrant. Never mind that he was born in Bethlehem, one of the humblest regions of Judah. Never mind that he was only a baby. Herod's image as a raging, out-of-control tyrant who goes so far as to slaughter infants to buttress his power is intended to jolt audiences. His volatile ways are pitted against the passive calm manner of Mary and Joseph and the awe-struck, but keen manipulations of the Magi. The evangelist builds on the tension the birth of the new boy king poses to King Herod by drawing the attention of foreign Magi to show that from the beginning of his life Jesus' ministry has been one of bringing outsiders into the fold.

EPIPHANY IS MEANT TO SOBER US AFTER THE EUPHORIA OF ADVENT EVAPORATES.

Epiphany is a sobering sequel to Advent. Now that manger scenes are packed up and stored in the garage until next year, now that melodies about shepherds, stable animals, and the little baby Jesus are automatically passed over when the search is on for music to accompany this week's lesson, and now that the portrait of the stoic, but dutiful carpenter and the passive and acquiescent virgin girl who give birth to the most special baby ever born are filed away in people's memory under a file labeled, "I wonder how I would have reacted if it happened to me, but thank God it didn't happen to me." Now what? How do you come up with a message that extends all the goodwill and euphoria of the past few weeks? You don't have to. Epiphany is meant to sober us after the euphoria of Advent evaporates. Now you have a chance to get down to brass tacks and concentrate on the unfinished business of Christ's coming. Now you can use an Epiphany lesson like Matthew 2:1-12 to encourage people to envision the world and the church Jesus and the prophets envisioned. What does it say about us that everyone in the church, everyone holds an important office of leadership, everyone we invite to church belongs to our same race, same generation, same class, and sees the world pretty much the same way we do? Tap into people's sincere resolve to start off the new year right and offer them the opportunity through the lessons of Epiphany to pack up last year's old cliches about people, rank prejudices about those different from them, and tired grudges from years ago and start the new year off by opening their hearts to strangers, foreigners, and the "others" God sends in their paths every day as they go about their daily business.

When Herod heard that a baby had been born in Bethlehem who could one day replace him and his sons as king, and uncertain about his exact whereabouts, the maniac king issued a decree that all male babies born that year be killed—in hopes of disposing of any future challenge to his household. Babies born to poor unwed mothers are easy targets for our worst prejudices and our ugliest political maneuverings. But was Herod's outburst fueled by more than his fear for his throne? Maybe one of the things he equally disliked about the newborn was his power to attract unwanted foreigners to Palestine. Maybe he resented the three Magi barging into his province inquiring as to the whereabouts of the baby born under the star, bringing with them their strange smells and quaint delicacies, coming from places with names no one could pronounce, doing everything according to their own strange rhythms, dressing differently from Jews and, worse, speaking with an accent thick enough to require one to listen hard and pay attention to them. Something had to be done. If these came, others may be on their way and pretty soon Jerusalem would be overrun with them! Members of the community to whom the Gospel of Matthew was written would have picked up on the story's larger premise: the Messiah whose very birth attracted foreigners was forced to flee to live among foreigners to escape death from his own people.

This Epiphany we are invited to look around in our daily comings and goings and consider some of the ways in which we have mistaken cultural homogeneity for national peace, conformity with unity, and difference with deficiency. And then we are invited to take a new look at the Star shining above our heads and ask ourselves what gifts we have as individuals and as a body to offer that show that we are willing to look past difference and see what really matters, namely, a commitment to do the will of heaven.

THE BAPTISM OF OUR LORD

JANUARY 7, 2001
FIRST SUNDAY AFTER THE EPIPHANY

REVISED COMMON	EPISCOPAL (BCP)	ROMAN CATHOLIC
Isa. 43:1-7	Isa. 42:1-9	Isa. 40:1-5, 9-11
Ps. 29	Ps. 89:1-29 or 89:20-29	Ps. 104:1b-2, 3-4, 24-25, 27-28, 29-30
Acts 8:14-17	Acts 10:34-38	Titus 2:11-14; 3:4-7
Luke 3:15-17, 21-22	Luke 3:15-16, 21-22	Luke 3:15-16, 21-22

We learn today that sometimes the road home, to where God is beckoning, will lead us through deep, uncertain waters. But the God who creates is the same God who is able to protect and deliver us from the raging uncertainties. Jesus' baptism at the Jordan manifests him to the world as redeemer and deliverer. The message is aimed at those who a couple of weeks after his Advent still can not make out the redeemer. He is there in the waters waiting for us to step in and be made new.

FIRST READING

ISAIAH 43:1-7 (RCL); 42:1-9 (BCP); 40:1-5, 9-11 (RC)

Interpreting the Text

The prophet we turn to this first Sunday of Epiphany is yet another anonymous voice of ancient times who was content to blend his voice with that of his ancestors to show how Yahweh can take the old and make something brand new. The name Second Isaiah is one scholars have given him to distinguish his proclamations from those of his predecessor, Isaiah of Jerusalem (Isaiah 1–39) and those of his successor, Third Isaiah (Isaiah 56–66), whom we encountered on the day of Epiphany. Typical of his proclamations of salvation are God's assurances that Israel will no longer stumble around in doubt but will now know for certain that Yahweh is God (41:17-20; 43:8-13; 49:24-26; 52:3-6). His preaching is filled with energy and imagination, his tone is bold and scrappy, and his vision of Yahweh's plan for Jerusalem is lofty and irresistible.

Sketchy details of his own call are provided in Isaiah 40:1-5, 9-11, where he is commissioned to cry out on Jerusalem's behalf, consoling her that, while her punishment admittedly exceeded her crime, at last it was all over (40:1-2).The way of the Lord comes to restore the fortunes of the people, and the glory of the Lord shall return (40:3-5). He clearly sees himself as a "herald of good tidings" (40:9) and declares his good news from the mountain top where he can proclaim for those who had grown cynical in exile where and how Yahweh was moving on Israel's behalf (40:10-11).

This would prove to give just the kind of preaching needed to ruffle the feathers of those who had resigned themselves to Babylonian captivity and had grown cynical about any hope of Jerusalem rebounding. In Second Isaiah's oracles one finds grand first-person speeches by Yahweh describing Israel's deliverance from exile and Yahweh's stunning defeat of her captors. With bold dramatic strokes of the poet's imagination, the picture we get in 43:1-6 is of God escorting desert-weary returnees safely back to their homeland. He insists to his listeners that the God of Israel is not some impotent despot who commands people to abandon the places where they have settled and move to a new destination but is powerless to protect them from the dangers that await them. His message to the wary, weary exiles is that no matter what kinds of dangers lay ahead, Israel will survive. How? At every step, Yahweh will be with them. The command to "fear not" is sprinkled throughout a number of Isaiah's salvation speeches (cf. 40:9; 41:10, 13f.; 44:2; 54:4) to allay the fears of those who protested that it would be impossible to cross the tumultuous rivers of Babylon. To those who envisioned all of them collapsing in the desert under the Arabian sun, the prophet argued that Yahweh would see to it that the heat would not consume them. This is how Israel will be able to recognize Yahweh as God: by Yahweh's power over history and over the natural order.

YOU WILL RECOGNIZE CHRIST AS THE ONE ONLY AS YOU ARE CROSSING STORMY WATERS AND FIND YOURSELF WONDERING WHAT'S KEEPING YOU FROM DROWNING.

By rattling off the names of nations and lands from which Yahweh has ransomed Israel (Egypt, Ethiopia, Seba, and beyond), the prophet is not contradicting the prior lectionary readings that envisioned the gospel gathering all nations together. The prophet is not trying here to stir up nationalistic or chauvinistic pride in the people. Instead, Yahweh stands in sovereign dignity above every nation, directing and governing over them for the glory of Yahweh's own purposes (43:7). The God who creates is the God who delivers. Like a reprimanding but reassuring mother, God asks Israel, "Why didn't you recognize me as the I who was there with you all along?" (40:21-24).

Nowhere was there more debate about exactly how Yahweh was going to bring about Israel's release from Babylonian captivity than when the question of who then or in the future would most likely emerge as Yahweh's spokesman, arbitrator, and servant. Second Isaiah had opinions on the topic, although he sometimes remains unclear about that person's identity and on other occasions seems quite explicit. For example, in 42:1-9 one finds one of four "Servant Songs" among the oracles of Second Isaiah (cf. 49:1-6; 50:4-11; 52:13—53:12). Although the prophet certainly sees the Persian King Cyrus as serving Yahweh's purposes (44:28; 45:1, 13) in issuing his edict in 538 B.C.E. allowing all exiles to return home and to rebuild their cities and temples (Ezra 1:1-4), in 42:19 he is ambivalent about who the servant is, his only description being that he will be a soft-spoken, tireless person who, chosen by Yahweh, enjoys Yahweh's favor.

Responding to the Text

Listening in on God describing how the returnees will be protected and guided through the perils of the desert as they journey back home to Jerusalem is enough to comfort anyone who has ever wondered how they will face an uncertain future. To hear God say that we belong to God should warm our hearts. To know that we are known by God, individually by name and collectively as a community is important to hear as we cross the threshold into a new year. What will the year bring? How will any one of us know what to do when adversities come? Now that Christ has come, how will I recognize him? How will I know which voice is his? These are some of the questions on the minds of those listening to sermons the first Sunday after the Epiphany. The answer today is the same as it was in Isaiah's day. The strange thing about the Anointed One is that you will recognize Christ as the One only as you are crossing stormy waters and find yourself wondering what's keeping you from drowning or as you are sojourning through hot arid places and find yourself wondering why you haven't collapsed from the heat.

Responsive Reading

PSALM 29 (RCL); 89:1-29 or 89:20-29 (BCP); 104:1b-2, 3-4, 24-25, 27-30 (RC)

Psalms 29 and 104 have been classified by commentators as hymns, whereas Psalm 89 is considered a royal psalm. Whether Yahweh is being celebrated in the psalm as a king in the royal psalms or as a creator, as in many of the hymns, the message is clear: the Redeemer God is enthroned in the natural order of the universe clearly visible for all to see. Psalms had the dual role of being both prayers and songs. The congregation's deepest longings were expressed in their prayers, and in their songs one overhears their greatest expectations. Whether it's

Psalm 104 or Psalm 29, the congregation acknowledges that they can experience the presence and glory of the creator God in the beauty of the natural order. In the case of Psalm 29 the congregation confesses that they can "hear" the voice of the creator God through thunderstorms that plague the region, leaving behind the terrifying sound of a chaotic sea (29:3-4), felled trees (29:5, 9), and crackling lightning in the wilderness (29:7-8). It may not always be possible to "see" the Holy One of Israel, but it may just be possible through the forces of nature to experience the King and Creator who sits above it all in majestic peace (29:11).

Second Reading

ACTS 8:14-17 (RCL); 10:34-38 (BCP); TITUS 2:11-14; 3:4-7 (RC)

Interpreting the Text

New converts to the Christian faith living in Samaria needed confirmation that their decision was right to risk persecution and loss of family ties to abandon their traditions and follow the teachings of the new movement arising out of Jerusalem (of all places!). It was common knowledge, as the woman at the well pointed out to Jesus, that Jews and Samaritans had no dealings with each other. But we see in the book of Acts that the gospel was beginning to arrive at the far reaches of non-Jewish regions, thanks to the evangelistic efforts of Philip (cf. Acts 8:4-8). The leaders of the apostolate in Jerusalem knew that the converts in Samaria needed and deserved special assurances not only that this new faith was real but that Jewish Christians in Jerusalem were willing to close the chasm between Jews and Samaritans. Peter and John, two important leaders in the apostolate, paid a visit themselves to the Samaritan converts. They came embodying the message of their founder as one of peace and unity. It was a bold move on their part to lay hands on the Samaritans so that they might receive the Holy Spirit, just as it had been a bold move on Peter's part to preach to Samaritans. They came to make certain that their Samaritan brothers and sisters were properly baptized and initiated into the new community of fellowship that was taking root everywhere.

Believers usually received the Holy Spirit as part of their baptism. This is the case in three accounts recorded in the books of Acts: on the day of Pentecost (2:38), at the baptism of the believers at Ephesus (19: 5-6), and here for the Ethiopian (8:14-17). But there had been some delay for the Samaritans in receiving the Holy Spirit. The author of Acts, Luke the physician, offers no explanation. A self-righteous group of Jewish-Christians might have been tempted to see the delay in receiving the Spirit as evidence of some inherent weakness in the Samaritans. But it might just be possible that the delay was not as a result of any flaw in the Samaritans. Perhaps it was those in Jerusalem who needed to travel to Samaria. They needed to come as much for their own sake as for that of the Samaritans. And when they came, they laid their hands on a people they once (based on ritual customs) believed were defiled. By coming to Samaria the apostles showed themselves open to God's working in all people. Then, and only then, could the Holy Spirit come down to confirm what should have been obvious all along: God's Spirit is as much a seal of God's peace as it is a sign of God's favor.

Peter's commitment to seeing the wall dividing people broken down is clear in his speech to Cornelius in Caesarea, where he admits to finally understanding that "God shows no partiality" (Acts 10:34). He sums up God's ministry through Jesus Christ beginning with his baptizing in the Jordan to his preaching and teaching of the gospel—especially the gospel of peace (Acts 10:36).

Likewise the writer of the book of Titus, presumably Paul, sums up the universal mission of Christian faith when he describes God "bringing salvation to all . . . while we wait for the blessed hope and manifestation of the glory of our great God and Savior, Jesus Christ" (Titus 2:11) and admonishing that God saves not according to works, but "according to his mercy" through the baptism of water and the Holy Spirit.

Responding to the Text

The story of the Samaritan's baptism of the Holy Spirit in Acts 8 should serve as a caution to modern interpreters not to be too quick about making bold proclamations about who is fit and who is unfit to belong to the family of faith. The Lord of the whole universe decides that, and from all indications available in Scripture, it appears that Jesus welcomes all. Can we say the same about our own individual communions? Are they representative of Christ's ecumenical vision for the church? If they are not, then how will the world know that we practice what we preach? How will they know that God is in our midst?

Ask your listeners to envision the most objectionable person they know sitting next to them in worship this morning, sharing the hymnal with them, listening and nodding to the same sermon, shaking hands and passing the peace alongside them. Better yet, as a minister imagine your worst nightmare coming through the door this Sunday. (Perhaps you don't have to. He stares grimly at you without fail every Sunday from the third pew.) Without such a person or persons in our midst it is difficult to appreciate the depth of Christ's gospel. Without that person it is also impossible to understand the breadth of Christ's grace. You are his enemy and—admit it—he is yours. But here you are together standing before a holy God working together, however imperfectly, toward a vision that in the end is larger than both of you. Now see Christ seated somewhere in the midst visible to all but the two of you, observing both of you, shaking his head in disapproval, scratching his head in amazement, and sometimes smiling in amusement. What must be going through his head: "For this purpose I came into the world."

The Gospel

LUKE 3:15-17, 21-22 (RCL); 3:15-16, 21-22 (BCP/RC)

Interpreting the Text

John the Baptist had no qualms about his role. His task, like that of Isaiah during the exile, was to prepare the way for the Messiah (Isa. 40:3). He set about his job adopting a preaching mode meant to level pride, sift through motives, and ready the hearts of people for the coming of the Christ. He saw his mission as to baptize believers as a ritual act of cleansing (Luke 3:15-17). But before he baptized those who came out to hear his desert sermons he gave them a good tongue-lashing: "You brood of vipers! Who warned you to flee the wrath to come?" (Luke 3:7). See him in the desert attire worn by radicalized desert priests who ministered in the tradition of Elijah and Isaiah before him, bolting out from the desert brushes looking crazed and convinced: "Repent, for the kingdom of heaven has come near" (Matt. 3:2). The portrait one gets from the tidbits of tantalizing biographical material found in all four Gospels is of someone who called things as he saw them. He wasn't shy about insulting his listeners by calling them vipers. He didn't mind calling down the wrath of God on nonbelievers (Matt. 3:7). He was quick to denounce those who came out to hear him if he sensed the least bit of duplicity about them in coming out (Matt. 3:8). Describing the judgment to come in uncompromising terms as an "unquenchable fire" (3:17), he denounced those who claimed Abraham as ancestor and therefore privileged standing with God. (One can only guess what more he said beyond the uncharacteristically tame comment, "It is unlawful for you to have her," when he rebuked Herod for his relations with Herodias, his brother's wife; Matt. 14:3-4; Mark 6:17-18.)

For all his zeal for his ministry, however, John was not taken with the limelight. He willingly surrendered that light to the one destined, whose baptism with the Holy Spirit and fire would be greater than John's baptism with simple water. The Gospel writers differ about exactly when John pinpointed Jesus. Matthew is the only who claims that, as John saw Jesus approaching from Galilee, he recognized him as the one he had been preaching about. But Mark and Luke stop short of making such a claim. Both agree that it wasn't until he had baptized the Galilean—and only after the heavens opened up, a dove descended, and he heard the voice saying from heaven, "You are my Son, the Beloved; with you I am well pleased"—that John's eyes were opened to Jesus' identity (cf. John 1:29-34). The opening of the heavens, the appearance of the dove, the voice from above were confirmation. Before that moment John just baptized those who came to him.

Finally, we have no hint that John was discriminating about who he baptized. For certain his preaching sifted out those who were insincere or skeptical. But there is no evidence that he privileged any one group over another. In Luke 3:21 one finds the words, "Now when all the people were baptized," which suggests that John baptized as many as were possible for one man and made no difference among them (Jew and non-Jew, rich and poor, elite and marginalized, women and men, Galilean and Bethanite, fishermen and tax collectors, fellow desert priests and members of the Sanhedrin). John leaves it to Jesus to be the final judge. And it was precisely this openness to whoever came to him to be baptized that allowed him to gaze at the Messiah for himself. Had John discriminated, he might have missed the chance to baptize Jesus. Had he allowed his prejudices get the best of him, he might have missed the theophany of a lifetime.

FOR ALL OF HIS HARSH, COARSE WAYS JOHN BELIEVED THAT IT WAS POSSIBLE TO REPENT AND START ANEW.

Responding to the Text

The themes from the readings from Isaiah 43, Psalm 29, and Acts 8 come together and are reinterpreted in new ways when juxtaposed with Luke's Gospel for today. John's "baptism unto repentance" helps prepare the hearts of everyone who listens to us this first Sunday after the Epiphany. A clean heart is one of the first conditions for being able to behold the Savior. Isaiah goes to great length to assure his audience that they will recognize the Savior by the protective care they will experience through the perils of making their way out of captivity and back home to Jerusalem. The perilous elements of water and fire they will encounter in their journey become elements of salvation in the work of the Holy Spirit and the rite of baptism by the time of Jesus.

The thunderstorm described in Psalm 29, with its terrifying lightning (fire) and stormy waters, also comes full circle in Luke 3. In both, the King of the Universe conquers the forces of nature to show his power and to reveal his identity. Moreover, John's ministry set in motion the ministry the apostles would later continue in the book of Acts, the major difference being that the apostles would travel well beyond the region John frequented (the Jordan) baptizing and preaching repentance as conditions for belonging to Christ. Another difference may be that while the apostles, because of their numbers, were able to draw strength from one another when they faced hardships in their ministry, John worked alone in the desert doing the same type of work, admittedly on a much smaller scale. He doesn't appear to be have been interested in building an institution around his preaching (although there is evidence in Luke 7:18 that he had his share of devoted followers). He suffers as a rejected prophet like prophets before him and after him (including Jesus).

I am a bit embarrassed to admit it, but I for one would not want to have to take up the mantle of John. I can't count John as one of my role models for ministry. Too radical. Too hermetic. Too unpopular. Too brash. Too single-minded. Give me someone like the prophet Huldah in 2 Kings 22:24, who is sought out for her opinion and, after saying what she has to say, gets to go home, close the door, and sit down in quiet to read the rest of her favorite book in peace. Not many ministers I know can match John's nerve. Not many ministers I know share his single-minded focus. Even fewer for that matter are comfortable enough with themselves and their gifts to give up willingly their command of the spotlight for someone with a more celebrated future ahead of them. But the truth is that John was radical before he met Jesus. He's the only boor I've known who wasn't also a bigot. I wonder how many marvelous, wonderful, life-changing, sacred experiences we have missed out on and how many people we have misjudged because we assumed that all boors were bigots.

Baptism with water signals in Scripture a new beginning, and Christian churches for centuries have used this ancient rite to initiate converts into their new life as members of the household of Christian faith. In ancient times the ritual of baptism took place once a year, usually some time around the first Sunday after the Epiphany. All new converts over the past year gathered to be baptized. John's baptism initiated converts into new beginnings. Ironic, isn't it, that he who preached, dressed, and modeled himself after prophetic figures from the past staked his ministry on a belief in new beginnings. For all of his harsh, coarse ways John believed that it was possible to repent and start anew, begin again, and change completely the way you do things after twenty, thirty, forty, fifty years of doing them one familiar way. What an appropriate time at the beginning of a new year to invite your listeners to think about the new journeys God will be beckoning them into this year, strange and unfamiliar territory, threatening and scary paths we will be asked to follow. The temptation will be to stay put and stick with what you know. But if you open yourself up to the unknown and follow where the Spirit leads, who knows? You may just find yourself standing waist deep in waters with a stranger, hearing voices, seeing doves, feeling an odd glow within, and discovering things about others and about yourself your soul has yearned for years to know.

SECOND SUNDAY AFTER THE EPIPHANY

JANUARY 14, 2001
SECOND SUNDAY IN ORDINARY TIME

REVISED COMMON	EPISCOPAL (BCP)	ROMAN CATHOLIC
Isa. 62:1-5	Isa. 62:1-5	Isa. 62:1-5
Ps. 36:5-10	Ps. 96 or 96:1-10	Ps. 96:1-3, 7-10
1 Cor. 12:1-11	1 Cor. 12:1-11	1 Cor. 12:4-11
John 2:1-11	John 2:1-11	John 2:1-12

THE READINGS FOR LAST SUNDAY offered important insights into the depths of God's saving revelation. The emphasis was upon recognizing the divine in our midst, perceiving the holy throughout our comings and goings, and unmasking the fears and prejudices we harbor that prevent us from having an authentic encounter with the sacred. Today we move beyond the abstract to the truly personal to see how Christ manifests himself to us in intimate place and in intimate ways, opening our eyes in unexpected ways to the sublime.

FIRST READING
ISAIAH 62:1-5

Interpreting the Text

Even after some took the leap of faith to return home, reviving Zion did not prove easy. Vindicating her before other nations was slow in coming. Yahweh speaks in Isaiah 62, promising to take things in hand "for Zion's sake." Yahweh will give the fallen lady a "new name" and hence a new reputation. Yahweh will make her legitimate again, and not leave her a forsaken and desolate woman. Once again we see the prophet employing imagery of light to characterize salvation, and we notice the powerful pull that divine revelation has on the imagination.

The tradition of portraying cities as female derived from the larger world of ancient Near Eastern mythology. The notion that capital cities were somehow uniquely attached to, protected by, and accountable to the patron god was a common way of thinking for prophets and audiences. While one finds instances where cities are portrayed positively (e.g., Zion the Beloved in Isaiah) in some instances and negatively (e.g., Jerusalem, the unfaithful wife, as in Ezekiel 16 and 23) in others the inspiration of this figurative way of capturing Zion was in its ability to arouse sympathy for a helpless ruined city or to justify condemning and ravaging a city of rebellious, degenerate inhabitants. Isaiah 62 offers the image of a Zion who is on the verge of becoming reunited with her benefactor (62:3–5).

Responding to the Text

Marriage is probably the closest thing on earth to the realization of what it ought to mean for people to coexist together. It is not just a sign but is supposed to be a spiritual, social, and political example of what is otherwise unknown in other areas of human interchange, and that is what it means to love, to be patient with, and to forgive one another. Some may recoil at talk about God marrying localities as the prophet does here in Isaiah 62, for it can lead to notions of God favoring one land more than another and some people more than others. This kind of thinking is at the basis of some of the founding rhetoric upon which the United States came into being, providing a basis for many of its imperialist measures in foreign lands and the pilfering and burning out of native inhabitants that took place on its own shores. And while this kind of talk should be avoided, the image of God as bridegroom and Zion as his bride does have one very important benefit. (That benefit may not be able to compensate for its risks, and each speaker will have to decide on that.) Borrowing from cultural thinking out of which it emerged, the image of a city as wife of the patron god was chiefly meant to convey how utterly helpless most cities and populations were to defend themselves against aggressive encroachments and how completely dependent everyone was upon the God of the Universe for its protection. Isaiah's message allows us to step back and look out beyond the pews to "the rulers and the authorities" that have the power to make our daily lives convenient or miserable: municipalities that determine what our ZIP codes will be, governments that determine our tax bracket, and the corporate forces who refuse certain ones of us health care and others the right to a decent education.

That Christ has come is a reminder to principalities not to overestimate the strength of their technology (chariots), weaponry (shields), and military budgets (horses) to protect them and not to prioritize them when assessing a nation's virtues. After all, history is replete with examples of what were once mighty empires crumbling and all but forgotten and capital cities burned to the ground and generations later no one remembering their exact site. In the end, all rulers govern at the behest of *the* Ruler of all rulers, says Third Isaiah's predecessor, for "all authority rests upon his shoulders; and he is named Wonderful Counselor, Mighty God, Everlasting Father, Prince of Peace. His authority shall grow continually" (Isa. 9:6b–7a).

Responsive Reading

PSALM 36:5-10 (RCL)

From whom does the source of all blessing, protection, abundance come? "Why, from Yahweh God, of course!" replies the psalmist in Psalm 36. "For with you is the fountain of life; in your light we see light" the psalm goes on to say in v. 9. After contemplating Yahweh's steadfast faithfulness (*hesed*) in the created order, the psalmist turns to the realm where humans can witness that *hesed* in a more personal manner, namely, in the gracious care Yahweh extends to those who intimately "know" the Savior. The psalmist acknowledges that such loyalty is precious and rare, barely heard of among the known gods of the period, and erratic in human bonds. No wonder the psalmist trips over himself in these verses with adoration and adulation. Modern audiences could stand to follow suit. Who can trust the love of another human being after all that we have seen and heard on tabloid television about what goes on in the backrooms of love, marriage, and vows? Despite all that they know, someone is falling in love this very moment. They can't help it. What wouldn't any of us give for the chance to be loved? After all, "love is strong as death" (Song of Sol. 8:6). It makes the beloved trip over herself and the lover do cartwheels on the mountains.

PSALM 96 or 96:1-10 (BCP); 96:1-3, 7-10 (RC)

The Hebrews were forever receptive to new ways of lifting their voices in praise to Yahweh. Key saving acts on behalf of the patriarchs and matriarchs of old may have been the foundation upon which Hebrew religion was formed, but each generation insisted upon telling its own history with Yahweh's day-to-day saving power (Ps. 96:2).The whole earth is invited to blend its voices (v. 1) in this hymn celebrating Yahweh's kingship over the earth (v. 10). The Hebrews did not deny the presence of other gods, but they were convinced that theirs was the creator God who made the heavens (v. 5). Other gods may exist, but Israel's god reigned over them all (v. 4b). Commentators have seen this as an example of the kind of psalm that may have been used at the New Year festival, at which the celebrating community gathered in the sanctuary from throughout Israel to rehearse their common belief in Yahweh as a God who uniquely creates, reigns, intervenes, and judges. Notice: Israel is boasting something pretty important here. Israel boasts that she recognizes the hand of her God from all the other gods of the earth. Israel knows her God in that intimate sense of a lover and beloved, once you have experienced your beloved, you can never step back and be separate from, detached from, and independent of each other again.

SECOND READING

1 CORINTHIANS 12:1-11 (RCL/BCP); 12:4-11 (RC)

Interpreting the Text

"Now concerning spiritual gifts brothers and sisters." So Paul begins this chapter (12:1). What had he been talking about before? He had been addressing the matter of the new covenant and admonishing the congregation at Corinth against the split across class lines that was beginning to take hold among believers during, of all things, the Lord's Supper. If that weren't bad enough, there is rivalry among them about whose spiritual gift is superior. The sense is that Paul is addressing a number of issues addressed to him by Chloe's people, presumably one of the families in the church, who wrote about the divisions that were beginning to develop in the church at Corinth. The city, one of the most cosmopolitan cities in Greece, was swarming with religious and ethnic diversity so that the church at Corinth was a hotbed for religious and ethnic divisions as members of the different factions tried to bring together free-thinking lifestyles as well as other rigid observances and intolerant attitudes under the church's one roof. The church is too much in need of all spiritual gifts to privilege one spiritual gift over another, argued Paul. All the gifts, "activated by one and the same Spirit," work in tandem with each other "for the common good." Paul applies the material image of the body to the factionalism at Corinth. His goal is to end the *schismata* or "divisions" within that body (12:25) by arguing that each person has a *charisma,* not for his or her advantage over someone else, but for profit to the community as witnesses to the manifest Christ.

Responding to the Text

No one who has pastored a church more than a week has to rack his or her brain trying to imagine how things had deteriorated to a degree at Corinth that questions of sexual immorality, hair styles, how to act in worship, idol meat consumption and the resurrection had to be addressed *ad seriatum* in a letter. Any one of these issues alone has been known to send factions scattering for cover. All them being disputed back and forth under one roof in one lifetime make you wonder how the church at Corinth ever survived.

The problem was not that the members held different opinions about one thing or another. The problem was that their different opinions were leading to conflict and divisions within the church. Paul appeals to them in "the name of Lord Jesus Christ" to come together in unity and to put aside their divisions and disagreement (1 Cor. 1:10-11). Evidently there were some who felt so marginalized and ostracized by the highly abstract tone in which these differences were handled that they felt they had no course of action but to drop a letter to their founder and friend Paul. Yahweh was the undisputed source of all their *charismata.* But in the meantime they needed a spiritual friend. What a lovely image to lift up this Epiphany season: every church needs a friend. There are times in the life of the church when the church could benefit from the wise and prayerful counsel of a friend—someone who stands outside the fray of raging opinions and personal ambitions, someone who listens and advises, someone who in times of disagreements can step in and remind the church of its first love and its greater witness, someone who will pray for the church when the church cannot pray for itself. "It is a great advantage for us to be able to consult someone who knows us, so that we may learn to know ourselves," wrote Teresa of Avila. Churches need the friendship of someone who is able to speak to its heart about the things that really matter, love and unity. If that friend is not Paul, then certainly it can be Jesus, who lived, died, and was raised for the sake of the church's witness.

The Gospel

JOHN 2:1-11 (RCL/BCP); 2:1-12 (RC)

Interpreting the Text

A friend's wedding at Cana, a village in Galilee, became the occasion for Jesus' first public miracle. The host was not rich and ran out of wine. Jesus' mother, Mary, was there and urged her son to do something. After some protest, Jesus relented and instructed the host's servants to pour water into six stone jars standing nearby. After they did this, he instructed them to draw off some and take it to the chief steward for a taste inspection. Not knowing the source of the new wine, the steward marveled at the superior quality of this batch compared to the first batch of wine. It happened, according to John's reckoning, the third day after Philip was called. The Evangelist doesn't bother to say whether anyone other than Jesus, Mary his mother, his disciples, and the servants found out about the miracle. It concludes simply, "and his disciples believed in him," which suggests that the miracle was for the disciples' benefit alone. That would make sense, because they were new disciples. Their faith in him needed to be confirmed. But John is the only one to report the story of the miracle at Cana. Why do the others fail to mention such an event if indeed it was at the wedding feast at Cana that Jesus first displayed his unusual powers? That is the more difficult question. The easier question is why John includes the story. How does it fit in with the larger literary and theological framework of John's Gospel?

The story of the wedding feast at Cana belongs where it does from a literary point of view because Cana is the home of Nathanael, one of the new disciples who has just been called in the previous chapter (1:43-51). John includes it here because the miracle confirms what Jesus has just told Nathanael earlier, "You will see greater things than these" (1:51), which was Jesus' reply to Nathanael when the latter questioned how Jesus knew him when he had no recollection of their meeting before (1:48). The miracle at Cana introduces Jesus' powers to Nathanael and to the rest of the disciples. It is the first of his miracles—a minor miracle, if there is such a thing, compared to the ones that follow in the Gospel of John. But it does the trick. Jesus' disciples are impressed.

The miracle at Cana also fits in with John's larger theological agenda. The miracles that Jesus performs not only amaze but also serve as signs to show Jesus as Messiah. Miracles strengthened belief in Jesus as the Messiah, Son of God—so John claims in 20:30. The miracle at Cana was the manifestation of his "glory." The first miracle involved turning water into wine. The second would be a long-distance healing of the Capernaum official's son (4:44-54). From there he feeds five thousand with five barley loaves and two fish (6:14), after that he walks on water (6:16-21), and on and on until the climax of his resurrection from the dead, which is confirmed by his three subsequent appearances to his despondent, and in some cases, doubtful disciples (20:19—21:14). The objective each time is shore up faith and to see to it that people believe (a word frequently used in John's Gospel) that Jesus is the Son of God.

TAKE THOSE EMPTY STONE JARS, FILL THEM TO THE BRIM WITH THE WATER OF HOPE, PRAYER, AND PERSISTENCE, AND DRAW FROM THEM.

All of this explains why John would decide to include in his Gospel the story of the miracle at Cana. But why does Jesus' first miracle take place at a wedding, of all places? Because that was the way God planned it, you may respond. True. But let's see if God will help us fill the pages of this book with a few more curious possibilities, and in so doing keep going the conversation between heaven and earth.

The wedding metaphor as we have already seen in Isaiah 62 symbolizes in prophetic tradition a time of fulfillment where God redeems the nation and restores its dignity and honor before the other nations (cf. Isa. 54:4-8; Hos. 2:16-20). Likewise, wine in prophetic tradition symbolizes the joy that accompanies God and the nation's reconciliation (Amos 9:11-14; Hos. 14:4-7). For John a wedding feast was an appropriate occasion for Jesus first to manifest his powers as the Messiah, Son of God. After all, he came to the world "not to judge the world, but to save the world" (John 12:47).

Finally, there is the matter of Jesus' mother. Catholic commentators, because of their interest in Mary, have written a lot about the dialogue recorded here between Jesus and his mother. Unsurprisingly, the lection for Catholics this week differs from the Protestant and Episcopal tradition, which stops at v. 11, and includes v. 12, which describes Jesus' family, namely, his mother and brothers, as taking part in his ministry at least in the beginning. In contrast, Protestants have generally ignored the dialogue between Mary and Jesus "as if it were unthinkable that Mary played a role in Johannine theology."[1] Protestants have generally sided with the Synoptics, which have Jesus responding rather harshly to any notion of maternal persuasion in his ministry (Luke 2:49; Mark 3:33-35; Luke 11:27-28). Catholics have taken their cues from John who is not so reactionary about Mary. She appears here in chapter 2 as the one who prompts her son to save a friend's wedding from disaster. She persists when Jesus protests that his hour had not yet come to publicly manifest himself by instructing the servants, "Do whatever he tells you" (John 2:5). Hers is a mother's confidence that her son will do the right thing. Matthew and John agree that Jesus could be won over with persistence (Matt. 15:21-28; John 4:47-50). Mary shows up again in John's Gospel as a model Christian at the foot of the cross, long-suffering and prayerful. For her patience, her prayers, and persistence, she is rewarded with an offspring, the Beloved Disciple, a representative of the church, someone to nurture and oversee in this new phase in the life of the ministry.

Responding to the Text

Ordinary Time—that's where this Second Sunday after the Epiphany belongs, liturgically speaking: Ordinary Time. That's that seven-month period of the year when life is lived outside the feasts and fasts of the Christian calendar. It's the longest period in the liturgical calendar in the Orthodox, Anglican, and Roman traditions, where no particular mystery of Christ is celebrated, and humans are left to their own to calibrate and celebrate mystery. This is actually the second Sunday in Ordinary Time, but last Sunday, focusing as it did on Jesus' baptism with all of its cosmic significance, kept the semblance of sacramental mystery before us. Switching our attention to a marriage feast on the second Sunday in Ordinary Time hurls us back to earth quickly. Exit kings and Magi, enter a woman and a man. Exit baptismal doves, enter wedding doves. Exit voices from heaven declaring divine Sonship, and enter voice from heaven sealing the vows made between two people. Exit factionalism and division, enter oneness and love. One of the inferences that can be drawn from Ordinary Time is that human beings can only take so many high holy days (Good Friday, Easter, Pentecost, Christmas) before they must return to the routine and the banal for air.

Nothing symbolizes our fleshly humanity like marriage. Think of wedding, marriage, and human love and, on the one hand, images come to mind that have little to do with the holy: revelry, passion, tears, intoxication, blood, semen, slamming doors, screams, soiled diapers, scraped knees, accusations, mortgages, tuition, betrayal, dentures in a cup of water, receding hairline, pecks on the cheek, and rosaries. Think of wedding, marriage, and human love and, on the other hand, a flood of images come to mind that have everything to do with the sacred: love, passion, a vow, loyalty, disappointment, repentance, forgiveness, and renewal. In the ordinary ebb and flow of human life, devoid of high feasts and fasts, we learn a lot about our Lord and ourselves by keeping to the ordinary routines of our lives. Christ manifests himself in mountain-top experiences, for certain, but he has been known to show up in miraculous ways on more than one occasion in the simple day-to-day activities of drawing water from wells, preparing food, tending sheep, and trying to figure out what to do when the wine runs out at a wedding celebration.

Perhaps the choice to manifest himself as the Son of God at a wedding feast was more his mother's choice than Jesus', as many have pointed out. Perhaps Jesus was trying to tell his mother that he was unwilling to start his public career at that moment when he protested to her. Perhaps she was being presumptuous, pushy, and impulsive. But sometimes mothers know best. For one thing, what's a wedding without wine? But, more importantly, what's a marriage without Christ's favor? In the years ahead there will be plenty of occasions when the couple will turn to each other and wonder whatever made them make so preposterous a vow—what did they see in each other in the first place, where did the love go, and is it possible for this marriage to be revived? The spiritual journey is much like marriage. It hits highs and lows, goes through seasons of ecstasy and ennui, and you find yourself wondering whether it's possible to regain the passion, the conviction, the spiritual momentum you once enjoyed. The message of this second Sunday after the Epiphany is yes. Take those empty stone jars, fill them to the brim with the water of hope, prayer, and persistence, and draw from them. You're apt to find upon drinking the second batch of wine—the one you drink in your middle and later years after the blush of youthful love has run its course, after you've experienced the betrayal of love, flesh, and ministry, after you've walked away from your first love and tearfully experienced the miracle of forgiveness—that the second batch can be better than the first batch of wine. That is the real miracle that took place at Cana. That is how Christ manifested his glory at the wedding at Cana. He showed us that it is possible to utterly give yourself away in love only to discover that the more you give yourself away, the more you find yourself.

THIRD SUNDAY AFTER THE EPIPHANY

JANUARY 21, 2001
THIRD SUNDAY IN ORDINARY TIME

REVISED COMMON	EPISCOPAL (BCP)	ROMAN CATHOLIC
Neh. 8:1-3, 5-6, 8-10	Neh. 8:2-10	Neh. 8:2-4a, 5-6, 8-10
Ps. 19	Ps. 113	Ps. 19:8-10, 15
1 Cor. 12:12-31a	1 Cor. 12:12-27	1 Cor. 12:12-30 or 12:12-14, 27
Luke 4:14-21	Luke 4:14-21	Luke 1:1-4; 4:14-21

LAST WEEK'S FOCUS WAS ON THE PULLS AND TUGS of human relations and what we learn about ourselves and Christ in the ordinariness of living together in marital love and working together as people of God. This week we focus on ways in which God encounters us and we encounter God by reading and hearing God's written word.

FIRST READING

NEHEMIAH 8:1-3, 5-6, 8-10 (RCL); 8:2-10 (BCP); 8:2-4a, 5-6, 8-10 (RC)

Interpreting the Text

We leap out of the sixth century B.C.E., where we have been for the past few weeks with Second and Third Isaiah, to the fifth century to catch up with a reformer at the time of the Second Temple who was preoccupied with rebuilding from ruins. It *is* possible. Those who returned under from exile to rebuild the Temple and the city walls can testify to that. One of those who led a party back to Jerusalem was the priest Ezra. He comes to us in our lesson at what is probably the inaugural of his ministry. The period is somewhere around 458 B.C.E. It is the seventh month, Tishri (September–October), the time for the Festival of Booths (Lev. 23:33-43). Considerable scholarly attention has been devoted to the way the narrative of Ezra and Nehemiah (two books which are combined as one in the Hebrew Bible) jumps back and forth between the two characters and confuses their role. The contents of Nehemiah 8 seem to fit best with the narrative flow of Ezra 8 and probably originally belonged after that chapter, which describes Ezra having been entrusted by the Persian king Artaxerxes I to bring the Jewish province in line with the law of God and with the law of the kings (Ezra 7:26).[2] Ezra's first act of business on returning to Jerusalem was to gather all the returnees together in the square before the Water Gate, where he read to them the words of the Torah, that is, some version of the first five books of Hebrew scripture. What bears pointing out here is the people's response.

The people wept. According to the story, the women and men of Judah cried when they heard Ezra read to them the words of God (Neh. 8:9). Had it been that long since they had heard God's word? Or was it the overwhelming emotion of it all—returning to their ancestral home, the sight of ruin all around, hearing the promises of God, the priest's moving reading of select portions of the Pentateuch/Torah? Or might the people have been overcome by something that rarely gets discussed by commentators, namely, that the assembly (*qahal*) that comes out to hear God's word is made up of women and men. Women and men were gathered together, women and men heard the word of God together, women and men were allowed to enjoy several days of festivities and rededication ceremonies.[3] The inference in Exodus 19:15 ("do not go near a woman") is that only men were allowed to show up for God's appearance on Mount Sinai. What made them weep? It was probably a combination of all three, and many more things we will never know about.

Responding to the Text

The heading for this section is "Responding to the Text," but I doubt anyone will weep as they read the contents of this book. I would be touched to know that my words had such an effect on someone, but I doubt that they will. I would be content simply if readers testified that reading this book opened them up to new ways of thinking and talking about old sacred texts. But the women and men in Ezra's day wept upon hearing him read the word of God. Now if scripture has never moved you to tears you probably find the returnees' response a bit excessive and perhaps would rather focus your remarks on Ezra's admonition, "Do not be grieved, for the joy of the Lord is your strength" (v. 10b). But the "strength" Ezra is referring to here is for those who are weak or faint with emotion. It's pretty obvious that these were not fainthearted people or people easily discouraged, judging by their willingness to take on the task of rebuilding Jerusalem. But hearing the word of God amidst the reality before them stirred up a well of emotion in them. Hope. Joy. Love. Resolve. Faith. They both heard God's word and felt God's presence in a radically new way.

Sometimes it's a matter of the right text read at the right time. A text that speaks comfort when one has experienced the loss of a loved one can offer overwhelming reassurance. A text that offers the possibility of new beginnings just when someone feels professionally that they have hit a brick wall can offer exactly the needed strength to press on. Hearing the story in Nehemiah 8 that books can retain their beauty and passion even when they are read to you just when you have begun losing sight in both eyes can bring tears to those same eyes. Sometimes it's a matter of the right text read at the right time.

Responsive Reading

PSALM 19 (RCL); 19:8-10, 15 (RC); 113 (BCP)

According to the psalmist, nature does not alone bear witness to the glory of God. God's law also reveals wondrous things about this glory. Perfect and full of wisdom, that law has the power to "revive the soul" (v. 7) and cause "rejoicing [in] the heart" (v. 8a). God's wisdom is disclosed both in the splendor and order of creation (Ps. 19:1-6) and in the wisdom of the Torah of Moses (vv. 7-14). Called a wisdom psalm because it praises the glory and insights of the Torah and admonish listeners to order their steps according to its wisdom, texts like Psalms 1, 19, 37, 113, 119, referred to as wisdom psalms, have been criticized by some as literature created to reinforce conformity and the status quo. But those who argue this way miss the potentially subversive power of music and song lyrics. As we can see in a psalm like 19, the psalmist does not advocate mere conformity to the way things are. The psalmist feels empowered to see, to think, and to speak up for herself or himself, concluding with the secret prayers of ministers of the gospel the world over:

Let the words of my mouth
and the meditation of my heart
be acceptable to you,
O Lord, my rock and my redeemer.

In a culture where only a minority of people was able to read and write, and that minority belonged to the elite class, most of the citizenry learned the words of the Torah by reciting in them worship and at home in times of family devotions. The heart-warming stories of faith and faithlessness, trials and triumph, hope and adversity were taken to heart, rehearsed, discussed and debated, and passed down from generation to generation (as the writer of Deuteronomy admonished in Deut. 6:6-9). Wisdom psalms remind us as speakers and teachers that after all our high-minded abstractions have evaporated into thin air, people will probably only remember the plain, simple, commonsense truths about love, hope, joy, and faith that we took the time to relate to their daily lives.

SECOND READING

1 CORINTHIANS 12:12-31a (RCL); 12:12-17 (BCP); 12:12-30 or 12:12-14, 27 (RC)

Interpreting the Text

We return today to the same epistle, with a few more verses added. The focus of the epistle last week was on the importance of the various members (spiritual gifts) working in harmony for the benefit of the body (the church). On the surface it may not seem that juxtaposing the same epistle lesson with Nehemiah, Psalms, and Luke today gives it any new twist of meaning. But look again. This week's reading causes the interpreter to address the hierarchies that emerge in the church when some people boast greater wisdom and knowledge than others. All gifts derive from God (1 Cor. 12:6), argues Paul, which means that no one can boast of creating the gift herself or himself. We discover elsewhere in the epistle that speaking in tongues was esteemed over other spiritual gifts (14:1-24). Perhaps its esteem was due in part because its spontaneous and strange utterances sounded mystical and other-worldly. The tongue speaker could claim some special powers, some special connection to the angels, or some special divine wisdom that was not available to others. Paul rebukes privileging tongue speaking over other gifts even though he was no stranger to ecstatic experiences himself (cf. 2 Cor. 12:1-4). No gift should be esteemed over another. And in v. 13 he seems to negate everything said before, or so it seems. There is a hierarchy of gifts, says Paul, but the supreme gift of all is available to every one: the gift of love. Strive for this gift. Second to love would be a gift that benefits everyone: prophecy, not tongues (14:1, 5, 39). A gift that makes some people stand apart from others as having deeper access to the divine is not the gift to covet. In other words, God imparts spiritual gifts and insights not for the benefit of any one individual, but for contributing to the common good (v. 7).

Responding to the Text

The late dean of the chapel at Howard and Boston Universities, Howard Thurman, a mystic and philosopher, tells the story in his book *Jesus and the Disinherited* about his grandmother, a former slave who, because she could not read, made him read the Bible to her in the evenings. He was free to read any portion of the Bible, except one. For years she wouldn't permit him to read anything from Paul's epistles. Her favorite portions were the Psalms and the Gospels—from these two he could read as many times as he liked. One day he timidly asked his grandmother why she disapproved of Paul's epistles. She told him that for years the overseer on her slave master's plantation would read to the slaves how Paul enjoined slaves to be obedient to their master, and she decided that if she lived to be freed from slavery she would never again read or have read in her hearing anything from Paul. The overwhelming evidence from the Gospels, the first five books of the Torah, and the Psalms was that God aimed for people to be free. God did not confine them to a permanent state of slavery. God was a God of love, Thurman's grandmother insisted, and love does not enslave the beloved. Love frees the beloved. Unable to read the Bible for herself, having heard the stories of the Bible read to her all of her life, Thurman's grandmother proves that encountering God's truth takes place in many ways. The overseer thought that because he could read, and because he was, he thought, better than slaves, he had the power to filter the truth to the slaves any way he saw fit. But the story of Thurman's grandmother proves otherwise. God's truth is not bound to texts, and neither is it tied to any one interpretation or doctrine. Rather God's truth is conveyed by means of the heart to those who yearn to receive it.

The Gospel

LUKE 4:14-21 (RCL/BCP); 1:1-4; 4:14-21 (RC)

Interpreting the Text

Here is where Luke the Evangelist felt Jesus' public ministry properly began: in his hometown synagogue debating with the leaders there. As was his custom on the Sabbath, Jesus went to the synagogue; but this time it would be different. He stood, was given the Isaiah scroll, read from portions of what now has come to be known as chapters 61 and 58, rolled up the scroll, gave it back to the attendant, and then remarked that today those portions were fulfilled (the inference being that he fulfilled them). Notice the custom of standing and reading the scripture (4:16), presumably out of respect for the word of God.

The Galilean carpenter's unusual insight into holy scripture amazed everybody. How did he come upon such knowledge (cf. Matt. 13:53-58; Mark 6:1-6)? But it was more than his divine insight that interested Luke when he recorded the story of Jesus reading from the Isaiah scroll in a hometown synagogue. It was also his boldness, his confidence, his self-possession in declaring himself to be the one spoken of in the Servant Song in Isaiah 61. It may have been a common text that apprentice rabbis read from at their initiation into the rabbinate. No one seemed to protest what he said. It was that *he*—Joseph the carpenter's son—who said it (4:22). Commoners did not normally spawn such obviously learned rabbis. From as far back as his youth Jesus had been hanging out in synagogues listening to, debating with, and learning from rabbis (Luke 2:41-52). Like most Jewish males he owed what education he had managed to get to the rabbis in the synagogues. But now the carpenter's son was claiming superiority over his teachers!

Judging from the response of those listening, Jesus was claiming to be more than a rabbi. He claimed that he was God's agent of promised salvation. What a boast! What a revelation! How very much like Luke's portrait of Jesus! Luke is as much interested in disclosing the soteriological side (the side having to do with his saving people from their sins) of Jesus' identity as he was the christological side (his lordship as the Son of God). In other words, Luke is very interested in the historical perspective of Jesus' ministry, the effects of what Jesus has done for humanity, which leads him frequently to use words like "salvation," "forgiveness of sin," and "life."[4] Preaching salvation is his purpose for coming into the world, as he discloses later in chapter 4: "I must proclaim the good news of the kingdom of God to other cities also; for I was sent for this purpose" (4:43). Part of what being the Savior entailed was reading scripture—oral proclamation—and trying to find language that would persuade his audience. After reading from the Isaiah scroll, everyone was "amazed at the gracious words that came from his mouth" (4:22).Their response was much like that of Ezra's audience upon hearing him read portions of the Torah in their hearing. It doesn't say that anyone wept, though some perhaps did who remembered the boy they first had encountered in a class on rhetoric and another in a class on interpretation who was now standing before them as a man convinced of his purpose.

EVERY WORD IN THE BIBLE WAS WRITTEN WITH THE EXPECTATION THAT MOST OF THOSE WHO ENCOUNTERED IT WOULD HEAR IT AS A TEXT READ TO THEM IN A GATHERING OF BELIEVERS.

Responding to the Text

Centuries ago the uneducated thought that those who could read were akin to gods. Reading was seen as a mysterious gift, on a par perhaps with being able to predict the future. It required special gifts—or so it was believed. Those who can and do read know that it doesn't take giftedness to be able to read, just practice. Judging by the declining number of books sold each year and the number of newspapers and magazines that fold every year, reading is falling on hard times. There are just too many other ways in the world these days to stay abreast and to be entertained. In those churches where time is taken every Sunday to read the scripture lessons aloud, have you noticed how many in the audience use this time to divert their attention and do other things like read the bulletin? Have you noticed how uninspiringly texts get read from the lectern—as though it's the seminarian or elder's first time reading the Bible? Public reading of the Bible today would scarcely move anyone to weep or even to look up from reading the bulletin or filling out the offering envelope.

Every word in the Bible was written with the expectation that most of those who encountered it would hear it as a text read to them in a gathering of believers. This explains the lyrical, poetic, engaging style of much of the language found in the Bible. Paul sent his letters as encyclicals to be read from church to church. Psalms were passed down from one generation to the next generation by choral singers through memory and imagination. Like almost all of the stories of the Old Testament, story traditions about Jesus' ministry were passed down and passed around orally by communities who met and rehearsed and reinterpreted these stories in light of their circumstances and their needs. "Reading" involved staying open to new meanings and messages in old cherished stories and verses.

Reading is a form of prayer in some traditions—certainly in the Hebraic tradition in which Jesus grew up, with Psalm 1:2 as its focus ("and on his law they meditate day and night"). By reading from the scroll Jesus was also praying. Every time God's word is uttered, knowingly or unknowingly a prayer is being uttered. Prayer opens us to new ways of thinking. Prayer makes understanding possible. Prayer makes study a sacrament. "What we glorify," writes Abraham Heschel, the Jewish philosopher, " is not knowledge, erudition, but study and the dedication to learning."[5]

Not all responses need be as extreme as weeping or becoming speechless. But you know the people have begun to glimpse the meanings of the morning scripture when they come up to you after you have preached, taught, or simply read the scripture as the morning lesson, and they say, "You know, I think I *see* now what you mean." Ultimately, speakers and writers alike hope they use words in such a way as to help their audiences get a mental image of the topic under discussion.

Jesus stood to read from the scroll of Isaiah, and his reading left those around him amazed. He had probably heard the text read out loud hundreds of times as he sat in worship all those years staring out at nothing in particular, never thinking what that text might mean to him. But something changed all that. One day he heard it differently. Sometimes it takes the right text finding the right person at the right time in her or his life. He saw himself differently after reading the scroll. So did those who heard him read that day.

There's always the chance that this Sunday might be the right Sunday for the man staring grimly at you from the third pew to hear the text read in a way that he cannot avoid seeing his life on its pages. Remember: just because you can't see him weeping doesn't mean that he isn't weeping inside.

FOURTH SUNDAY AFTER THE EPIPHANY

JANUARY 28, 2001
FOURTH SUNDAY IN ORDINARY TIME

REVISED COMMON	EPISCOPAL (BCP)	ROMAN CATHOLIC
Jer. 1:4-10	Jer. 1:4-10	Jer. 1:4-5, 17-19
Ps. 71:1-6	Ps. 71:1-17 or 71:1-6, 15-17	Ps. 71:1-6, 15, 17
1 Cor. 13:1-13	1 Cor. 14:12b-20	1 Cor. 12:31—13:13 or 13:4-13
Luke 4:21-30	Luke 4:21-32	Luke 4:21-30

LAST SUNDAY WE SAW HOW GOD IS DISCLOSED through the word of God, and how reading that word opens us up to new and wonderful possibilities. But we have been speaking here for the past few weeks as though the world eagerly awaits God's disclosures. We wish it was so, but it isn't always the case. This week's lesson admits that, like our Savior before us, Christians risk rejection every time they challenge the rulers of this present age. People can see the beauty of the light and still choose its opposite.

FIRST READING

JEREMIAH 1:4-10 (RCL/BCP); 1:4-5, 17-19 (RC)

Interpreting the Text

Because his ministry spanned Judah's last decades as a sovereign nation, the prophet Jeremiah witnessed firsthand the terror, paranoia, plotting, and refusal to hear the truth that erupt when power is being dismembered. Although only three kings are mentioned in the superscription to his book (Jer. 1:1-3), the prophet Jeremiah saw four Judean kings rise and fall during his lifetime: Josiah, the beloved king; Jehoiachin who ruled only three months before being taken off into exile by the Babylonians; Jehoiakim, his arch opponent; and Zedekiah, the puppet king. The prophet died sometime after 587 B.C.E. in Egypt after fleeing there along with other Judeans to escape further reprisals by the Babylonians against Jerusalem.

Jeremiah's calling took place during a relatively calm time in the tiny kingdom of Judah (ca. 627 B.C.E.) when the Camelot king, King Josiah son of Amon, was busy putting into place political and religious reforms that would strengthen his control of all the regions bordering Judah. But paranoia was beginning to set in as rumors flew throughout the kingdom and beyond about the political disturbances taking place in the north. The great empire Assyria was on the verge of collapse as its resources were being depleted from all the energies it had to expend fighting off mounting intrusions from its old enemy Babylon. Rulers of states under Assyrian rule from Damascus to Judah to Egypt were busy speculating about what all this might portend for struggling kingdoms in the south like themselves. Josiah set about taking advantage of Assyria's preoccupation by reinforcing his borders.

It was the worst time in the world to be called a prophet, especially a prophet that would be appointed "over nations and over kingdoms, to pluck up and pull down, to destroy and to overthrow, to build and to plant" (Jer. 1:10). Rulers don't take kindly to big-mouth prophets standing in the marketplace, outside the palace, or inside the Temple gates denouncing their policies.

Like the prophet Moses before him, Jeremiah was not eager to be a prophet. We can see in his official call narrative that he protested to God that he was both too young and much too unsuited for speaking publicly (1:6). That he understood his message to be God's word is evident from the numerous occurrences of the phrase "the word of the Lord came to me" here in the first chapter and throughout the book. The phrase was a prophet's refrain (cf. Hosea 1:1; Joel 1:1; Jonah 1:1; Micah 1:1). But God's call could not be avoided. God commanded Jeremiah not to speak of himself as a boy and not to be afraid of the powers he would confront. God would be with him, for his calling was not the result of some spontaneous, impulsive act on God's part but had been set in motion since he, Jeremiah, was an embryo in his mother's womb (1:5). God's tone borders on rebuke later in v. 17 when God warns the prophet against falling apart when the time comes to confront the powers that be, but then it softens as God assures Jeremiah that he's stronger than he thinks (v. 18), which is good since the prophet would be going up against "the kings of Judah, its princes, its priests, and the people of the land" (v. 18). Rejection was certain. For as often as God's word threatens the security they have built for themselves, people will refuse to hear the word of God. They will fight you as a prophet, God warns. But they will not be able to prevail over you, promises God "for I am with you . . . to deliver you" (v. 19). Such a narrative and call experience would become important in the coming decades when the prophet would need to prove to his increasingly agitated listeners that he didn't ask for this call and took no pleasure in being a prophet of doom. But God's word must be uttered and fulfilled.

Responding to the Text

"Don't get mad at me! I'm just doing my job!" How many times have we heard traffic cops or bill collectors, and others with irritating tasks say those words after we've just about bitten off their heads in protest? How many times have we said or thought the same thing when it was our time to say something unpleasant to someone who didn't want to hear it? No one likes being the messenger of bad news. Rejection stings. The comment that you're just doing your job may be accurate, but it doesn't help soothe the hurt you feel when you have been blasted and what you have to say has been rejected. At the many low moments in his ministry, for example when the chief priest Passhur struck him for preaching his ominous prophecies in the courts of the temple and had him bound and placed in stocks (20:1-6), Jeremiah had plenty of time on his hands to remind himself and to complain to God that he hadn't asked for this job.[6] But there he was, being obedient. Because that's all he could do. That's all any of us can do. Be faithful to our calling, and let God vindicate us. It's the clause in the minister's job contract that makes the job doable: "for I am with you . . . to deliver you." The story of the prophet Jeremiah's call teaches us that with God's call comes God's promise to remain with us. Therefore, if you must endure rejection as part of the job, it is reassuring to know that your employer steadfastly stands behind her side of the contract.

Responsive Reading

PSALM 71:1-6 (RCL); 71:1-17 or 71:1-6, 15-17 (BCP); 71:1-6, 15, 17 (RC)

The suffering psalmist's comfort is that since birth—and even prior to birth—God has been the source of the psalmist's hope. Persecution hurts, but you can endure it with someone by your side who believes in you. Rejection stings, but you get over it with time and the assurances of a companion. Absent from the prayer of this psalmist is the image of the quiet, stoic, longsuffering saint who stands alone in the face of danger. The psalmist has the good sense to know that sometimes in battle the wisest course is to run for cover. Seek refuge. Get behind a rock (Ps. 71:3). Stay put until you can regain your balance, see your way clearly, or spot some reinforcement coming. "In you, O Lord," cries the psalmist, "I take refuge" (Ps. 71:1). The psalmist cries out to God for deliverance from his enemies. But this is one of those many instances in Hebrew psalms where faith is present even in lament. This is not the outcry of an infidel who lashes out in anger and frustration. The psalmist cries out to God *because* God is his hope (v. 5).

Second Reading

1 CORINTHIANS 13:1-13 (RCL); 12:31—13:13 or 13:4-13 (RC)

Interpreting the Text

It would have been enough had the first epistle to the Christians consisted solely of this great hymn to love. But, set as it is in its context, between two chapters about diversity within unity, showing in chapter 12 why the body requires a diversity of members (gifts) and in chapter 14 how diverse gifts serve to build up the community, chapter 13 is a rhapsody to the transforming power of love (*agape*) within community. This chapter is one of Paul's finest moments as a prophet. Love is not self-seeking, but builds others up. Fifteen verbs here show concretely what love accomplishes. Above all, love unifies. It doesn't pit gifts against each other, it privileges the other over self. Even prophecy, a gift Paul himself thinks highly of for reasons that should be obvious (14:1, 5, 39), is worthless if it is not accompanied by love (13: 2). Paul is trying to show here how the Corinthians' zeal for tongues and for wrangling over the gifts of the Spirit are completely at odds with what is the fundamental basis of the Christian faith, namely, the supremacy of love. Thus, for Paul this is not just a matter of spiritual gifts. With the words, "And I will show you a more excellent way" (12:31), we see that for Paul it is a matter of Christian ethics. Love is the only context for gifts. Why love? Because love is permanent whereas the *charismata* (gifts) are temporal and relative (1 Cor. 13:8-10).

Responding to the Text

The temptation is to overanalyze 1 Corinthians 13, when the wisest thing to do would be to let the chapter's beauty and power speak for itself. But one may wonder how this epistle fits in with the other lessons this Sunday that focus on prophetic conflict. No one was more aware than Paul how difficult it was sometimes to keep up the appearances of love when you're angry at your followers! He manages a calm, patient, and paternal tone in writing his first epistle to the church at Corinth. But as the issues keep cropping up and as news keeps coming back to him that his work at Corinth is threatened, his patience wore thin. He hints in 2 Corinthians 1:1-4 of another letter he had to write to the church at Corinth (which we do not have a record of) one where his tone was evidently harsh and impatient. By the time he writes 2 Corinthians he is back to his composed self. Too bad we never get to see the harsher side of his dealings with the Corinthians. But we have proof in Galatians of how testy Paul could become when his back was up against a wall. If Galatians is any indication of how vicious he could become when dogged and pushed in a corner, then we can take comfort in its portrait of someone who reminds us of ourselves when the pressure is on to defend your honor, clarify your teachings, safeguard your work, and prove your credentials. Who would think that the same person who wrote, "Love is patient; love is kind; love is not envious or boastful or arrogant or rude" (1 Cor. 13:4-5) could have hurled against those who opposed his teaching on circumcision, "I wish those who unsettle you would castrate themselves!" (Gal. 5:12)? Did the prophet really mean that? Nah, of course not. He was just venting. Gulp.

1 CORINTHIANS 14:12b-20 (BCP)

Writing to a church that had become overzealous about spiritual gifts, Paul turned his attention in chapter 14 to trying to regain order in worship. The whole point of spiritual gifts, Paul argues, is not personal gain but building up the church. If the gift leaves the one with the gift looking mystical but leaves everyone else in the church confused and ignorant about what's being proclaimed—then the gift is counterproductive for worship. Utterances that are not understood, even if they issue from the Spirit, do not benefit worship. The point of corporate worship is to worship God corporately. What applies to the Corinthians, the same applies to Paul. He admits to having had his share of ecstatic experiences—even more than most—but he reserves this ecstasy for private praying (14:18). He argues for intelligent utterances during public worship so that everyone can understand what is being said and can assent to it with "Amen" (v. 16). For Paul prophecy outranks tongues because prophecy is intelligible and does not require an interpreter and because it is for the benefit of the whole church (v. 3). For those who were simply unable to constrain themselves from speaking in tongues Paul has one word of advice: "pray for the power to interpret" (v. 1).

Paul's motivation in chapter 14 for trying to quiet the tongue speakers at Corinth falls outside the lectionary but begs to be mentioned. In 14:23 he quips, "If, therefore, the whole church comes together and all speak in tongues, and outsiders or unbelievers enter, will they not say that you are out of your mind?" In other words, don't give people a reason to reject the gospel when there is a better way to win them to Christ. Paul reminds the church this season that not all rejection of the gospel is because the unconverted are hopeless infidels. Sometimes the church and its members are guilty of being poor witnesses. Sometimes it takes stepping back and looking at your worship and your witness through the eyes of the outsider and honestly admitting that there are places and instances where the church has become so inbred, so spiritual, so cliquish, so unintelligible, so mystical that it turns people off. It has become "so heavenly minded that it is no longer any earthly good."

A cartoon appeared some years ago that made its way into many Christian publications and was reprinted in quite a number of Sunday bulletins across the country. It shows a man standing at the heavenly gate talking to a figure who is supposed to be Jesus and pointing downward at earth in the direction of a church of quarreling people. The man explains why he never became a Christian when he had a chance: "It's not you that I had problem with," he says. "It's those darn followers of yours that got on my last nerve!"

The Gospel

LUKE 4:21-30 (RCL/RC); 4:21-32 (BCP)

Interpreting the Text

At first the synagogue crowd was amazed by Jesus' reading of the Isaiah scroll. "Is this not Joseph's son?" they asked among themselves when he had finished. Here he was a carpenter's son reading like a learned man when everyone knew that only those with rabbinical training read as he did. But as he went on that day in the synagogue, their awe turned to hostility. His arrogance was insulting. How dare a son of a carpenter presume to be able to read their thoughts! He spoke of knowing that they were hoping that he would repeat at home the miracles he had performed in Capernaum. But he refused to do so. Like Elijah and Elisha before him (1 Kings 17:1, 8-9; 18:1; 2 Kings 5:1-14), he said, who were only able to perform miracles among non-Israelites because their own people rejected them and despite the many needy in their midst, Jesus knew that his hometown folks would never accept him. When they heard this, the listeners became incensed and led him out of town to the edge of the city to throw him over a well-known cliff there (Luke 4:30). He did for others what he refused to do among his own, they were probably thinking to themselves.

This is not the first story in Luke where Jesus' powers are challenged and put on the spot. Nor is it the last. A few verse earlier, before his hometown could ask in their hearts, "Do here what you did in Capernaum," there is the temptation scene in 4:9 where Satan dared Jesus, "If you are the Son of God, throw yourself down from here." A similar challenge would be hurled at him while he hung from the cross in 23:35, "He saved others, let him save himself." Rejection in his hometown of Nazareth becomes one in a string of rejections that he endures as God's messenger. For Luke rejection is part of a prophet's

EPIPHANIES ARE POSSIBLE ONLY IF THE WAY HAS BEEN CLEARED AND THE HEART HAS BEEN OPENED TO NEW REVELATIONS.

lot (cf. 6:23; 11:47, 48-50; 13:33-34; 20:9-19; Acts 7:52; Acts 28:25). Jesus is rejected, and so will be his followers after him. The rejection scene in Nazareth portends and climaxes with Jesus' ultimate rejection in Jerusalem where he will be crucified. But, according to Luke, neither rejection nor crucifixion can, in the end, discredit Jesus. He escapes being thrown over the cliff, and he conquers death by getting up from the grave, proving, according to Luke, that God's purposes may be frustrated but they cannot be averted.

Rejection may be a prophet's lot in Luke's Gospel, but being able to discern the hearts and motives of audiences is the prophet's best defense. John the Baptist detected that fear more than repentance was the motivation of some of those who came out to hear him (3:7). Part of Jesus' mission as foretold by Simeon would be to discern the hearts and motives of audiences (Luke 2:35). In fact, Jesus is repeatedly presented as exposing the thoughts of opponents and wavering disciples (5:21-22; 6:8; 9:56-47; 24:38). He exposes them not to humiliate them but to show that his mission was not only to save them from an unjust world but also to save them from their own sinful thoughts. In the end, Luke argues, Jesus would endure the same rejection as that of prophets before him. After all, his rejection had been foretold in Scripture, just as it had been foretold that God's work of salvation—comprehensive, glorious, and universal as it is—would not come about without conflict and tension.

Responding to the Text

The early church had a keen interest in stories about the repeated rejection Jesus experienced as he went about his ministry. They took great comfort in knowing that they were sharing in his suffering, for they knew firsthand the price that went with confessing Jesus as Lord and Savior. Luke's account is in two parts (Luke and Acts), to show Theophilus and others reading the account how Jesus' ministry prefigured the trials and persecution then being experienced by the stubborn little post-resurrection movement and how Hebrew scripture foretold the Messiah's rejection (cf. Acts 4:11, 25-26; 13:40).

Jesus reads the scroll of Isaiah and in so doing reminds us during Epiphany of the importance of dwelling on the word of God. Deep in some monastic traditions is a belief in the value of seeking intimate communion with God through dwelling with and in the Word of God. Catholics call this form prayer *Lectio Divina* (Divine Reading). It is spiritual reading, reading with the divine, inner eye. It is reading with the desire to be transformed totally by God's word, rather than just by facts about God. Had Jesus' audience that day "read" the Isaiah scroll along with Jesus with an open instead of a closed heart, they might have heard what he heard and known what he knew. For he was doing more than just reading

Scripture. He was also allowing Scripture to read him. His critics were too busy sizing him up, however, to hear what he was saying.

But Jesus left a prescription for dealing with scoffers: shake the dust of their towns off your feet (Luke 10:10-12; cf. Acts 13:51; 18:6) and go on to the next town. If only it were that easy! If only your scoffers would be content to see you gone and out of their midst. Perhaps then you could rest. But they rarely are. Some are not happy until they have dogged you from town to town, hurling their taunts and accusations at you. In the beginning you are amazed at their tenacity. Then one day you come to accept it for what it is, namely, the barks and ravings of a tormented spirit. You take the proper measures to protect yourself and to protect your loved ones from its fits, and you leave it to the Spirit of God to keep the promise made to the prophet Jeremiah, "'They will fight against you; but they shall not prevail against you, for I am with you,' says the Lord, 'to deliver you'" (Jer. 1:19).

In the meantime you shake the dust off your feet, even though that too is not easy to do. Rejection hurts. Most of us would do anything not to be rejected. Ministers are the worst, it seems. We find rejection especially hard to take. After all, we were drawn into the ministry as a vocation because we wanted to help people and because we believed that we had gifts to offer in healing the world's hurts. And when that rejection is from those close to us, those whom we opened our hearts to, we feel crushed. But stories like this one of Jesus' reception in his own hometown synagogue in Nazareth remind us that people can see the light and still choose its opposite, see the high road and choose the low road, know the truth and prefer a lie. Epiphany is about Jesus' manifestation of himself not just once, but—thank God—repeatedly to the world. And epiphanies are possible only if the way has been cleared and the heart has been opened to new revelations. The Nazarenes were not prepared to hear him. Thank God he did not stop "preaching, teaching, and sharing the good news of the gospel" because of his experience at Nazareth. (It remains unclear whether he ever visited Nazareth again.) There in the next town—see, there on the map, a place you never imagined in a hundred years you would be—there in Capernaum is a man possessed with a spirit and others sick with various kinds of diseases just waiting to receive the good news of the gospel.

Finally, an ancient collect in the Book of Common Prayer reads: "Almighty God, unto whom all hearts are open, all desires known, and from whom no secrets are hid: cleanse the thoughts of our hearts by the inspiration of the Holy Sprit, that we may perfectly love thee, and worthily magnify thy holy Name; through Christ our Lord. Amen." Not even our secrets thoughts are hid from God, says the ancient collect, even if they are hid from us. God knows. And even if they are hid from us, they do not remain hidden forever. Eventually they tell on us. They slip out without our knowing and without permission. They have been content to lie buried just beneath our rationalizations, our excuses, and our desire not to know. But one day they show up demanding a hearing. A memory. A habit. A fear. A truth we never got around to telling. They appear demanding an honest conversation with us before our end. They nearly crush us with their demand to be dealt with. And we are left to cry out before them, "Lord, have mercy."

FIFTH SUNDAY AFTER THE EPIPHANY

February 4, 2001
Fifth Sunday in Ordinary Time

Revised Common	Episcopal (BCP)	Roman Catholic
Isa. 6:1-8 (9-13)	Judg. 6:11-24a	Isa. 6:1-2a, 3-8
Ps. 138	Ps. 85 or 85:7-13	Ps. 138:1-5, 7-8
1 Cor. 15:1-11	1 Cor. 15:1-11	1 Cor. 15:1-11 or 15:3-8, 11
Luke 5:1-11	Luke 5:1-11	Luke 5:1-11

Not everyone's heart is closed to the good news of the gospel, as we saw last week. Why some hearts remain closed to God, we cannot always understand. But today's lessons remind us and those to whom we preach that for every one who rejects and scoffs at the gospel, there will be others around the corner, in the next town, down at the seashore receptive to the Redeemer's instructions.

First Reading

ISAIAH 6:1-8 (9-13) (RCL); 6:1-2a, 3-8 (RC)

Interpreting the Text

At last we meet Isaiah of Jerusalem, whose preaching in the eighth century set the foundation for theological talk about Zion and whose ministry could still be felt three and four centuries later in the oracles of his prophetic followers, Second Isaiah (Isa. 40–55) and Third Isaiah (Isa. 56–66). Not much is known about the prophet except that he was the son of Amoz, was married to prophetess, had two children both of whose name symbolized Zion's doomed future, and lived and preached during the second half of the eighth century. His call from God came in 742 B.C.E., the year the king who reigned during the southern kingdom's most prosperous and stable times died, King Uzziah. The king's death signaled the end of an important era in Judah and marked the beginning of a succession of weak, acquiescent kings (Jotham, Ahaz, and Hezekiah) none of whom could muster the strength to stave off Assyria—"the rod of (Yahweh's) anger"—

who was beginning to scout out vulnerable nations beyond its borders to conquer and to annex to its empire. Isaiah entered the sanctuary that Sabbath, hoping for some sign from Yahweh.

Isaiah had served and worshiped God in the Temple every Sabbath for all of his life, but this particular day was different. Today Isaiah caught a glimpse of the heavenly court. Today he saw the Lord "sitting upon a throne, high and lofty" (Isa. 6:1). Whether the Lord appeared to Isaiah in a vision or in a dream or face-to-face, Isaiah does not say explicitly (although the latter seems unlikely since directly looking upon God with the naked eye was excluded by Hebrew scripture [Exod. 19:21; 20:19; 33:20; Deut. 18:16; Judg. 13:22]). Like Moses before him (Exod. 33:12-23) and Ezekiel after him (Ezek. 1:28), the prophet Isaiah refrains from describing the deity. That would have been blasphemous. The most he brings himself to say beyond that Yahweh was high and lifted up was that "the hem of his robe filled the temple" (Isa. 6:1). That is it. In deference to Yahweh he describes instead the other sights and sounds taking place in the heavenly court.

Cherubs, or seraphs, were believed to be messengers or agents of God. The winged creatures accompanied the deity in the heavenly court, each with three pairs of wings: one pair covered their face in the awesome presence of God; one pair covered their feet (genitals) as a sign of their commitment to purity; and with the final pair they flew about to fulfill the commission of God. The cherubs' threefold cry of "holy" and their ascription of the deity as the "Lord of hosts" acknowledged Israel's God as free from earthly limitations (Isa. 6:3). Part of their commission was to take a live hot coal off the altar and to touch Isaiah's mouth with it and in doing so to purify him from his sins and commission him for his new vocation as a prophet (6:6-13).

Isaiah came seeking solace in the rituals of Temple worship. And behold, there in worship he found more than he was looking for. He came mourning the loss of a beloved king, but that day in the Temple, Isaiah found the Holy One of Israel! Yahweh's holiness contrasted sharply with Isaiah's uncleanness (unworthiness to serve) but, thanks to the act of the seraphs, Isaiah was empowered to be Yahweh's instrument. Because of what Isaiah saw that day in the Temple, the eyes of the world would for centuries to come become open to the redeeming glory of the heavens.

Responding to the Text

Isaiah fails to say whether anyone else in the Temple that day saw what he saw, heard what he heard, or felt what he felt: the robe, the seraphs, the voice, the awful shaking. Surely there must have been others present that day in 742 B.C.E.—prophets, priests, scribes, rabbis, courtiers, and the like. Perhaps they were singing the psalm along with him or listening to the same Torah text read by the priest. Yet, it seems, only Isaiah was receptive to what happened next. The others went through the motions without giving much thought to what they were doing. But Isaiah caught a glimpse of heaven that day.

Visions like the one Isaiah experienced were and are rare. Although the emphasis during the Epiphany season is upon appearances by the holy in our midst, we find ourselves compelled to admit to our congregations and to ourselves that most encounters with the divine are not on the scale of that of the prophet Isaiah. The truth is that most of our most memorable encounters are those that erupt into the daily details of mundane, ordinary life, while we are dressing our children, tidying up the office, driving in the hustle and bustle of holiday shopping, sitting next to a stranger on an airplane, visiting parents in nursing homes, or as in biblical days drawing water from a well, tending sheep on the backside of a mountain, or cleaning up after a night of unproductive fishing. The covers are pulled back, for perhaps only a second, and it is as if we see the truth about ourselves, our pasts, our fears, our hopes—and then it is over. And we are left stammering to consciousness. But we see it, however fleetingly.

Describing her routine as a writer, Flannery O'Connor wrote once that every morning she dutifully made her way to her desk in her study whether she knew what she was going to write about or not. She stationed herself predictably at her desk in front of her typewriter faithfully every morning, waiting and open, *in case* an idea came to her mind. This was a ritual for Flannery O'Connor much as Isaiah's appearance in the Temple that day in 742 B.C.E. was for him. It was an act of obedience, faithfulness, and devotion that is done even when you do not feel like doing it and even if you cannot remember anymore why you do it. You show up, and you remain open. To what? To whatever happens. Mystery. Revelations. Voices. An awful shaking. The touch of angels. *Just in case.*

JUDGES 6:11-24a (BCP)

While on the surface the focus of the story of Gideon is ultimately on Gideon's commissioning as a judge and military leader in a campaign against Israel's enemies, the Midianites, it describes on another level how the divine can and does gloriously manifest itself in the profane realm of everyday existence so as to get human attention.

It is an ordinary day, and Gideon doesn't appear particularly worried about anything. But when the angel calls to him from under the oak tree ("The Lord is with you, mighty warrior" [Judg. 6:12]), Gideon's response betrays his worries: If the Lord is with us, why has the Lord sat by and allowed us to be overtaken by the Midianites?—to paraphrase his question to the angel (vv. 13-14). When the angel responds that he has been selected to lead Israel in battle against the Midianites (v. 14), Gideon protests that he is the least worthy since he comes from the weakest (smallest) tribe of Israel. Gideon asks for a sign that God is calling him to this role—and he receives one: fire springs from a rock and consumes the meat and cakes he has presented as an offering to God (vv. 19-24). Gideon cries out in wonder and a bit of disbelief when it dawns on him that he has been in the presence of heavenly beings (6:22). The story narrates not only Gideon's commissioning. It also functions as an aetiological tale, explaining the origins of an altar that had been erected and left standing near the oak at Ophrah. The author of Judges draws on the legend of Gideon to explain how the altar came to be where it was. The altar is a reminder of God's self-manifestation as a God of peace, says the author.

There is no hint that Gideon was doing anything out of the ordinary as he stood threshing wheat in the wine press that day. Out of the ordinary, the commonplace, the *saeculum*, the Holy One appears, scripture teaches. But amidst the ordinary, the commonplace, and the *saeculum*, human beings devise for themselves rituals, routine acts, patterns of behavior that keep them accountable and on task. Worship is one of them. Threshing wheat at the wine press faithfully every day is another. Celebrating the liturgical seasons every year is one more. Waiting faithfully outside your child's school every day at the same time to take her home, to dance lessons, or to wherever is yet another. Standing on your feet for hours every month serving meals to hundreds of homeless at the downtown shelter is another. They prove that we are serious in our intent to keep our word. They prove that we are dependable. They prove that we intend to show up regardless of whether the other party will show up. Above all, rituals show that we are receptive to whatever happens or doesn't happen.

Responsive Reading

PSALM 138 (RCL); 138:1-5, 7-8 (RC)

Interpreting the Text

A typical feature of psalms of thanksgiving is thanking God for answering the prayers of people or individuals and delivering the nation or the individual out of trouble. This feature stands out in Psalm 138. The psalmist celebrates what God had done even while waiting eagerly for God to do even more for the psalmist (vv. 7-8). Thanking God for God's merciful acts and bearing witness to others about what God has done are constituent elements of divine worship. For those unable to worship in the temple as a result of travel or illness, the simple act of bowing down in the direction of the house of God suffices as an act of adoration and humility before God. While kneeling in the sanctuary, perhaps gazing up at the splendor and grandeur of the Temple facade as perhaps Isaiah was doing that day in 742 B.C.E. during worship, such a song takes on special meaning. The point is that God "appears" and makes God's self known by answering the prayers of wearied petitioners (v. 3). No angels, cherubs, or heavenly intermediaries are mentioned as agents of the deliverance the psalmist experiences. The psalm celebrates a theophanic manifestation of the divine through works and wonders on behalf of the "lowly" (v. 6). Even kings have to sing the praises of the Lord upon hearing the word and ways of the Lord, says the psalmist (vv. 4, 5); they will do this even though in the end it is the lowly whom the Lord favors over the haughty (v. 6).

PSALM 85 or 85:7-13 (BCP)

Underlying both Psalm 138 and Psalm 85 is a belief in the Divine graciously attaching itself to temporal profane spaces. In Psalm 138 the divine is associated with the Temple: in Psalm 87 it is Zion. The mood switches in Psalm 87, however, to lament and grief. The community begins by calling on Yahweh's favor toward Zion in times past (vv. 1-3) as a way of petitioning the national God to show the same favor in the present (vv. 4-9). Zion is in danger. The nation asks whether Yahweh's anger is forever (v. 5). They ask for Yahweh's *hesed* and salvation (v. 7). They wait to hear what Yahweh will say to them (v. 8). We wait with them. Together we stand as a community of believers confident that Yahweh's glory will prevail.

Second Reading

1 CORINTHIANS 15:1-11 (RCL/BCP); 15:1-11 or 15:3-8, 11 (RC)

Interpreting the Text

Prior to chapter 15 Paul's attention has been upon restoring orderly worship in the community, urging the women at Corinth to cover their heads for the sake of keeping peace in the church (even though he admits to relying here more on custom than scripture for this injunction: 11:1-16), warning against class prejudices and social jockeying at the Holy Communion celebration (11:17-34), and exhorting the congregation to love and unity and not to esteem any gift in worship above another (12: 1—14:39). He climaxes the epistle by addressing doctrinal errors circulating about the resurrection of Christ. Those in the church with a Greek background had no problem with belief in the immortality of the soul, since Greek philosophy had already introduced them to such a notion. But talk of a resurrected body or the immortality of the body was preposterous to some of them, coming as they did from a background that denied the value of the body. Paul recognized that no sooner had he left Corinth that false theology began to emerge which over-spiritualized everything and urged members to deny the deeds done in the body because of its inferiority to the spirit. Paul reminds the church of the gospel that was first proclaimed to them (by Paul) and that first saved them (15:1-2). Simply put, Christ rose from the dead in body and in victory. The finer points of his argument are beyond our purview in this lesson, but the whole weight of Paul's argument for Christ's bodily resurrection rests on one central piece of evidence presented in vv. 1-11.

How can we believe that Christ rose in body from the dead? Paul says that we believe because Christ showed himself first to Cephas (Peter), then to the twelve disciples (v. 5), then at one time (!) to more than five hundred other believers (v. 6), then to the James the brother of the Lord and to the apostles (v. 7), and finally to the least of them all, Paul (vv. 8-10). For those who questioned Paul's leadership because he was not a part of the original twelve, he concludes the section by saying that whether they believe his proclamation that he had seen Christ or that of the others who confessed to having seen Christ—the point is the same: reliable people have claimed to have seen the resurrected Christ in the flesh, and upon that confession we have all come to believe (v. 11). The good news or *euangelion* rests on just such a confession which Paul first proclaimed at Corinth and which at that time they readily received, and upon which they are being saved: Christ is risen.

What in the world is going on over there that causes you to question the basic claim of the faith? Paul all but asks.

Responding to the Text

Lawyers will tell you that nothing seals a case like an eyewitness to the event. The same holds true for religious belief. Nothing convinces the person wavering and weighing whether to become a Christian, whether to join a particular church fellowship, whether to believe, like the personal testimony of an eyewitness who can relate her own experience in these areas. Seeing is believing. And belief is to be shared with others who will in their own time "see" for themselves.

Paul admits that the generation that had originally seen the resurrected Christ was dying out (1 Cor. 15:6). When that happened, no more eyewitnesses would be around to testify to what they have seen and heard. It would be left to the church at Corinth and those elsewhere who received the proclamation to be Christ's witnesses. The church would have to content itself with the stories passed down to it, the memory entrusted to it. Each generation has to see him, feel him, hear him, and come to know him—through the gift of the Holy Spirit—for itself. So it has been down through the generations: the story our spiritual ancestors first proclaimed has had to suffice. And it has, it does, it will—until each one of us is able to see, hear, and feel Christ for ourselves.

That brings to mind a story about the power of story—but it is also a story about the importance of remaining open to belief. It is one of the legends of Baal-Shem, which means "the master of God's name," told by his followers, the Hasidim, a Jewish sect of eastern Europe that arose around the middle of the eighteenth century and lives on to this day. Hasidic teaching centers on rebirth, believing that renewal is possible.

Perceiving that he was dying, the Ba'al Shem Tov called for his disciples and said, "I have acted as intermediary for you, and now when I am gone you must do this for yourselves. You know the place in the forest where I call to God? Stand there in the place and do the same. Light a fire as you have been instructed to do, and say the prayer as you learned. Do all these and God will come."

Shortly afterwards, the Ba'al Shem Tov died. The first generation of followers did exactly as he had said, and sure enough God came as always. After this generation passed, the second generation had forgotten how to light the fire the way the Ba'al Shem Tov had instructed. Nevertheless, they faithfully made the pilgrimage to the special place in the forest and said the prayer they had been instructed to pray. And, sure enough, God showed up.

A third generation came long who had forgotten how to light the fire and no longer remembered the place in the forest where they should stand. But they said the prayer as the Ba'al Shem Tov had instructed. And again God showed up.

By the fourth generation, no one was around who remembered how to light the fire nor where the special place was in the forest. Neither was anyone alive who could recall the prayer the Ba'al Shem Tov had instructed his followers to pray. But there was one person who remembered the *story* about the fire, the forest, and the prayer, and delighted in telling it over and over. And sure enough, God came.

The Gospel

LUKE 5:1-11

Interpreting the Text

Having suffered rejection in his hometown, Jesus proceeded to Capernaum, a city in Galilee, and from there to a small fishing village on the coast of the Lake of Gennesaret (otherwise known as the Sea of Galilee). He was unknown in these parts, presumably. Luke uses the story to contrast the receptivity to Jesus on the part of strangers in the next town to that of his hometown people of Nazareth. When Jesus came to the lake he found fishermen busy washing their nets after a long unproductive night at work. The only thing on their mind was cleaning up, eating, and getting some sleep. An epiphany was the last thing on their mind. Jesus hired Simon to take him out in his boat a little away from the shore and from there the crowd who had come out to hear him could get a better view of him as he taught them, sitting. The narrator trusts here that the reader will pick up on the irony of it all: Jesus hires the boat to catch humans while Simon uses it to catch mere fish.

Simon's name has already been introduced to the reader by Luke in 4:38, where while in Capernaum Jesus enters the house of the mother-in-law of a certain Simon. Unaware of who the stranger was but eager to make money and not let the night be a complete waste, Simon agreed to hire his boat out to Jesus (5:2-3). After he finished teaching (and when possibly it was time to pay Simon for his time), Jesus suggested that Simon and his men let their nets down there in the deep water. Because he had just been out in those very waters all night, Simon was not eager to waste his worker's time unraveling the heavy gnarled nets all for nothing: "Master, we have worked all night but have caught nothing" (v. 5a). Peter addressed Jesus as "Master" possibly because he was impressed with what teachings he could hear from where he stood barking orders to his associates. "Yet if you say so, I will let down the nets" (v. 5b). He didn't believe Jesus any more than did the hometown folks in Nazareth, but something in him relented despite his better sense. The catch his men pulled up was so hefty that they had to beckon other boats over to help them pull the fish into the boat. Each boat that came became so filled with fish that each looked as if it was about to sink. Upon seeing Jesus' power, Simon Peter fell down in submission saying, "Go away from me, Lord, for I am a sinful man!" (v. 8).

THERE IS PRECIOUS LITTLE IN SOME OF OUR PREACHING TO SUGGEST THAT AS MINISTERS WE HAVE EVER BEEN OVERWHELMED WITH AWE AND WONDER IN CHRIST'S PRESENCE.

Luke refrains from calling what Jesus does at the Lake of Gennesaret a miracle, but Peter's response along with that of his associates does not differ from that of those in the miracles stories strewn throughout Luke's Gospel (compare the response of those who witnessed Jesus' healing of the paralytic in the story that follows, 5:17-27, especially v. 26). On the one hand, it wasn't a miracle in that the laws of nature were not defied. After all, fish were there in the sea; they simply were not biting the night before when Peter and his associates were out with their nets. But, on the other hand, it was a miracle in that it challenged Peter's expectations and beliefs.

Luke uses several different Greek words in his opening chapters to capture the stir and astonishment Jesus evoked in audiences (*thambos* [4:36; 5: 9], *thauma* [4:22; cf. 9:43], *ekstasis* [5:26]). What seems certain in 5:1-11 is that Luke is contrasting Peter's initial disbelief with his subsequent confession (v. 8). Peter was convinced now after seeing the magnitude of this unexpected catch. Jesus' manifestation of his power not only convinced him but also convicted him. As with Isaiah of Jerusalem's Temple vision, which left him filled with self-loathing (Isa. 6:5), and Gideon's cry after encountering the angels (Judg. 6:22), Peter responds similarly to Jesus' power with awe and revulsion (5:8). Beholding the divine one's power over the universe each man came face-to-face with his own limitations and unworthiness. But Luke is quick to point out that Peter was not the only one to witness Jesus' power over nature that day at the Lake of Gennesaret. His fishing partners James and John, sons of Zebedee, also saw what happened and were amazed. As a result, all three left their boats and their fishing business to become fishers of men instead.

The story describes how the three disciples came to follow Jesus, just as the story of Isaiah's vision describes his call to be prophet. For both parties it started out with them going about their ordinary routine, doing what they knew to do, expecting the minimum, but willing to trust God for something more; and for all parties it ended with an extraordinary encounter that left them departing forever changed.

Responding to the Text

Long after his first appearance to the world, Jesus is still showing up in our midst and defying our expectations. He appears, and our response is one of amazement, wonder, and marvel. But before we as ministers can proclaim such a message, we have to be able to testify that we have experienced just such a message. Ministers run the risk of ceasing to be witnesses to the presence of Christ in their own lives. In fact there is precious little in some of our preaching to suggest that as ministers we have ever been overwhelmed with awe and wonder in Christ's presence like Peter, James, and John. Members can only assume that their ministers have had such moments, although their ministers don't talk about them. But why don't we speak of them? Is it because we think the experiences are too private? Too difficult to put in words? Too muddled with other things going in our lives at the time that we're no longer certain how much of it was born out of our neuroses back then and how much of it was God's initiative? The temptation is to stick to what we know, namely, the dry homiletical pronouncements we pasted in our mind that evaporate in the sanctuary air as soon as we utter them because they are spoken devoid of passion and personal witness. We have learned to speak about belief, joy, hope, Jesus, faith, with what often seems like "a maximum of authority and a minimum of vital personal involvement."[7] Like Peter and his associates who were professional fishermen, we have mastered the technique of our craft and we labor all night reinforcing our nets, but when the morning comes we find that we were unable to catch fish.

But now and then, at unforeseen moments, a divine mystery breaks into our routine and makes us drop our nets and bow before its presence. We feel unworthy to stand in its presence. But even more we feel incapable of finding words to describe it. "Ineffable" is the term we in religious circles have settled on to describe those miracles that were not miracles after all but felt like miracles nonetheless. But "ineffable" does not release us as ministers of the responsibility to testify to our personal experience with the Holy. Even if they scoff at our descriptions and question our experience, we must speak about them regardless. For the souls that await you in the pew do not want your dry descriptions; they yearn for testimonies of what you felt and what you perceived. Whether they believe you is not the point. The point in sharing your personal experience is not to convince people but to stir up people's interest and prepare their hearts for their own now-and-then, here-and-now encounters that break into their midst and defy their expectations. We share our personal testimonies of our encounters with God, if not for their sake, then certainly for our own—so that we may relive the moments and per chance reexperience the wonder.

SIXTH SUNDAY AFTER THE EPIPHANY

FEBRUARY 11, 2001
SIXTH SUNDAY IN ORDINARY TIME; PROPER 1

REVISED COMMON	EPISCOPAL (BCP)	ROMAN CATHOLIC
Jer. 17:5-10	Jer. 17:5-10	Jer. 17:5-8
Ps. 1	Ps. 1	Ps. 1:1-4, 6
1 Cor. 15:12-20	1 Cor. 15:12-20	1 Cor. 15:12, 16-20
Luke 6:17-26	Luke 6:17-26	Luke 6:17, 20-26

LAST WEEK'S LESSONS FOCUSED ON THE WONDER and amazement that fill the heart at beholding Christ's glory. Today's readings peer more closely into that same heart to ponder what lay hidden within it. The heart is the seat of the will in the Jewish-Christian tradition. Christ comes not only to discern the hearts of human beings but also to inspire the hearts of those who remain steadfast in him and to offer them a glimpse of the kingdom that is to come.

FIRST READING

JEREMIAH 17:5-10 (RCL/BCP); 17:5-8 (RC)

Interpreting the Text

This text is from a section of the book of Jeremiah filled with "oracles of judgment and renewal" (16:14—17:13). Both outbursts of condemnation and promises of restoration can be found within a few verses of each other. Commentators never fail to mention the deeply emotional tone underlying Jeremiah's oracles, dubbing him the "weeping prophet." The book's profound emotional edge can be detected as early as the book's opening, where one gets the feeling of listening in on a private conversation between God and prophet, the latter begging to be spared God's call and God demanding the prophet to pull himself together and get on with it. The prophet evidently obeyed, but not without complaining and railing against God from time to time. That seems evident from collection of oracles found in the book that have come to be known as the "laments of Jeremiah" or borrowing, from Augustine's memoir, "the confessions of

Jeremiah" (11:18—12:6; 15:10-21; 17:14-18; 18:12-23; 20:7-13, 14-18). In all fairness to the prophet, however, a conscious effort has been made by the Deuteronomic editors of the book to draw parallels between this sixth-century prophet, who urges Judah repeatedly to repent and obey to avert God's judgment, and the prophet Moses, who centuries earlier first laid down the Torah calling for obedience. Both were reluctant prophets, both harangued God, and both appealed to the Torah as the ethical basis for Israel's existence. Similarly, both describe the consequences of obedience and disobedience to the Torah by contrasting a life marked by "blessings" and one marked by "curses" (cf. Deut. 28).

Trust is at the heart of the blessings and curses that Jeremiah speaks about in 17:1-10. Simply stated, those who put their trust in mortals rather than Yahweh are cursed; those whose trust in Yahweh are blessed. There is nothing complicated about that. Those who trust in mortal flesh never flourish any more than a parched shrub in a desert, needing water. But those who trust in Yahweh are like a tree planted by water whose roots are long and deep, sprouting out into the stream. The description of blessing is exactly like the one found in Psalm 1. The notion of the blessed life being like a robust tree is found in three places in Hebrew scripture: Proverbs 3:18, Psalm 1:2, and here in Jeremiah 17:7. Who is borrowing from the other and which one is original cannot be determined. But contrasting one thing with another is a favorite literary device of ancient and modern poets when trying to shed light on the essence of something. The assumption is that you understand what a thing is by understanding first what it is not, and vice versa. In this case, where the prophet is trying to point out for his listeners the dangers of trusting in idols and the pitfalls of placing one's confidence in human beings and not in Yahweh, he contrasts sharply the plight of the parched shrub with that of the flourishing tree. The shrub languishes parched and alone in the desert, whereas the robust tree is able to flourish even in intemperate weather because its roots run deep. To reinforce his point he asserts that trust is an issue of the heart (v. 9). Only Yahweh can discern its true motives, and an individual's actions are the best indicator for discerning the heart (v. 10). Unfortunately, the prophet does not hold out much hope for Judah. Sin has already inscribed itself unalterably on Judah's heart (17:1; cf. 4:18).

Responding to the Text

The heart's motives are knowable only to God, says the prophet. Its slippery, shifty ways go undetected even to the one to whom the heart belongs. God asks for the heart, yet our greatest failures as human beings issue from our hearts. It confesses trust in God, but then it negotiates with idols. It calls on the name of God, but then it refuses to obey God's ways. The prophet throws up his hands in exasperation, as many of us do when our hearts betray us: "Who can understand [the heart]?" Judah's stubborn heart has blinded her to Yahweh as the true source of her sustenance (5:23, 24). Not surprisingly, the word "heart" shows up more than fifteen times in the book of Jeremiah. The weeping, reluctant prophet refers to his own heart several times to describe his grief at what was happening in Judah (4:19; 8:18). But it is his understanding of the heart as the seat of one's will that makes him appeal again and again to the inhabitants to turn to Yahweh with their whole heart (Jer. 3:10; 24:7; cf. 4:14). He is certain that if they were to seek Yahweh with their heart and not just with their mouths, the inhabitants could avert the disaster heading their way from the Babylonians. But people do what is in their heart to do (9:8). The prophet believes that only God can know the heart, and only God can change the heart. In his vision of the new covenant that will be cut with God's people, Jeremiah describes God carving the Torah on the very hearts of God's people, where it can never again be supplanted nor taken away (31:31-34).

Responsive Reading
PSALM 1 (RCL/BCP); 1:1-4, 6 (RC)

This is one of the best-known psalms in the Psalter, second only to Psalm 23 perhaps. Its prominence as the first of 150 psalms has a lot to do with the weighty consideration given to it by commentators. Categorized as a Torah or wisdom psalm because it describes the ideal believer as the one who meditates on the Torah day and night, it fittingly opens the psalm collection, beginning as it does with the beatitude "blessed," "happy," or "fortunate" (*asher*) to describe the ideal believer (the translation "wise" can probably also be applied although there is a precise Hebrew word for that). The person who routinely fixes her or his mind upon the Torah is compared to "trees planted by streams of water" that never fail to bear fruit in their proper season (Ps. 1:3). In contrast, the foolish or wicked person is like the chaff that lacks the substance to stay put and can be easily driven away by the wind (v. 4).

Here is an appropriate place to point out that the English word "law" is an inadequate translation of the Hebrew *torah*. The latter is a term rich in meanings, and a number of meanings can be present or implied when it is being used. The word *Torah* should certainly not be reduced to refer to some inhibiting legalism. Two meanings are relevant for our purposes. *Torah* can refer to the broader story narrated in the first five books of the Old Testament of the actions Yahweh took to create a people and to guide them into the future. It can also refer to the responsibilities that shape the identity of the people who repeatedly rehearse the story of the actions Yahweh took on their behalf. The Torah mentioned in

Psalm 1 refers to both the story of Yahweh's deeds on behalf of Israel and the deeds or obligations Yahweh expects Israel to perform in return. The blessed or happy person is the one who meditates routinely on the inseparability of the two.

As we see in this Torah song, wisdom or happiness does not come from contemplation for contemplation's sake. Happiness is not a state of bliss but a devotion to a certain way of life, a life committed to a certain course of action and behaving (or not behaving) (v. 1). Seen in this way, Psalm 1 becomes all the more a proper psalm with which to introduce the whole of the book of Psalms. For the songs and prayers found within express more than just Israel's personal feelings and responses to Yahweh's gracious deeds. They reflect Israel's answers to the one who asks them to live a certain way.

Second Reading

1 CORINTHIANS 15:12-20 (RCL/BCP); 15:12, 16-20 (RC)

Interpreting the Text

Imagine Paul working tirelessly every day to get a new church off the ground there in Ephesus but obsessing over the letter he was still composing in his head to the church over in Corinth (1 Cor. 16:8). Tonight, before lying down, perhaps he would get Titus or Sosthenes (1 Cor. 1:1) to do some dictation for him. Tonight he planned to shift the discussion to the resurrection which required some concentration on his part since he planned it to be the climax of the letter. He resented all the time and energy this letter was taking, and the way it was keeping him from giving his undivided attention to this work at Ephesus. The same work required to get the Corinthian church off the ground (Acts 18:1-11) was required in Ephesus: teaching about and conducting baptisms, laying hands on the sick, casting out demons, being dragged into lecture halls, synagogues, and marketplaces defending the faith, rescuing himself and followers from riots, training apprentices, being dragged in and out of synagogues and courts every day defending the faith, stopping to answer the questions of passersby (cf. Acts 19:1-40). Ephesus needed his undivided attention, but he couldn't let sinners come in and triumph over his work at Corinth. Besides, he couldn't stop thinking about this latest round of disturbing news from Chloe's people about all the quarrels and divisions taking place at Corinth. Serious aberrations had arisen there concerning disorderliness at the Lord's Supper, spiritual gifts, speaking in tongues, sexual immorality, and a host of other things. He resented the wicked intruders who came into his churches as soon as he departed, spreading bad doctrine and raising doubts in people's minds about his credentials. Was he a fool for thinking that being this itinerant missionary thing could work? He couldn't be two places at one time! Darn those Corinthians with their free-thinking ways!

Paul was anxious to take a boat over the Aegean Sea to give the church at Corinth a piece of his mind, but he decided to postpone it. The Ephesus ministry was too young to leave unsupervised. After months of hard labor the ministry was just beginning to pick up speed and gain some momentum. So Paul settled on dictating a letter instead, being sure to include a greeting in his own handwriting to assure those in Corinth that this letter was authentic (16:21). On occasions like these he was grateful for both his rabbinic background and the passion it had aroused in him for *Torah* and rhetoric. All those years meditating on *Torah* served him well when it came time to defend the gospel and prove that Christ fulfilled *Torah*. He was also glad for the knowledge of Greek philosophy which he picked up here and there in Tarsus, his hometown. He needed the passion of the one and the orderliness of the other to help him craft the finer points of Jesus' resurrection, which was a thorny issue for largely gentile churches where the notion of the immortality of the soul was perfectly acceptable but that of bodily resurrection was a stumbling block. He would show those Greeks a thing or two tonight: he was no country, uneducated Jew. He could argue the subtler points of philosophy with the best of them!

THROUGH THE CHILD WE HAVE BECOME THE FAMILY OF GOD.

He would start off tonight's dictation with a simple point: "Are we to believe that all the eyewitness accounts to Jesus' resurrection are a lie?" is the way he was thinking about opening. *No, no, no,* he told himself as he walked through the square that day, *That's putting the matter too bluntly. Don't scoff at them—not just yet. Soften it a bit:* "If there is no resurrection of the dead, then Christ has not been raised; and if Christ has not been raised, then our proclamation has been in vain and your faith has been in vain" (15:13-14).

Responding to the Text

Sometimes our zeal for Christ can blind us to our own shortcomings. The prophet Jeremiah was correct: "The heart is devious above all else." In the quasi-journalistic reconstruction above of what may have gone through Paul's head as he composed his first letter to the church at Corinth, we see how Paul's own ego-needs may have blinded him to some of the ways in which he was more like his detractors than unlike them. Sometimes we do the right things for the wrong reasons, and sometimes we do the wrong things for the right reasons. Even in our zeal to be devoted followers of Jesus we can swell with pride and self-righteousness and violate the very *Torah* we profess to cherish. Jesus was fully aware of this when he warned his disciples how easy it is to become self-deluded: "Indeed an hour is coming when those who kill you will think that by doing so they are offering worship to God" (John 16:2).

Reinhold Niebuhr pointed out that "the possibilities of evil grow with the possibilities of good,"[8] meaning that evil is much more inextricably bound up with good than most religious thinkers are willing to acknowledge. He goes further to warn against dividing ourselves into "a contest between God-fearing believers and unrighteous unbelievers."[9] This kind of dualistic thinking divides the world into "us" versus "them," making us reach back and rely on language and imagery that conceals more than it reveals where talk about "light" vs. "darkness" and "the forces of God" vs. "the forces of Satan" is used uncritically, blinding us to the partial truth in our adversaries' position and the partial error in our own.

Our only protection against self-deception, if that is possible, is found in what the psalmist understood was the true blessing of meditating routinely on the *Torah*. For one thing we are reminded of how utterly dependent we are upon God to reveal to us not only the evil that lurks out there in the world if we do not properly order our steps. Keeping our ears attuned to God's commanding voice keeps us potentially aware of and honest about the evil that lies just beneath the surface of our own good deeds. "[God] knows how we are made; [God] knows that we are dust" (Ps. 103:14).

The Gospel

LUKE 6:17-26 (RCL/BCP); 6:17, 20-26 (RC)

Interpreting the Text

Earlier Jesus had been gathering followers from town to town. Among those who followed him were Peter, James, and John, who left their fishing boats at the Lake of Gennesaret (5:11); then there was Levi the tax collector, who abandoned his tax booth (5:27-28); and there were others whom Luke doesn't mention by name. By 6:13 he distinguishes between disciples (followers) and apostles ("appointed representatives"). Peter, James, John, and Levi belong to the latter along with nine others: Andrew, Philip, Bartholomew, Thomas, James son of Alphaeus, Simon the Zealot, Judas son of James, and Judas Iscariot.

Using the general term "disciples" to refer to everyone (6:13, 20), Jesus now turns his attention to outlining some of the demands that come with being a follower in this new kingdom movement. His speech here becomes in Luke's Gospel Jesus' first extensive teaching. Luke is less concerned this time about his audience's response. Whether the disciples respond with amazement or hostility to Jesus' words, Luke does not bother to say. The diseased and infirm come out to hear Jesus, but their interest chiefly is in being healed (6:19). Whether they bother to stay around and listen to Jesus' teachings is not certain. Luke's concern at this moment is to portray Jesus as shifting his ministry from being simply an itinerant miracle worker to being a leader and a visionary.

Luke makes use of speech material that has already been gathered together by Matthew the Evangelist (Matt. 5–7), but he borrows it and adapts for his own purposes. Most notably, Matthew's Sermon on the Mount (Matt. 5:3-12) turns into Luke's Sermon on the Plain (Luke 6:17-49), where Jesus stands on a level place rather than an elevated place to address his audience. Before him are people with very little to offer beyond their enthusiasm and their devotion. But they are the beginnings of his new movement who, despite their poverty and need, recognize the presence of something new and powerful happening around them. Jesus' teachings in 6:20-27 will help give this new thing some clarity. He is about to explain to them the purpose for his coming.

The teaching unfolds in a three stages: (1) Jesus declares the disciples blessed (*makarioi*) (vv. 20-23) for their willingness to accept a rejected, reviled status in order to follow him. Their sacrifice will not go unrewarded, for the kingdom belongs to them, and when that eschatological kingdom dawns, the revulsion and rejection will change to fulfillment and joy. (2) But he warns those who are rich and who seek only the approval of others (vv. 24-26), for they will be the ones who will lose out in the kingdom and experience their laughter turn to weeping and mourning. And then he calls his disciples to an attitude of love for enemies and nonretaliatory behavior (vv. 27-30) that will presumably serve as the basis for their admittance to the kingdom.

Commentators have observed that Luke is more willing to address the concrete socioeconomic circumstances of his followers than is Matthew. The latter spiritualizes their circumstances by talking about the "poor in spirit" in contrast to Luke's (economically) "poor," and "those who grieve over sin and evil in the world" compared to "those who mourn" in Luke. Nevertheless, Luke has tinkered and tampered with the blessings (and woes) in his own way as well when he speaks to his disciples in the second person ("Blessed are you . . . ," rather than "Blessed are those who . . ."). Luke's second-person address reinforces the picture of Jesus as someone who speaks intimately and compassionately to the crowd, someone who identifies with the crowd by standing with them rather than above them. We saw in the judgment oracle in Jeremiah 17 and in the wisdom speech of Psalm 1 how the beatitude served to commend the path of good or wisdom over evil and folly. But in Luke's Gospel, beatitudes express confidence in a future day of divine reversal where those who are poor will enjoy all the privileges that come with possessing the kingdom, those who are hungry will eat until they are filled, and those who weep will be able to laugh again (Luke 17:20-23). In their sharp contrast to the blessings, the series of "woes" help to reinforce the notion of Jesus' ministry as inaugurating an era of reversal, turning things on their head, a new order of things. He stops the healing and begins to teach the poor and meek, the persecuted, and those hungry in order to inspire the motley band he has gathered around him that day and to motivate them for the days ahead. They do not know at this point what lies ahead. They are eager to sign on to any revolution that promises them a share in the world in which they live. That Jesus is promising them that and more won't dawn on some of them until later (and never does for others). Nevertheless, Jesus takes the time at the beginning to try to set his followers' sights higher, where they might glimpse the better and more powerful kingdom that is to come, one that has some things to do with power, and everything to do with the reign of God. They couldn't see it fully at the moment, but if they pay attention they may be able to catch glimpses here and there as they follow Jesus closely.

Responding to the Text

People eager to pursue a spiritual path are always asking the question, "How do I know the will of God?" They ask that even though there are scores of laws, precepts, admonishments, and promises scattered throughout both the Old and New Testaments to guide them. They ask despite the volumes of books that have been written by mystics, clergy, laypersons, travelers, and seekers over the centuries, but especially over the past twenty years, about every aspect of the spiritual journey. They ask even though they have been members of your churches for decades. One day a certain man ran up and posed the same question to Jesus, admittedly in a different manner, but seeking the same kind of information: "Good Teacher, what must I do to inherit eternal life?" Before going further Jesus answered him bluntly, "You know the commandments" (Mark 10:17ff.). Jesus knew that this man was asking for more than information. He was asking for what T. S. Eliot speaks of as "the knowledge that gets lost in information." The man had grown up hearing the commandments recited all his life. He perhaps had occasion to read the commandments, sing the psalms, and repeat the proverbs for himself. So it wasn't information that he wanted. He had information. He wanted certitude. And certitude is what the world craves. Be assured this Epiphany season that the world is not interested in just a glimpse of Jesus. Neither will it be content simply to meet Jesus. The world demands to know for certain that in following Jesus they are on *the* right path. They want to be certain of God's will before they step out. They want to know this even though it is the very thing none of us who proclaim the gospel can offer. We cannot give them certitude but only a *way*, a journey of faith. It is only when they have accepted Jesus' invitation to follow and embarked upon the journey that they will come to know the things they need to know about Jesus and about themselves. Writing about what she has learned about the will of God, Wendy Wright confesses:

> If you think you sense the will of God in your life in some long-range, highly detailed plan, something you can see stretching out with clear goals and successes into the future, *that* is *not* the will of God. If, however you have an insistent sense that the next, very hesitant step beyond which you can see nothing is in fact the step that must be taken, *that* is most likely the will of God for you.[10]

SEVENTH SUNDAY AFTER THE EPIPHANY

February 18, 2001
Seventh Sunday in Ordinary Time; Proper 2

Revised Common	Episcopal (BCP)	Roman Catholic
Gen. 45:3-11, 15	Gen. 45:3-11, 21-28	1 Sam. 26:2, 7-9, 12-13 22-23
Ps. 37:1-11, 39-40	Ps. 37:1-18 or 37:3-10	Ps. 103:1-4, 8, 10, 12-13
1 Cor. 15:35-38, 42-50	1 Cor. 15:35-38, 42-50	1 Cor. 15:45-49
Luke 6:27-38	Luke 6:27-38	Luke 6:27-38

Last Sunday's readings helped us see the difference between those who trust in God and those who refuse to do so and the different futures that await them. Today's readings go a step further to push those who trust in God to see what should be their attitude toward those who do not trust God and who persecute them. Christ invites us to join him in more than a journey of being kind and affectionate toward those who mistreat us. He invites us to change the way the way we view ourselves and each other. He urges us to show compassion even to our enemies as a way of ushering in God's grace upon us all.

First Reading

GENESIS 45:3-11, 15 (RCL); 45:3-11, 21-28 (BCP)

Interpreting the Text

The first reading is part of a larger short story or novella that recounts the coming of age of one of Jacob's sons, Joseph, the last in the line of patriarchs who earns for himself special mention in the book (Gen. 37, 39–41, 42–45). The larger story has all the trappings of a family story, which begins with favoritism and tensions among Jacob's sons (37:4, 11, 18-23, 33-35) and moves through tension to climax and resolution (45:1-15). Resolution brings forgiveness, reconciliation, and promises as we can see in chapter 45, which is the theological center of the *novella*. Joseph's action in 45:1-15 restores *shalom* to Jacob's family, healing the breach that resulted from his brothers' jealousy of him as their father's favorite and that led them to sell him to a caravan of Ishmaelites who were passing through at the time. The caravan would eventually take Joseph to Egypt and sell him to Potiphar, the captain of the Egyptian guard (Gen. 37).

By the time we meet Jacob again, he has endured thirteen years in slavery and imprisonment in Egypt and now, as a result of a number of divinely maneuvered circumstances, has been elevated to an office equivalent to viceroy in the Pharaoh's court, having charge over the royal household and all the affairs of the people. Famine forces his brothers to leave Canaan and their father's household in search of food in Egypt. There in Egypt they meet up with the brother they had left for dead years ago who has not only motive but by now the means to make them pay for their crime against him. But in Genesis 45:4ff, as his brothers stand by in dismay and shock, Joseph tells them that, despite their intentions to undo him permanently by selling him into slavery, God was at work throughout, providentially using their misdeeds to put him in a position years later to preserve their family. He climaxes with the words, "So it was not you who sent me here, but God; he has made me a father to Pharaoh, and lord of all his house and ruler over all the land of Egypt" (45:8). Joseph's mention of God stands out here in the novella—unusual, because there is comparatively little mention of God's agency in the Joseph story beyond the oblique statement, "The Lord was with him" (39:2, 3, 5, 21). That God was orchestrating Joseph's release from prison and his subsequent rise in Pharaoh's court was always assumed but never explicitly stated. But here in chapter 45 Joseph credits God with his preservation and the subsequent preservation of the whole family in Canaan. And he decides to show his family the same steadfast love that God had shown him (39:21).

Instead of punishing his brothers, Joseph uses his elevated status as viceroy in Egypt to help his family. Their having to come to him for assistance only served to confirm the first dream he had recounted to them in 37:5-11, which was of him being elevated to greatness and them bowing before him. Joseph's act of forgiveness initiates what arguably is one of the most moving scenes in the Bible—brothers collapsing into each other's arms, weeping, kissing each other, and begging each other's forgiveness. Joseph's act restores and reunites Jacob's family, and with that Jacob the patriarch can now die in peace (45:28).

Responding to the Text

The natural impulse is to strike out when we are hurt by someone. By the time Joseph encounters his brothers, the narrator has seen to it that all of the reader's sympathies rest with Joseph, who would be perfectly justified in punishing his brothers for selling him into slavery. We wait for him to blast them. We look forward to him having them bound in chains and carted off to the same prison where he had to languish for thirteen years. We expect him at least to remind them that he was right all along in what he dreamed years ago that he was destined to be great and that one day they would have to bow to him. But Joseph refuses to satisfy the reader's base desires. He misses his family in Canaan and yearns to be reunited with them, and he chooses to forgive them instead. He leaves his bloodthirsty readers to satisfy their lust for revenge elsewhere. He attributes everything in the end to God. The dream about him rising to greatness was never about him in the first place. It was always about God—God standing in the background of human history bringing about God's larger plan and purposes, saving lives, disrupting plans, effecting change, turning evil purposes to a good end, and keeping promises God made to ancestors years ago: "I will make of you a great nation." (12:2).

1 SAMUEL 26:2, 7-9, 12-13, 22-23 (RC)

Interpreting the Text

David spares Saul a second time in 1 Samuel 26. The battle between their two camps for control over the tribes and their occupied territories has grown more fierce and the stakes have gotten higher. Samuel the prophet and judge has died (1 Sam. 25:1), leaving a vacuum of leadership that must be filled. Just before Samuel's death, Saul, upon discovering David's compassion in not killing him when he had the chance, seemed prepared to accept Samuel's judgment against him and to accept the choice of David as his successor (24:16-22). But everything changed upon Samuel's death. Saul became more determine than ever to put an end to David.

By 1 Samuel 26 Saul has doggedly pursued David into the wilderness of Ziph, but David remains hidden and out of Saul's reach in the wilderness. See the image of David, a former harp player surrounded by a ragged band of soldiers drawn from the desperate, despised, and disenfranchised elements of the population going up against Saul the king over Israel and his well-trained army. After sending out spies to discover Saul's whereabouts, David manages to sneak past Saul's guards and penetrates Saul's camp to where Saul lay sleeping with his spear stuck in the ground at his head. Abishai, his attendant, begs for the chance to put an end to David's archenemy. But David refuses to murder Saul there in his sleep. "Do not destroy him; for who can raise his hand against the Lord's anointed, and be guiltless?" Although he attributes saving Saul's life to not wanting to provoke God's wrath, he actually shows himself to be a superior strategist when he decides to take Saul's sword and to brandish it before Saul in front of his troops in 26:22-23, causing Saul's troops to lose confidence in his leadership.

Responding to the Text

Twice David has the chance to kill his enemy Saul, and twice he spares Saul's life. Both times he expresses profound respect for Saul's position as God's anointed, namely, as God's chosen leader over Israel. Whether he spared Saul for political reasons or whether he did so on moral grounds, the point is the same: murdering someone has consequences. David belonged to a universe of thinking (as did Saul) that believed that every deed carried within it the seed of its own retribution. Murder begot murder. Conversely, mercy begot mercy. David knew that murdering Saul would not only trigger a storm of conspiracies and plots throughout the tribal confederacy, each tribe seeking power and domination over the others. He also knew that murdering the king of Israel could also threaten his own bid for power. Killing Saul would undermine the moral confidence of the tribes making it open season for assassinating leaders of tribes. Whether secular or moral in its reasoning, the point is the same. Deeds have consequences. Although David knows better than to expect Saul to reward him for showing him mercy, it is evident from what he says in vv. 22-23 that he believed that God would reward him for sparing Saul.

Responsive Reading

PSALM 37:1-11, 39-40 (RCL); 37:1-18 or 37:3-10 (BCP)

Wisdom or Torah psalms like Psalm 37 affirm that the person whose lifestyle is based on the fear of Yahweh and the teachings of the *Torah* is "happy" or "blessed," whereas the person whose lifestyle is not based on these things will never enjoy the good fortune that comes with serving Yahweh. But psalmists were not demagogues who reduced life to simplistic equations, denying the many instances in society where things haven't panned out the way we were taught to believe they would. For example, despite all the teachings about the wicked being those who will not be acquitted by God and who will therefore perish (Ps. 1:5-6), anyone with eyes then and now could and can look around and see the many instances where the wicked were and are prospering and flourishing. The writer of Psalm 37 confronts this enigma of life and tries to answer the question that invariably arises, "Why is it that things often work out so badly for the God-fearing person and so well for the one who is careless about, or defiant of, God?"[11] Along with Psalms 49 and 73, Psalm 37 tries to answer this question that has haunted people of faith down through the centuries. The psalmist takes seriously the economic disparities between the just and the unjust, and does not pretend that the disparities do not exist. While we would hope that the psalmist would have used this as an occasion to launch a full-scale protest against poverty and injustice on the order of the prophets, we take heart in the fact that the psalmist addresses the issue at all. Psalm 37 offers the posture of patient waiting and promises that the wicked one's prosperity is temporary and lacks deep rootage, unlike the meek who will inherit the earth and enjoy life's abundant prosperity in perpetuity. *Why should anyone trust this promise?* hecklers may ask out loud. Because the Lord will see to this, says the psalmist in vv. 39-40.

PSALM 103:1-4, 8, 10, 12-13 (RC)

It would go a long way in explaining why he spared Saul's life those two times in 1 Samuel if we could prove that David was the author of Psalm 103 or if we could prove that he was at least familiar with this hymn as we now have it. But the truth is that we don't know for certain which, if any, of the 150 psalms we now have David actually composed himself. Some seem to allude to circumstances that match some of what we know about David's life, such as Psalm 23 and 51. But it is precisely their lack of specific historical details that has lent to the psalms their universal, timeless appeal. Here in Psalm 103, however, the psalmist's whole being is summoned to praise the Lord for "all his benefits" (vv. 1-2).The psalmist goes on to enumerate at least a few of those benefits: iniquities forgiven, diseases healed, a life redeemed from the Pit, love and mercy extended, and a life satisfied with good. Even if David did not compose the psalm, it is obvious that David's actions fit in with the theology expressed in it. God is merciful and slow to anger, so we should be the same. God neither deals nor repays us according to our unrighteous acts, so we should not repay others according to those measures. God is compassionate and forgives us our transgressions, and so should we be with each other. David may or may not have written Psalm 103, but it's obvious that he was heir to its ethical vision of showing to others the same love, compassion, and forgiveness that God extends to you.

SECOND READING

1 CORINTHIANS 15:35-38, 42-50 (RCL/BCP); 15:45-49 (RC)

Interpreting the Text

Paul's defense of Christ's resurrection has shifted from merely arguing for it as the basis for Christian faith to answering specific questions some in Corinth had about the notion of bodily resurrection. Paul tackles their question head-on by quoting the question the way it has been posed to him: "But someone will ask, 'How are the dead raised? With what kind of body do they come?" (15:35). He answers it by contrasting a seed with the plant it produces, arguing that the human body has within it already the seed of its transformed resurrected body which God has appointed. Paul is making it clear to the Corinthians that God has already provided a body, a spiritual body, one that is imperishable and incorruptible and suitable for the resurrection. This is not for Paul just a question of setting the Corinthians right about the kinds of corpses God has established for the resurrection. Rather it is a matter of proving that God has made all the necessary preparations for the day of judgment when the dead in Christ are raised from the grave and the righteous and unrighteous are judged.

Responding to the Text

Of all the topics hotly debated in churches today that threaten the unity of the church, the question of the kind of body the righteous will have at the time of the resurrection is not one of them. Unlike our Corinthian ancestors, some contemporary Christians have no problem believing in bodily resurrection, assuming as we do that one body is as good as another. Conversely, for others, the concept of bodily resurrection is so inconceivable that they don't even bother trying to fasten their postmodern minds around it and so dismiss Paul's wranglings here with the Corinthians as one of those many arcane cultural debates that show up in the Bible that contemporary Christians can safely ignore. Whichever position you take, there are stakes involved in Paul's argument, for the resurrection is a keystone of Christian witness. If Christ was not raised, then Christian faith is baseless, there will be no resurrection of believers at the end time, and the daily risks Paul and other Christians were taking on behalf of the gospel were for absolutely nothing (15:23-34). If this is all there is to life, with no reward for faithfulness and no punishment for sins, then what is the point of it all (v. 37)?

Paul's point here should give us pause whether we agree with it or not. There is no denying the strong eschatological origins of the Christian faith with its belief in an end-time reckoning of the just and the unjust, good and evil. Even those who have abandoned any belief in an afterlife and find the apocalyptic notion of a final judgment day wishful thinking and extraneous to their faith should take another look at Paul's argument here. If all we have to look forward to as those who are taught to love, forgive, be meek, reconcile, and refrain from violence are occasional successes here and there, a convert here and an apology there, with no lasting triumph over the powers of wickedness, and if those who crush and mock the poor and needy never have to account for their cruelties, then what is the point? Then why not throw up our hands and simply eat, drink, and be merry, for tomorrow we die (v. 32)? If Christ is as impotent as we are to right the world's wrongs, then why do we suffer? Such questions deserve to be asked, even if they leave the church stammering.

The Gospel

LUKE 6:27-38

Interpreting the Text

The call to do good to one's enemies did not originate with Jesus, as some today would like to believe, but can be traced back to the Old Testament, where in Exodus 23:4-5 and Proverbs 24:21-22 justice is seen as extending even to one's enemy. In the new kingdom that Moses envisioned, like in the one Jesus envisioned here in Luke 6:27-38, justice was to prevail in all areas of life, even in dealing with those who hate you. Do not take advantage of your enemy even when you have the chance to do so by pretending not to notice that their property is in jeopardy (Exod. 23:4-5) or that they are hungry or thirsty (Prov. 24:21-22). Even the love Moses commands his followers to have for one another in Leviticus 19:18 is not some sentimental call for kinspeople to get along with each other. For certain, he enjoins them against seeking revenge and bearing grudges that are so typical of intimate relations. Loving one's enemy, whether that enemy is a despised family member or a hated non-family member, involves rising above personal animosities and doing what is in the interest of the community, which sometimes involves absorbing hurt rather returning it. This is the manner of life expected of the disciples. It is evident from Luke 6:22-23 that Jesus is trying to prepare the disciples for the days ahead when they will encounter hatred and persecution. He calls them to live in accordance with God's mercy—loving enemies, giving, and not judging. There will be plenty of occasions for them to refer back to his teachings.

LUKE, PERHAPS MORE THAN THE OTHER GOSPEL WRITERS, IS EMPHATIC THAT LOVE AND GOODNESS HAVE THEIR REWARD FROM GOD.

Luke, perhaps more than the other Gospel writers, is emphatic that love and goodness have their reward from God (vv. 35-36), just as those who are rich, full, and who are laughing now have their reward (vv. 24-25). He stops short here of saying concretely what that reward will be and whether they will receive it in their lifetime or in the time to come. It is enough for Jesus to say that those who keep his teachings about loving enemies, giving, and not judging will become "children of the Most High" (v. 35).

Responding to the Text

In the kingdom that Christ proclaims, everything is topsy-turvy. This is imperative to make clear this seventh Sunday after the Epiphany, as it was important to make abundantly clear at the beginning of Jesus' ministry, so that people are not mislead into thinking that the whole purpose of Christ's coming is to satisfy their creature needs. Of course, Luke makes it abundantly clear that the poor, hungry, the marginalized, and the diseased were the focus of his ministry and that his vision of the coming kingdom included their material relief. But he also makes clear that his purpose in coming was not simply to feed, clothe, comfort, and heal. Christ comes to invite us into a totally different valuation of ourselves and of each other. He invites us into imagining with him a new community. He invites us to join him in ushering in this new kingdom where our individual interests are of less importance than those of the community. He leaves us with what no doubt are just glimpses into what that new kingdom will be like. Everything we have been taught about viewing ourselves as individuals who have a right to look out for number one, whose needs come first, and who are within our rights to nurse grudges until we are ready to let them go will be turned on its head. "Be merciful, just as your Father is merciful" is the concise version of his teachings. To the generous will be given liberally, for this is their reward. Finally, Jesus' command to love, give, and not judge is less a command than a promise. Loving, giving, and not judging is not simply the way to earn God's forgiveness. It is the way to open our lives to receive God's glorious grace.

THE TRANSFIGURATION OF OUR LORD

FEBRUARY 25, 2001
LAST SUNDAY AFTER THE EPIPHANY /
EIGHTH SUNDAY IN ORDINARY TIME

REVISED COMMON	EPISCOPAL (BCP)	ROMAN CATHOLIC
Exod. 34:29-35	Exod. 34:29-35	Sir. 27:4-7
Ps. 99	Ps. 99	Ps. 92:2-3, 13-14, 15-16
2 Cor. 3:12—4:2	1 Cor. 12:27—13:13	1 Cor. 15:54-58
Luke 9:28-36 (37-43)	Luke 9:28-36	Luke 6:39-45

WE WERE INVITED LAST WEEK TO VIEW OURSELVES and each other differently by reordering our priorities and by radically altering the way we treat each other—to do good to each other, even to those who mistreat us. The Transfiguration of our Lord shifts our attention this week from doing to being. We are reminded by each lesson that to enter into God's communing presence, that is, to really experience a face-to-face encounter with the divine, is to risk having one's priorities reordered and to be permanently changed from within. That's because to recognize Jesus is to enter, if only for a moment, into the mysteries of the divine realm and to depart with a radical, new way of understanding the divine-human connection.

FIRST READING
EXODUS 34:29-35 (RCL/BCP)

Interpreting the Text

Exodus 34 is a fitting text for contemplating what it means to encounter the Holy, because it seeks to describe the difficult task Moses faced trying to reenter ordinary human existence after some wondrous encounters with the divine. Moses is the messenger par excellence who speaks to God on behalf of the people and to the people on behalf of God (20:18-21; cf. Deut. 34:10-12). After this second meeting on the mountain is completed, Moses descends with his face shining and aglow (Exod. 34:29). Aaron and all the Israelites had to be reassured by Moses that it was safe to approach him because the dazzling light all about him caused them to recoil in dread (34:30). From then on, it seems, whenever Moses appeared before Israel after devoting time with God, he wore a veil; and whenever he was in the presence of God he unveiled himself (34:33-35).

A common belief in the ancient Near East was that gods were always surrounded by a luminous glow, indicating their power and heavenly character. The prophet Moses is suffused with God's heavenly glow as he descends the mountain to speak with the people—making his reentry into ordinary human life no easy matter. The priestly scribes who are responsible for a great deal of the material in the book of Exodus stop short of saying that Moses beheld God directly. (The deuteronomic school of scribes does not seem to share the priests' squeamishness about the matter; cf. Deut. 34:10-12.) The most Moses was permitted to see according to the priests was the backside of God's glory (33:22-33). But even the sight of God's backside was enough to leave Moses radiating with light when he finally descended the mountain, signaling his absorption in that divine encounter.

Interpreters are typically baffled by this quaint story in Exodus because the writer never bothers to say what the problem was with Moses' radiating face. The story's mystery might be cleared up, however, if it is interpreted within the larger focus in the book of Exodus upon God's "glory." The radiant glow upon Moses' face becomes yet another display of the inscrutable glory of God in all of its mystery, danger, and power. To encounter God, to really commune with God, and to enter into God's mysterious glory, is to be changed like Moses in such a way that radically alters one contact with and understanding of ordinary life.

Responding to the Text

Is it really possible to enter into the mystery of God's divine presence in such a way as to be permanently changed? Who would want to enter such a mystery and risk, becoming so altered by that experience as to become unapproachable by the rest of humanity? While one thinks of ministers as those who routinely scurry off to lofty spiritual planes to commune with God, the truth is that the soul can bear only so much of the lofty. In fact, some of the most memorable encounters with grace are those that erupt into the daily details of mundane ordinary life. The challenge is to not confine God to the spectacular and to take delight in the joys and rewards of everyday fidelities. By putting a veil over his face, Moses sought a way to remain approachable to the human community to and for whom he was responsible. The point of having a transfiguring experience with the Holy, then, is not to be permanently lost to the world, but to be able to move back and forth between the sacred realm of the divine and the common realm of relationships and obligations with a fair amount of humility and awe.

SIRACH 27:4-7 (RC)

Interpreting the Text

This passage describes metaphorically the manner in which speech discloses one's inner character and being. The book—a collection of proverbial recommendations for living—brings to mind the contents of Proverbs. The book's author, "Jesus son of Eleazar son of Sirach of Jerusalem" (50:27; 51:1), claims in his prologue to have translated his grandfather's collection of poetic observations in order make it possible to draw from them and "[to] make even greater progress in living in conformity with the divine law." In the ancient world, where your word was your bond, where words were believed to have power of their own, your speech was believed to be a window into your inner character. Just as the sieve separates the husks and dung from the grain, so does your conversation bring your flaws to the surface (27:4). Just as the kiln tests the vessels the potter carefully shapes and molds, so do the words we say confirm what we *really* believe and how we *truly* feel about life (27:5). The well-tended fruit tree will produce fruit that reflects the sound care it has received; in similar manner what comes out of our mouths reflects what we have had put into our hearts (27:6). The author concludes that it would be wise to reserve praising someone until you've had a chance to learn the contents of that person's heart (27:7).

Responding to the Text

Transfiguration Sunday is not just about encountering God in all of God's saving mystery but also about being profoundly changed by that encounter with the sacred. What might be a sign of someone's transformation? Listen to that person's conversation. It should not be taken as the *only* indication of one's transformation and inner person. But if you listen carefully and long enough to the words that issue from a person's conversation you will discover along with Sirach that eventually the mouth will disclose the arch of one's heart.

Responsive Reading

PSALM 99 (RCL/BCP)

Psalm 99 reminds us that human revelation is just one side of the encounter in a theophany. God enters the human realm ("shows up") in theophanies typically to deliver God's people from danger. But human beings play their role in theophanic encounters in the way they respond and behave in response to what they have experienced. Exorbitant descriptions of God as ruler, one enthroned upon the earth, and concerned about justice and righteousness are common refrains through the Enthronement Psalms (Psalms 93, 95–99). This author of Psalm 99 takes great care to link the psalm verbally with Exod. 15:1-18, the song of praise Moses and the Israelites sang when they were delivered from Egypt. Both rhapsodize about God's reign over the earth, declaring God to be "great," "awesome," "mighty," and deserving to be "exalted."

The psalmist's mention of God's "holiness" in vv. 3, 5, and 9 harks back to the description of God's awesome presence throughout the book of Exodus. That presence is both entrancing and terrifying. It causes people to "tremble" (or recoil as Aaron and others did at the sight of Moses descending the mountain) and makes the earth to "quake." This is the same holy presence that guides, instructs, and—thankfully—condescends to commune with common humanity (Ps. 99:7).

PSALM 92:2-3, 13-14, 15-16 (RC)

The worshiper's obligation, insists the psalmist, is to make known through musical praise God's "steadfast mercy" (*hesed*) and "faithfulness" (*'emunah*). Even though most theophanies in scripture take place on mountains and are usually prompted by crisis and danger, God is capable of being revealed on those occasions when the community comes together and erupts into praise and worship (Ps. 22:3). Israel's spontaneous praise in Exodus 15 testifies to the Holy One's fundamental character as a mighty Redeemer. By delivering them and causing them to prosper and by planting the righteous in the sanctuary where they produce fruit far into old age, God is disclosed as one who is forever upright, as reliable as a rock, and as inherently righteous (92:13, 14, 15).

SECOND READING

2 CORINTHIANS 3:12—4:2 (RCL)

Interpreting the Text

The veil covering Moses' face had no particular negative connotations in Exodus 34:29-35. For Paul, centuries later, it becomes a symbol of Israel's blinded stubbornness. In fact, it's no longer the prophet who wears the veil, according to Paul, but the people, that stiff-necked, stubborn audience that refuses to accept the gospel Paul preaches. The radiant light that shined when the law was given through Moses protecting (presumably) both prophet and people is no longer necessary, says Paul, because a greater glory has been disclosed through the Spirit. In Christ the veil has been set aside along with the old covenant that Moses received on the mountain (2 Cor. 3:14).

With Christ comes the opportunity to behold the glory of the Lord "with unveiled faces" (3:18). But the Spirit offers more. We behold the Lord's glory and simultaneously are beheld by it as we find ourselves being transformed into the Lord's glorious image through the work of the Spirit. This is the inspiration for an audacious hope, says Paul, one that kindles boldness (3:12) and honest dealings (4:1–2) in believers.

Both Moses and the priests who preserved the tradition about his ministry to Israel would probably take great umbrage to Paul's reinterpretation of the veil that the prophet wore on his face. While it's true that Paul is probably guilty here of caricaturing the veil's meaning for his polemical purposes, it's probably also true that he is convinced that he is justified for doing so. He is attacking what he takes to be the blinded thinking of his opponents who insist upon the superiority of the old law (covenant) over the new. Paul goes so far as to suggest that Moses wore the veil because even he recognized the impermanence of the law and attempted to hide this fact from the people by failing to comment on its inadequacies. We can only guess how Paul's opponents reacted to his slanderous comments about one of their sacred traditions—especially by one who was a former teacher of the law himself! The point of it all was Paul's attempt to persuade his followers of the gospel's simplicity, accessibility, and sensibility, which was meant to tear down walls of division and to bring God's redeeming love to light for all to experience.

Responding to the Text

If Transfiguration Sunday taps into our deep desire to encounter the Saving One authentically and profoundly in such a way that it leads to transformation, then how do we explain the fact that different people see and experience the sacred differently? We claim to encounter the same God, but our experiences of our encounters sometimes differ so radically as to make one wonder whether we're talking about the same God. Why can't we see what the other sees? If we did, perhaps we could come together and agree on how to change the world. If different Christian bodies all claim to have had transforming encounters with the same Savior, then how does one explain the deep differences and divisions that exist among Christians?

A fundamental precept of our postmodern existence is that what you see depends upon where you stand and that all of us have been inescapably shaped by our contexts. The precept goes a long way to explain why people see and interpret life differently. What it cannot explain, however, because of its limitations is what makes people capable of changing their minds; it cannot explain what makes a person able to place another person's welfare above one's own and enter empathetically into that person's world and try to hear and see with their ears and eyes. Transfiguration Sunday holds out for us the possibility that people can experience the divine presence of God together in community with each other, and not just in isolated cloistered mountaintop experiences; for through the Spirit it is possible for people with radically different agendas and opposing perceptions of the world to be "transformed into the same image from one degree of glory to another" (2 Cor. 3:18).

1 CORINTHIANS 12:27—13:13 (BCP)

See the comments on 1 Corinthians 13 for the fourth Sunday after the Epiphany, above.

1 CORINTHIANS 15:54-58 (RC)

Interpreting the Text

Upon Christ's return at that final moment in history when all mysteries will be revealed, the last and most confounding mystery of all will be cleared up: the role the body plays in the realm of things spiritual. Paul is emphatic that it won't be the spirit alone that will be transformed upon the return of Christ. The body too will be "reconfigured"—despite what has been its indisputable power to frustrate human beings' effort to encounter God by fading away into death and physical decrepitude. Paul has seen the risen Lord, and based on that vision he issues a powerful taunt against death, promising that it will be—indeed has already been—swallowed up in Christ's death and resurrection. Death's deadly sting, which previously drew its strength from the power of sin, has been detoxified in Christ's victory over death in the resurrection. Hence, not just the spirit of humans but the body too will be fundamentally changed and redeemed at the eschaton. Christ's bodily resurrection marks a victory over death and decrepitude that allows the perishable body at the end time to put on a new imperishable body, one that will be immortal (15:53-54).

In light of the opposition he faced in the Hellenistic world to any notion of a raised, immortal body, it was imperative that Paul make a strong and convincing case for Christ's resurrection and for his victory over death. He pulled out all the stops on this one, citing Hebrew scripture (cleverly altering portions for his purposes; cf. Isa. 25:8; LXX of Hosea 13:14), quoting hymnic expressions, drawing on Greek philosophy, and tapping into a common fear among human existence, namely, the fear of death. Whether he was right about all the events that will take place at the return of the resurrected Christ remains to be seen. It is comforting to consider the possibility, however, that our bodies will accompany our souls into the divine realm, albeit a better, improved version of the body. After all, our bodies have been the only home for the soul that we've known. But exactly what all that will look like in the end remains a mystery (if only to this author). But, alas, there remains one component of Paul's argument about Christ and the eschaton in which we should forever take comfort, namely, that our efforts to do what we can to usher in the Lord's kingdom, despite decay, disease, and death (both ours and that of those we love), will not go unnoticed or unrewarded. "Take courage," says Paul, "your labor is not in vain" (15:58).

The Gospel

LUKE 9:28-36 (37-43) (RCL); 9:28-36 (BCP)

Interpreting the Text

A little more than a week has passed since Jesus' promise in Luke 9:27 that a few privileged disciples will be allowed to glimpse the glory of the kingdom of God. The scene is set to fulfill this promise when Jesus, like Moses before him, withdraws to a mountain for prayer and communion with God. He takes his three closest disciples along with him. Peter, John, and James could hardly have prepared themselves for the experience that awaits them. They are still, at this point in the narrative, fumbling, impressionable followers who are hopelessly joined to this itinerant ministry for reasons they don't quite yet understand, pleased to be counted among the intimates (Luke 8:19-21) of the man who has come to be known for his preaching and healing powers (8:1). Luke has already alluded in 8:51 to the privileged status of the three who would upon Jesus' death be elevated to positions of leadership and power in the early life of the church. But at this point in the narrative they will not conduct themselves as future leaders. They will show themselves to be fatigued, dim-witted mortals who are about to embark on an experience that will bring them face-to-face with the true identity of their master. This moment stands at the heart of the Transfiguration narrative. It is the moment when the main figure is recognized in the story for who he is.

Like Moses before him, Jesus' face and whole being become suffused with dazzling light as he prays (9:29). The disciples watch as two glorified figures from the past come into focus and began conversing with Jesus as he moves deeper into prayer. The reason for the appearance of Moses and Elijah is never commented upon by Luke. He didn't have to. By this time, Moses and Elijah had come to be associated with the messianic age (Deut. 18:15-18; Mal. 4:1-6; Rev. 11:3ff.). An informed audience would have picked up on the echoes tying Jesus' ministry to that of these two figures: (1) Moses and Elijah too were associated with meeting with God on Mount Sinai/Horeb (Exod. 24; 1 Kings 19). (2) Both are also the two who according to Hebrew tradition were taken up to God without dying (see Deut. 34:6 and 2 Kings 2:1-12). The two figures speak to Jesus about his imminent departure and the soon completion in Jerusalem of his ministry (Luke 9:31).

While Luke's account up to v. 31 focuses on Jesus' interaction with the figures, it isn't until v. 32 that the reader begins to see things through the disciples' eyes. But Luke seems to have his doubt about whether the three disciples make credible witnesses to all the events at the Transfiguration. They are, after all, sleepy and drowsy while all of this is going on, although they do manage to stay awake enough to overhear Moses and Elijah's conversation with Jesus. As the two are about to depart Jesus, Peter with typical ardor intrudes upon the heavenly scene and offers to build three tabernacles as monuments to what has taken place that evening. Luke points out that Peter is ignorant of the full implications of what's taking place and blindly risks blaspheming the hour by imposing upon the divine will. Luke sums up Peter's blindness by saying, "not knowing what he said" (v. 33). Not until the dazzling brightness of the glory cloud moves threateningly in on the disciples and almost overtakes them does Peter, along with John and James, recognize the moment as part of the divine mystery. The same divine cloud that brings instruction and deliverance is capable of leaving terror and dread in its wake. It admonishes the trespassers saying, "This is my Son, my Chosen; listen to him!" (v. 35). A voice coming out of the cloud is again reminiscent of God's speaking from Mount Sinai to Moses (Exod. 19:16; Deut. 5:21). Similarly, the disciples' fear evokes the memory of the Israelites' terror at Mount Sinai in Exodus 20:19-20.

WHENEVER GOD REVEALS THE DIVINE SELF TO INDIVIDUALS, IT IS FOR THE SAKE OF THE COMMUNITY.

The point of Transfiguration was not simply to confirm Jesus' true identity to his disciples, even though this was a much-needed component to the drama; his disciples had been chosen after the baptismal event, which was the last time a voice from heaven supernaturally boomed from above to confirm Jesus' identity. In fact, the Transfiguration scene stands close to the middle of Luke's Gospel, between the account of his baptism and his prayer at Gethsemane (22:39-53). Common to all three events are supernatural appearances (the voice and dove in 3:21-22; the figures of Moses and Elijah in 9:28-36; and the angel's appearance in Luke 22:43-44 as Jesus prays in Gethsemane). Taken together, the three reflect Luke's effort to show that divine guidance becomes visible as a supernatural event in the lives of followers. Luke emphasizes that Jesus' true identity as God's Son takes place in a situation of prayer rather than, as Mark suggests, while on a preaching tour (cf. Mark 8:27). Jesus goes up to the mountain to pray (9:28), and when the cloud recedes he is standing alone, presumably still in prayer (9:36). No attempt is made by Jesus to explain what happened in between. The disciples are in sufficient awe to not push Jesus to explain. Neither do they bother "in those days" mentioning to the others the things they'd seen and heard (v. 36). Besides, who would believe them? They certainly weren't able to understand everything right then, and neither could their other companions whom they had left behind.

We can only imagine that Peter, John, and James were forever changed by their experience. We assume that the divine admonition, "Listen to him!" was taken to heart by the three disciples and that from then on they, more than the others, pay special attention to their master whenever he speaks of his future sufferings and death (cf. 9:43b-45). They become acutely aware of their limitations in matching Jesus' power as healer as manifested in the story of the healing of the boy with a demon (9:37-43). While they are far from fully comprehending his ministry (9:44-45), they understand Jesus better than the others and the implications of his mission to the world. Undoubtedly they gain a clearer glimpse into what it means to be chosen and called to leadership in the kingdom. They had to know by now what lay ahead for them as select followers of and witnesses to that same kingdom.

Responding to the Text

Be grateful to Luke for describing the disciples' gallant effort to stave off drowsiness and slumber in order to take in the full impact of what they were witnessing. (Luke is probably trying to allude to their unformed, immature faith at this point in the itinerant ministry.) Surely there were moments on the mountain when they thought their eyes were playing tricks on them. If only one of them had been allowed to accompany Jesus he could have talked himself out of believing what he was seeing. "You're only dreaming," he may have told himself. But Jesus brought a company of three to accompany him in prayer. According to Hebrew tradition, in order for a charge to hold up it had to be corroborated by two or three witnesses (Deut. 19:15; cf. 17:6). Years later after their master's death, when their own identity would be called into question, the three disciples probably took comfort in the experience they had shared early in Jesus' ministry. The difference being that by then it wouldn't be Jesus' experience they would be reliving in their heads. It would be their common experience of God's tendency in times of uncertainty to assure believers in supernatural ways.

"It is not safe to pray alone," writes Abraham Heschel. "Tradition insists that we pray with, and as a part of, the community."[12] God is disclosed to communities of believers and not principally to individuals. Whenever God reveals the divine self to individuals, it is for the sake of the community, fully expecting the individual to belong to a community and prepared to take back to that community all that the individual has experienced. After all, God's covenant is with people and not with individuals. So, how do we avoid private, pietistic, idiosyncratic interpretations of what it means to encounter God? Create more opportunities for people of all backgrounds and stations in life to come together in worship and to behold God together. What we do as individual communions of believers is secondary to what we experience together as children of the one God. This is not to trivialize private, individual prayer. Instead it is to reclaim the power of corporate prayer. Praying and worshiping in community firmly grounds our thoughts and impulses in an endless chain known as eternity.

LUKE 6:39-45 (RC)

Interpreting the Text

The focus of this passage is upon what Jesus manifests about himself as a teacher of the law. He distinguishes himself by his urging that his followers go a step further and envision a radically new way of being human. He is no ordinary teacher. He insists that his followers distinguish themselves by their obedience to his teachings, that they love their enemies and show nonjudgmental generosity to all. Here Jesus draws on the ill-fated image of watching the blind lead the blind to point out the absurdity of following leaders who are incapable of setting an example (6:40-41). Moreover, it is pure hypocrisy to hold others accountable to ethical minutiae while failing to attend to these same matters in one's own journey as a disciple. If transfiguration is about being permanently changed by one's encounter with the Holy, then the best testimony to a transformed life is the way one treats those around her. No difference is made here in Luke between being and doing. The surest evidence of a follower's character is by the way he treats others. This lection harks back to the Sirach text with its collection of pithy observations about the orderliness of human life. In this case, to see something or someone, to *really* see something or someone is less about the image that is reflected back to you of the other. It is more about peering at others as they stand chatting on mountains with divine figures or gaining better insight to yourself and all the ways in which you have failed to live up to the grand ideals of your faith. Jesus cuts through the hypocrisy, self-deceit, and shallowness that lay just beneath the human heart. He reminds us on Transfiguration Sunday that we should be inspired to take out our hand-held mirrors and in the light of day hold them up to see the image of ourselves reflected back to us.

Responding to the Text

This passage prevents us on Transfiguration Sunday from appealing to private, pietistic language to describe who Christ is in our lives. A change that can't be verified or apprehended is no change at all. The character of our personal encounters with our Savior will rely upon our ability to be recognized by others as a follower. The Transfiguration disciplines us to see the connection between our confession and our obsessions. "Out of the abundance of the heart the mouth speaks" is the way Luke concludes this passage. Christ comes to reveal himself to us and to reveal us to ourselves. The light that accompanies him is capable of illuminating the truth while simultaneously piercing the darkness. We see the light and know immediately that if we submit and allow ourselves to be drenched in its rays we will find ourselves on a path of no return where even those who love us may not recognize us because of our radical commitment to Christ.

Notes

1. Raymond Brown, *The Gospel of John I-XII* (Garden City: Doubleday, 1966) 107.

2. The scribal editor tries to make heads and tails of the jigsaw of a narrative by including Nehemiah's name in the list of those present for the Torah reading convocation. As best as we can determine, Nehemiah arrived in Judah during a third phase of rebuilding, under Artaxerxes II (404–358 B.C.E.) and took an active part in the task of rebuilding the walls of Jerusalem.

3. Tamara Cohn Eshkenazi, "Ezra–Nehemiah," *Women's Bible Commentary*, ed. Carol A. Newsome and Sharon H. Ringe (Louisville: Westminster/John Knox, 1998) 129.

4. *The Oxford Companion to the Bible*, ed. Bruce M. Metzger and Michael D. Coogan (Oxford and New York: Oxford Univ. Press, 1994) 473, 474.

5. Abraham Joshua Heschel, *The Insecurity of Freedom: Essays on Human Existence* (New York: Farrar, Straus & Giroux, 1966) 237.

6. His editors would later include a number of his most anguished laments about God's calling upon him and sprinkle them throughout the collection of his oracles: 11:18—12:6; 15:10-21; 17:14-18; 18:12-23; 20:7-13, 14-18.

7. Frederick Buechner, *Telling Secrets* (San Francisco: HarperCollins, 1991) 37.

8. Reinhold Niebuhr, *An Interpretation of Christian Ethics* (New York: Meridian, 1956) 97.

9. Reinhold Niebuhr, *The Nature and Destiny of Man* (New York: Scribner's, 1941) 1:222ff.

10. Wendy M. Wright, *The Rising: Living the Mysteries of Lent, Easter, and Pentecost* (Upper Room Books: Nashville, 1994) 35.

11. Bernhard Anderson, *Out of the Depths: The Psalms Speak for Us Today* (Philadelphia: Westminster, 1983) 224.

12. Abraham Joshua Heschel, *Man's Quest for God: Studies in Prayer and Symbolism* (New York: Scribner's, 1954) 45.

THE SEASON OF LENT

JOHN STENDAHL

I WAS SITTING NEXT TO A FRIEND at the concluding liturgy of our church body's recent national assembly. When the time came to exchange the peace I turned first to greet my wife and then back toward David. He had begun turning toward me but seemed suddenly awkward, his hands fumbling in front of his body as if to catch something there that he could not find. It took me a moment to understand the cause of his distraction: colliding with his wife in order to share the peace of the Lord, he'd had his glasses knocked clean off his face. He quickly recovered both spectacles and dignity, but I, at least, was left with this memory, a moment of charming human clumsiness in the high festivity of inspiring worship.

I have thought of David's glasses several times since that day. It was such a trivial incident, but their dislodging by Christ's peace seemed in my musings an emblem of something that can happen—and sometime needs to happen—when the power of God works on us. Our glasses are knocked from our eyes and reality blurs out of focus. Some consequence of love leaves us off balance and fumbling, clear order and detail replaced by vaguer patterns and shapes before our eyes. Sometimes grace unfocuses us.

It would of course be a more familiar metaphor to speak of our gaining vision and clarity by grace or faith: "I once was blind but now I see." Thus the spiritual discipline of Lent can be thought a tool for focusing more intently and discerning more clearly. What we ignored or took for granted we now resolve to pay closer attention to. Whether it is the closer or the more distant that blurs for us, whatever our perceptual failings, now we are bidden to put on our corrective lenses and see what had been ignored or hidden.

These two metaphorical proposals for a Lenten agenda, donning our glasses and losing them, are not contradictory. Each, indeed, may need the truth of the other, and both are suggested by the classic simile for the season: Lent as intentional time in the wilderness. Forty years for Israel, forty days and nights for Jesus, time like the forty weeks of a pregnancy, time of a wilderness passage through strangeness to new life. The desert, undefined and uncluttered by social construction, literal or figurative, can be a place of greater clarity, of sharper lines and brighter light. Yet it can also be a place of shimmering heat and dubious perception, a landscape uncertain and unmeasured. And perhaps it is by that quality as well that it serves as the setting for preparation and recommitment.

Historically, of course, Lent has much of its genesis in the catechumenal journey toward baptism. The recently heightened consciousness of that theme as basic to the season's agenda—and indeed the recovery of ancient catechumenal practices in many churches—has been exciting and enriching. Yet attention to the movement of outsiders and seekers toward their incorporation in the Paschal community should not be thought contradictory to the penitential and pilgrimage traditions that run as parallel origins in the season's development. The community of the baptized does not simply stand as the company of those safe on the other shore of the river, encouraging the catechumens on their passage to join them in the settled land of milk and honey. They are not now those who have already arrived, who have it all figured out and under control (or at least who foolishly imagine that they do). This season becomes a time for the baptized to alienate themselves, to join the catechumens in the wilderness. Into these weeks of penitence and rededication, discipline and formation, the baptized march out in order to travel again the journey of their becoming.

LENT MAY BID US SEE BY THE UNFIXING OF VISION, TO FIND OUR WAY BY DISORIENTATION, TO COME HOME BY GETTING LOST.

Some years ago someone asked me to help her use Lent as a time to think more intensively about the problems and issues of her life. After trying to formulate a way to do so—thinking still more about the matters already so prominent in her consciousness and conversation—it occurred to me that perhaps the opportunity of the season could be just the opposite. To stop focusing and look away from her familiar troubles and terrors would not be easy, but it might be a better work of discipline than she had originally intended. Training her thought and imagination elsewhere, on different stories and other issues, might be a kind of sabbath time away from her own life. Afterwards, that life might have become different in her eyes. There was no prior certainty of what that difference would be or of the precise utility of the kind of Lent I proposed she observe—only my sense that she needed to go into new and unfamiliar spaces.

Since that time, this notion has come back frequently as partial but recurrent truth. We are called to sight and clarity, but also sometimes to this loosening of focus. Lent may bid us see by the unfixing of vision, to find our way by disorientation, to come home by getting lost.

What might we see when our eyes unfocus? Perhaps, as for that recently blind man in Mark 8:24, people will look like trees walking: then, our sight having blurred, maybe also the dangerous distinction between "humanity" and "nature" will loosen its hold on our minds. If we can't make out details so well, perhaps we will see common elements where before we were aware only of differences among us. Faces might appear gentler and unblemished. Unsure of perspective and distance, we might think attainable what would otherwise seem out of reach. Perhaps we will have to imagine new and necessarily humbler, more tentative explanations of reality in place of our lost clarities. Imagining what we cannot see for sure, perhaps we will see what God intends, choosing even "things that are not to bring to nothing the things that are" (1 Cor. 1:28).

ASH WEDNESDAY

FEBRUARY 28, 2001

REVISED COMMON	EPISCOPAL (BCP)	ROMAN CATHOLIC
Joel 2:1-2, 12-17 or Isa. 58:1-12	Joel 2:1-2, 12-17 or Isa. 58:1-12	Joel 2:12-18
Ps. 51:1-17	Ps. 103 or 103:8-14	Ps. 51:3-6, 12-14, 17
2 Cor. 5:20b—6:10	2 Cor. 5:20b—6:10	2 Cor. 5:20b—6:2
Matt. 6:1-6, 16-21	Matt. 6:1-6, 16-21	Matt. 6:1-6, 16-18

"REMEMBER THAT YOU ARE DUST and to dust you shall return." The simple imperative and declaration hardly sounds like good news. Even liturgies that use other words still speak the reminder with the ashes themselves; even those who eschew the ritual can recall the reality to which the name of this day points. Under the face of a friend or within the face in the mirror appears something like a death's head, a skeleton under the living skin and flesh. Yet that blurring vision is not a soft-focus uncertainty: it is the clear and ultimately inevitable truth about us. Lent begins by bidding us to remember our mortality and need, to look at it straight and honestly. Is there good news strong enough to reach and transfigure this place?

FIRST READING

JOEL 2:1-2, 12-17 (RCL/BCP); 2:12-18 (RC)

Interpreting the Text

The prophet's call sounds itself like a trumpet of announcement and alarm. The dread armies are coming, swarming over the hills and mountains toward Jerusalem, unswerving and terrifying. It is quite likely that the reference here is not to human conquerors but to the plague of locusts described devouring the countryside in the preceding chapter. The disaster is then "natural" rather than military. Human or insect, however, these numberless hordes are the Lord's soldiers, and they come not as vindicators or liberators of the people but as agents of a terrible judgment upon them.

Joel is most likely a postexilic work, but the evocation of Babylonian conquest and Zion's destruction here is not only memory but urgent warning and threat. The present hangs in imminent peril as the horizon darkens with the swarming army. Death is in the air.

Prophetic threat, however, is always just that. A threat, a warning that seeks to force what would otherwise not be done, that tries to compel a turning, some great change. And great it had to be now, if this terrifying "Day of the Lord" was to be averted or endured. Not just a private penance but the whole nation, priests and people together in a massive emergency action (vv. 15-17). Perhaps such dramatic and communal repentance, such turning back to the Lord as it says, would cause also God to turn back, and even leave behind a blessing rather than devastation. After all, God had relented before, and the language that Joel offered here as the people's only hope strongly recalls the drama of God's repentance in Exodus 32–34. Perhaps it was not too late.

It was not. Joel goes on to describe the Lord's favor and blessing restored. Within this pericope, though, there is still the perhaps, the note of uncertainty and alarm.

ISAIAH 58:1-12 (RCL/BCP alt.)

Interpreting the Text

This reading also gives us trumpeting words, words of prophetic warning. This eloquent call to national faithfulness, compassion, and justice rings out still with urgency. In 1997, Bill Clinton used the concluding verses of this reading as the theme and call for his second inaugural address; it is hard to read these words without yearning that both he and we as a people had done better at holding them before our eyes. They sound again with divine reproach for the inequities and squandering of our prosperity.

One striking aspect of this call to repentance is that the problem with the people is not that they are not religious. On the contrary, "day after day they seek me and delight to know my ways, . . . they ask of me righteous judgments, they delight to draw near to God." These are pious folks, not a "godless" or "secular" nation. Yet there is a deep emptiness and disappointment in their piety; it does not reward them with any sense that God notices them.

The prophet offers the diagnosis and remedy for this malaise. True religion is not this presumptuous attention to God without notice of the laborer, the poor, and the oppressed. Rituals of repentance or even sincere massaging of internal contrition brings no blessing. But if you attend to justice and to the needs of the afflicted, then will your religion have meaning and power for you, then will God answer when you call. The relationship with God that now eludes you, and the transformative, restorative power it is supposed to bear, depends on this righteousness.

Responding to the Text

On this day of Christian ritual penitence par excellence, both these lections warn (as our Gospel reading) of the danger of merely ritual action. "Rend your hearts, not your garments." Both texts call to deeper repentance. Or perhaps "deeper" is not quite the right word, for depth may suggest in our parlance intensity of feeling, an emotional contrition that does not merely go through the motions but really feels it. That, after all, is the way our culture uses the word "heart." It is in our day the locus of human emotion. Biblical imagery, however, more often identifies the bowels with feeling and the heart with thought and will. One traditional use of Lent is as a time to massage, with hymnody and prayer, deliciously deep Christian feelings, but the repentance called for here is not merely or primarily depth of individual emotion. In both these passages it is the whole structure of society that is disordered, and playing around with our private interiority will not save us.

In Joel there is a life-or-death peril, annihilation coming on like an inexorable army. We in our time may read of these locust-soldiers and sense some impending disaster, some historical or natural force that will sweep us away. Our nation, our culture, our church, our families, our very existence and this physical world: all in danger. Perhaps some disease is already at work in us, some sickness unto death that gathers force just out of sight. If only we all recognize it, sound the alarm, all together face it with some serious repentance, maybe then we have a chance. God may take pity. Such was God's way of old.

The reading from Isaiah may speak to a more subtle fear, that our religion just doesn't work, that much as we like its trappings and petty pleasures, it is a pretty hollow thing. God is not there. Our prayers seem unheard, our lives decorated but unchanged. It is striking to me that when the prophet describes the alternative and answer to such ineffectual religion the language is at once ethical and also what we in our Christian terminology call sacramental. The religion that is needed entails liberating and feeding, clothing and hospitality. It is the work of community. And it is "not to hide yourself from your own flesh." The NRSV translates that word "flesh" (baśar) as "kin." The interpretation is correct, I believe, but a valuable ambiguity and resonance has also been lost. Not hiding ourselves from our kinfolk, our sisters and brothers, has also to do with not fleeing our own flesh. It is our own mortality and vulnerability we may be tempted to flee as well as much as theirs. And then there is also our flesh made visible and common in Christ: our community is constructed on that level, in the flesh, the body.

We may not really believe that repentance of the kind that Joel describes will save the nation or the world or ourselves. We may not really believe that if we were just more sacramentally ethical God would come through for us with power and glory. But what else will work? We are in peril. In the prophets' words is a hope, a chance. It is better than despair, and it turns us from death toward life.

Responsive Reading

PSALM 51:1-17 (RCL); 51:3-6, 12-14, 17 (RC); 103 or 103:8-14 (BCP)

A psalm traditionally associated with David's repentance in 2 Samuel 12, Psalm 51 cries out with eager yearning that one might be made different. Purge me, cleanse me, make me right again. They who have made these words their own through countless generations know as the psalmist did how deep the sickness, the simple wrongness, of sin can sit in our being. It is neither just a feeling of guilt on our part or a verdict of guilty on God's part at stake here. It is sickness and stain and corruption. The words acknowledge the kind of dishonesty and shame that perpetuate themselves in secret, and they ask to be fixed. Please God, they ask, and they are willing to grovel, to plead, and even to bargain. Make me right and I will serve you. I will become a teacher, an example. I will bring others to you. See how broken-hearted I am. This strong pleading we make our own, but we are perhaps grateful that the language is formal and prescribed, liturgical play-acting that no one need think is really how desperate we are. Then again, perhaps we *do* find ourselves also in these old phrases, find ourselves longing to be made different, washed clean, born fresh.

Second Reading

2 CORINTHIANS 5:20b—6:10 (RCL/BCP); 5:20—6:2 (RC)

Interpreting the Text

In his two letters to the Corinthians, Paul devotes much space and energy to the problem of his own authority. If he is to teach and correct these gifted and fractious people, how is he to secure their hearing and respect? When dealing with the Galatians he had been able to pull rank, reminding them of his status as their founding apostle and warning that not even an angel should be permitted to lead them in a contrary course. With this community, however, "his" people are seen as only one of several factions. From the first chapter of 1 Corinthians he has therefore argued his counsel not from authority of office but in the context of a pluralistic community of the Spirit. Here, in this second letter, the problematic question may still be heard in the background: "Who is he to tell us anything?" People could see his weaknesses, both those in which he appeared strange and those in which he was so clearly ordinary. Paul was vulnerable.

What he does in 2 Corinthians is to take that vulnerability and turn it into a kind of authority. It is precisely in human weakness that divine strength is revealed, in the earthen vessel that the treasure is borne. This is the way God is working. Even the sinless one is "made sin" for our sake. And now is the time, the jubilee "acceptable time," when God's vulnerable ambassadors speak: "God is making his appeal through us; we entreat you on behalf of Christ, be reconciled to God" (5:20).

The almost rhapsodic passage that makes up most of this reading forms a description of the way in which now, in this time of reconciliation, Paul's life has been "transvalued." Even indignities and defeats are now commendations, sorrows cradle joy, and poverty bears riches.

Responding to the Text

These words speak, as do the texts for the first reading, of a critical time, an urgent now in which to act. The urgency here is in the entreaty: Be reconciled! The classic indicative-imperative progression operates in 2 Corinthians 5: God was in Christ reconciling. . . . Therefore be ye reconciled. For God's sake, don't accept this grace in vain. Make it something that works in you, that can be seen in your life. Paul's apostleship here has to do with a middle term in this progression, the "ambassador" of reconciliation who declares and entreats on behalf of Christ.

The urgent now here is not as dark a "Day of the Lord" as in the alarm sounded in Joel. It is a day of acceptance and favor, a salvation day the light of which transfigures the whole landscape of life. Yet here again, in jubilee as in judgment, there is the confrontation with our limitation and weakness. This day's ashen declaration, that each human creature is dust and to dust returns, is incorporated in Paul's answer to the question about his authority. Who does he think he is anyway? Headed for death, acquainted with grief as well as joy, disgrace as well as honor. Dust, yet now so alive. The intensely triumphant note of this passage is not a denial of death nor the pretense that failure is not an option. On the contrary, it is with the acknowledgment of his weakness—dignified and matter of fact, not pridefully wallowing in wretchedness—that he has anticipated and disarmed his scoffers. The earthen vessel of his own perishing human flesh is all the more a token of what treasure it has been honored to hold. The ashes are consecrated to a saving purpose: they make the sign of the cross.

THE GOSPEL

MATTHEW 6:1-6, 16-21 (RCL/BCP); 6:1-6, 16-18 (RC)

Interpreting the Text

These familiar words are drawn from the Sermon on the Mount. The Gospel of Matthew is increasingly being read as testimony and teaching from a portion and period of the Jesus movement that still understood itself as contending for the identity and faithfulness of Israel, proposing a "Judaism" (the term is anachronistic and must be handled with care) defined both in the teachings of Jesus and in the life of the messianic and exemplary community of his followers. The particularly sharp attacks on the Pharisees found in this Gospel might in fact best be understood in the context of that ongoing struggle for the definition of Israel. The Matthean church would likely have known the growing Pharisaic movement as its principal—and arguably also most similar—competitor in the work of reforming and inspiring the people of God to new faithfulness. The remembered and reported words of Jesus describe a lifestyle for the reign of God, or (as Matthew consistently phrases it, with pious Jewish avoidance of the divine name) the kingdom of heaven.

Even if Matthew's original community and audience was more Gentile or catholic than pictured in this scholarship, however, indeed even when it becomes what it now is, Jesus' preaching still carries this quality of proposal and call. Here is a way of life described, a faithfulness prescribed, as of old, upon a mountain.

The section set before us today picks up the day's themes of genuineness and humility. Here again is the recognition that piety can so easily become a pride, a way of showing off. It can all become a vehicle for inequity and sham. The pieties of charity, prayer, and penitence are treated here, each with its warning and counsel. Jesus stands (or, in fact, sits) here in the company of rabbinic sages in warning against the proud uses of religion. Almsgiving—the Greek word in the text is dikaiosyne, "righteousness," for already here, as in today's Judaism, the Hebrew word tzedekah means concrete generosity—too easily becomes self-glorifying, and prayer become ostentatious, and fasting not true repentance but a chic display of spiritual strength.

IN A CULTURE OF DENIAL AND FRANTIC FEAR, THE TRUTH HAS AT LAST BEEN SPOKEN AND SIGNED ON OUR FLESH. ITS INEVITABILITY COMES AS IMMENSE RELIEF AND A BEGINNING OF WISDOM.

They who delight in such earthly and immediate satisfactions of religious practice have, as Jesus says, already received their reward. The true reward to be sought is elsewhere—in heaven, in secret, in the future. The eloquent counsels to discretion and secrecy, unself-consciousness and simplicity, draw on a realism about the seductive vanity of "spiritual" as well as "material" riches: "Do not store up for yourselves treasures on earth, where moth and rust consume and where thieves break in and steal. . . . For where your treasure is, there your heart will be also."

Responding to the Text

We may be struck each time we encounter this text on Ash Wednesday by the incongruity of such counsel against any public sign of faith or penitence on a day when many come to take on just such a sign. "Wash your face," says Jesus even as we smudge our foreheads with ashes and wear them for the world to see.

Of course, we may conclude, as generally we have, that we need not take these dominical words as invariable mandate or literal prohibition. We may find beauty and blessing in the ancient emblem of the ashes, and we can receive both encouragement and community when we see that token of death worn in the public square. Nonetheless, or perhaps all the more, the ashes come with the warning that underlies Jesus words. It is in fact part of the ashes' meaning that they will not save us.

In many churches the ashes used on this day are the burned remains of palm branches that once were banners waved in joyous worship and faith. Even our worship perishes and turns to dust. The very best and most godly that we have, our faith itself, is as mortal and subject to sin as we are. Our hope is not there.

Except that, strangely, it is there, in this stark and ashen truth that we find true hope's beginning. For it is truth, calling us from the dominion of both lies and self-deceptions. Pious pride and venial greed, poses and secrets, all are doomed and hopeless. This despair spells first our freedom from false gods and then our communion as mortals of tender worth. "For he knows our frame; he remembers that we are dust," read the words of Psalm 103. A great compassion wells up from this place.

We are going to die. I am. You are. There is no need to hide from it any longer. In a culture of denial and frantic fear, the truth has at last been spoken and signed on our flesh. Its inevitability comes as immense relief and a beginning of wisdom.

The wisdom, the counsel of Jesus in these verses, naturally involves choosing what abides over what perishes: "For where your treasure is, there your heart will be also." There is, however, an important irony here: what perishes (what moth and rust consume or thieves break in and steal) is in this world considered treasure precisely because we think it will last, while that which is stored up in heaven tends to look more pitiably, perishingly human in our eyes.

It was said in ancient Greece that the immortal gods envied us human beings our mortality. They who would not die could not love with the same intensity nor see the world charged with the same glory as do we whose days were numbered. Yet our God has broken the bonds of immortality; our Lord has come to die with us. The ashes tell of his nearness to us.

FIRST SUNDAY IN LENT

MARCH 4, 2001

REVISED COMMON	EPISCOPAL (BCP)	ROMAN CATHOLIC
Deut. 26:1-11	Deut. 26:(1-4), 5-11	Deut. 26:4-10
Ps. 91:1-2, 9-16	Ps. 91 or 91:9-15	Ps. 91:1-2, 10-15
Rom. 10:8b-13	Rom. 10:(5-8a) 8b-13	Rom. 10:8-13
Luke 4:1-13	Luke 4:1-13	Luke 4:1-13

EACH LENT THE FIRST SUNDAY RETURNS US TO THE WILDERNESS. The forty days of Jesus' fasting are not just scriptural warrant for the length of the season we have begun. They themselves point to their own "back story" in the memory of Israel, the forty years of desert wandering. Pointing back, they point away as well, away from the settled and the safe. Away from ourselves, to find ourselves anew—or perhaps for the first time.

FIRST READING

DEUTERONOMY 26:1-11 (RCL); 26:(1-4) 5-11 (BCP); 26:4-10 (RC)

Interpreting the Text

The book of Deuteronomy itself is one that "goes back to the wilderness." It speaks to those who are settled, who have come into the land and who live in its prosperity, but it addresses them with the voice of a Moses still in the wilderness. It points Israel back—back first to the time just before they entered into this national enterprise they are living out, the time when their unmatched prophet "whom the LORD knew face to face" (Deut. 34:10) charged them with divine words in a final sermon of warning and exhortation. Back even further, then, to the recollection of Israel's sojourn in Egypt, and of the bondage under Pharaoh, and of the great liberation. A powerful aspect of this particular text as continuing commandment to the people is the insistence that the history be claimed as one's own: you are to say, "This happened to me, to us." The NRSV's use of the ungendered, "my ancestor," for 'avi, "my father," is eminently defensible, but it unfortunately blunts this aspect of the text. Slavery and liberation were not experiences that happened to distant ancestors. The wandering Aramean is here to be imagined as if just one generation away, and it is our generation now that knew oppression and ate the bread of affliction. God brought us out with a mighty hand and an outstretched arm. God brought us through the wilderness into this land. Remembrance and reclamation of that heritage are, of course, part of the Passover ritual, a ritual that reproves that child of Israel who denies that this happened to himself or herself. (Note how that seder rebuke underlies Jesus' dispute with hoi Ioudaioi in John 8:33, part of a chapter otherwise easily understood as the most poisonously anti-Judaic, even anti-Semitic, in the New Testament.) With each harvest, each renewal of bounty in the land, Israel is to remember and give thanks. The first fruits are to be offered with a recitation of the story, personalized and "owned" as a credo or a canonical history. This is cultic action, but it is interesting that the priest here seems to drop out of the action after v. 3. Before the priest the offering is set, but the action described is entirely that of the inhabitant. This action, moreover, is not only "liturgical" but social and ethical: "Then you, together with the Levites and the aliens who reside among you, shall celebrate with all the bounty that the LORD your God has given to you and to your house."

The reference to the "Levites and the aliens" is also vital. Remembrance of one's own history as a foreigner and a slave, of one's own vulnerability and dependence on others, entails compassion and hospitality. Repeatedly Deuteronomy returns to the law of responsibility and care for those on the dependent margins of society: widows, orphans, aliens, slaves. The deuteronomic version of the Ten Commandments (5:6-21) explicates the keeping of the Sabbath not as emulation of the divine pattern of creation (as in Exodus) but rather as a recurrence of a day when all workers, beasts of burden, slaves, and aliens "may rest as well as you" (Deut. 5:14). Why? "Remember that you were a slave in the land of Egypt and the LORD your God brought you out from there with a mighty hand and an outstretched arm; therefore the LORD your God commanded you to keep the sabbath day" (v. 15).

Our reading refers also to the Levites. This nongeographic priestly tribe was to be landless, dependent on the settled. In this context it makes sense to think of them not as an elite but rather those who are of the people yet also intentionally made alien in the midst of Israel. They insure that within the very body of the settled nation there will be those who are not quite at home, always dispersed and, to at least some extent, still wandering. Both the presence of Levites and hospitality to them are thus means for wilderness remembrance.

Politically and culturally, Deuteronomy's themes have seemed particularly resonant to Americans. They have often shaped our self-definition and have been rewoven into what one might call our "canonical histories." This land was seen as a place of promise, flowing with milk and honey, given by God but granted also with the errand to make here a place of righteousness and equality, a commonwealth of welcome for the stranger and refuge for the alien. Among the images from Anglo-American history which long functioned as the hegemonic norm for our nationhood was that of John Winthrop aboard the Arabella in 1630, charging the settlers of Massachusetts Bay with their responsibility to be "A Model of Christian Charity." Winthrop's sermon was given on the ship, before they landed on the shore, and he stood as Moses in the wilderness on the verge of the promised land, describing to his people the way of death and the way of life, bidding them choose rightly. They were to be "as a city on a hill" and to keep faith with their God after the counsel of Micah 6, "to do justice, to love kindness, and to walk humbly with your God."

We must recognize the cruelties and hypocrisies that can so easily be obscured, and even nurtured, by that deuteronomic reading of our history: The displacement and outright genocide of native populations, the pride of election, the careless arrogance that cannot see through other eyes— all mark our national history (and all might be read as historically implicit even in the scriptural narrative as well). Nonetheless, the words of Winthrop, like those of Deuteronomy, also read as warning and call to something better, a sobering reminder of what was intended, hoped for, meant to be—not only for Israelites nor for Americans, but for us all. Returning to the verge of the land, to the ocean or wilderness, we begin again. By remembrance before the altar with our gifts, we stand again at a threshold, slaves and beggars all.

Responsive Reading

PSALM 91:1-2, 9-16 (RCL); 91 or 91:9-15 (BCP); 91:1-2, 10-15 (RC)

This Psalm will serve as the devil's scripture in the Gospel reading, but we wrest it back from Satan's grip. We read it as our own and will not abandon its bold words just because they have been sullied by evil usage.

But, to be honest, the psalmist's words seem excessive, far too bold. This is not so much courage as bravado, an unrealistic promise of invulnerability. It is clearly unrealistic. How can we credit or commend so extreme a faith as would believe that one is safe, beyond the reach of disaster or death, no matter how close they come? Clearly Jesus was wise to push these words from him with the counter-scripture, "Do not put the Lord your God to the test."

Perhaps we should invoke against this Psalm's excessive confidence also a yet more familiar counter-text, praying as Jesus taught us not to be led into temptation, to be saved from the time of trial. The Lord's Prayer recalls us to humility and reminds us that we are not so strong and that evil is very powerful. We can fail and perish. Let us, dear God, not be tested too hard.

Yet of course sometimes faith and courage do take the form of bravado. Sometimes one should stand up straight and laugh at Satan's pomps and pretensions. Spit in his face and mock his vain power. Rage as he might, he will not have you. However bad things look, the victory will not be his. Humility and honest fear is not the only note to be sounded in the face of trial and temptation.

Martin Luther was particularly exuberant in such full-chested piety as this, but it is certainly not a uniquely Lutheran mode of faith. The immoderate confidence of this psalm has been an important element in the evening prayers and in the mutual encouragements of God's people of every generation. It is heady and glorious and sometimes just right. We should sing or say it for real, as a word of bravery and good humor, even if—or particularly because—on this day we acknowledge that the words can mislead or lie.

Second Reading

ROMANS 10:8b-13 (RCL); 10:(5-8a) 8b-13 (BCP); 10:8-13 (RC)

Interpreting the Text

Paul here reaches back to Moses' final sermon in Deuteronomy for textual warrant and/or resonance for his point that righteousness was attained not by those who strove for it but by those who did not (Rom. 9:30-31). In a bold exercise of interpretive freedom, Paul takes the nearness of the word in Deuteronomy 30:14 not as a reference to the attainability of the law but rather as a description of Christ's accessibility. It is here Christ rather than the keeping of the commandment that we need not ascend high nor descend deep to claim. The "word" (davar in Hebrew, rhema in Greek) is here no longer the call to an achievable deuteronomic law, but rather the speakable utterance of faith.

Paul thus sets the Torah text on its head as he applies it to the salvation of the gentiles. No longer is it the doing of the commandment that is the accessible Way of Life; it is rather the confession of Jesus' lordship from the heart that is seen as near and available righteousness. Glossing the "word" in this manner and proclaiming its proximity on lips and heart without its original reference to observance, Paul proceeds to cite a form of Isaiah 28:16 ("Every one who believes in him shall not be put to shame" is Paul's construction of the verse) that emphasizes the universality of this particular source of vindication. That scriptural reference that leads in turn to the affirmation of a new community in such reliance, a universality without distinction between Jew and Greek since either may call on this Lord, this Messiah who is so very near.

Before moving on to take up the issues of agency and apostleship so vital to the justification of his own work, Paul concludes this section with one more reference. It is the words from Joel 2:32, so familiar to us from the Pentecost kerygma in Acts 2. Alongside the references to Christ as Lord in the preceding verses, the Joel citation illustrates how freely the title of Lord as Israel's God has been allowed identification with the name and figure of Jesus. Scripture about the ineffable Holy One can be interpreted as teaching and promise about the Lord Jesus. Calling on that name is, Paul here claims, powerful enough to save.

Responding to the Text

The freedom and creativity with which Paul and other New Testament writers use scripture seem to violate our modern canons of interpretation, our attention to text and history. What we have here is a biblical sensibility and style of argument much more closely akin to the play of rabbinic conversation than to analysis of what the text historically or originally "meant." The Christian use of "the Law and the Prophets," or more largely of the body of writings that came among us to be called the Old Testament, is rightly a matter of some controversy, fraught with the issues of supersessionary appropriation and anachronistic distortion. Some among us have so recoiled from a perceived Christian hijacking of Jewish scripture that they not only eschew but censure all christological interpretation of the "Hebrew Scriptures." Complicating the problem for us, however, is that early Christian writings that read the Scriptures in such ways have themselves become canonical Scripture for us as Christians, scripture that binds itself decisively to the writings that preceded it. What is now often called "The Hebrew Bible," and the Tanach of Judaism, and the traditional Old Testament (with or without the so-called Apocrypha), and the graphai quoted by New Testament writers—none of these should be thought exactly the same entity as the others, particularly when such thought issues in warfare over who rightly owns or understands the Bible. Yet, of course, there are important ways in which all these are intimately related to one another.

Such complexities of canon and interpretation are probably not on the preaching agenda this day, but we may notice that this reading raises again the question of the use and misuse of Scripture. The devil and Jesus and Paul are all quoting

Bible verses today, each using the words cited as weapons in a conflict. In Paul's case, he is most likely aware that these verses from Deuteronomy 30 could be wielded against his argument for a righteousness apart from the Law. What clearer or more eloquent statement do we have of the Law's achievability and of its life-giving function? Instead of fleeing or hiding from this opposing text, however, he leaps to lay hold of it himself and then to wrest new meaning and implication from the words. He makes the words argue something that seems quite other than their plain meaning. These words no longer belong to Moses; they are now spoken by "a righteousness that comes from faith" (Rom. 10:5-6).

Yet Paul's bold appropriation of texts to argue what they had not intended may not be so mad a violation of the scripture after all. If what is at stake in Deuteronomy concerns God's covenant and relationship with the people, and if the keeping of the Law is then their sign and the enactment of that relationship, certainly Paul's words here make new and surprising sense. It is now Christ who is that sign and enactment, and it is the confession of his name that lays claim to the covenant anew. Faithfulness was not meant to be a striving for distant accomplishments but a living, in trust and devotion, with a God near at hand. Such was the intent all along. It was not about something distant and doubtful but someone near and trustworthy. This sense, which we later Christians might call "sacramental," is arguably also a fair representation of the commandments' actual function both in Deuteronomy and in much of living Judaism. On this day, moreover, it is a good weapon for us to have if we feel far from safety and the devil assails us with deadly words in the wilderness.

The Gospel
LUKE 4:1-13

Interpreting the Text

All three Synoptic Gospels follow the story of Jesus' baptism with the telling of his temptation in the wilderness. This sojourn in the wilderness is described as either caused or facilitated by the Spirit; in Mark, Jesus is "driven" or "thrown out," but Luke's description of the Spirit's action is typically gentler, a leading in the wilderness. Matthew writes of leading "into the desert," closer to the Markan description, but Luke's "in" reflects his emphasis on Jesus' ongoing relationship with God. Luke's narrative also interrupts the urgent drive from baptism to wilderness by inserting between them a genealogy, one that focuses not on the descent of Jesus from Abraham and David, as in Matthew, but rather on the filial line between Jesus and God.

For all those differences, however, these accounts may also each be drawing on an archetypal sense of the wilderness as the natural place of testing for the recipient of a vocation. Baptized and anointed as the chosen one of God, Jesus does not immediately begin his mission. Before hitting the roads of Galilee, he heads for the desert.

It may be a deep archetype, but the precise purpose of this retreat prior to the forward march of ministry is still open to debate and speculation. It might be a time for Jesus' personal testing of his vocation, or similarly for a kind of training camp, a physical and mental preparation or a purification for the rigors ahead. Luke does not tell us, but neither does he describe these forty days as primarily intended either for Jesus' being tempted or for his seeking out Satan in the first engagement of a longer war. Jesus is tempted by the devil in the wilderness, but it is unclear in Luke whether the devil's assaults were what either Jesus or the Spirit in him were seeking there. The temptations may indeed be the secondary consequences of Jesus' faithfulness to his Father, by-products of his spiritual commitment. Of course Satan would go after him while he is thus exposed and alone.

The intensive temptations described in this pericope are in fact designated as coming after the forty days of fasting. Luke makes a point of Jesus' famished state. What follows is not a summary of various temptations in the course of a long wilderness retreat but is to be understood rather in the context of a weakened condition. These temptations take place when Jesus is most exhausted and vulnerable, in extremis. The temptations accord with their setting in an uncertain, possibly hallucinatory landscape, charged with doubt and desire.

First the hunger for food, then the desire for power and glory, and finally the wish to be proven and vindicated—with each of these Jesus is tested. In each case, Jesus beats back the temptation with words of scripture. In the last temptation here—the middle one in Matthew—the devil also quotes the Bible, but Jesus shows that the point is not having a Bible verse, but rather having the right one. (So also, he tells the devil, "One does not live by bread alone," but he did not quote those words later, when hungry people needed feeding.)

There are various ways these temptations can be parsed, either as types of human temptation in general or as temptations for Jesus in particular, "shortcuts" that would in fact short-circuit the mission he had come for. A point noteworthy in Luke's version is the placement of the trip to Jerusalem as the last of the three temptations. Jesus will in fact go to Jerusalem for the culmination of his work. In time, when the kairos comes, he will drop into the void there, falling into death with a final faithful prayer of trust drawn from the Psalms. But not yet, not like this.

Headed into the wilderness with Jesus this Lent, we may imagine our way back to a deuteronomic sense of communal reconsecration. We may intentionally imagine ourselves outside the landscape of settlement, aliens and refugees despite whatever comforts we have accumulated. Such would be a salutary exercise, certainly true to the general theme of this day and season. If the clutter of our possessions seems to crowd us and our routines render us listless, we may welcome Lent's simplicity and discipline. Its barren landscape might more beckon than frighten us.

Yet all this, valuable though it may be for our edification, seems to miss the point in Luke's telling of the temptation story. This evangelist's concern is not so much, either primarily or ultimately, with the consecration of identity through symbolic return to the desert, nor even with the cosmic struggle between Jesus and the powers of evil. What Luke offers, I think, is rather an account of how Jesus, "full of the Holy Spirit," prevailed over the devil in the wilderness. He is able to be in a place of vulnerability and confusion, to be weak and hungry, and yet not succumb to the devil's seductions. It is there in the first verse: he carries the Spirit within, and that Spirit leads him when he is in the wilderness. This Jesus is not led or thrown or driven into temptation by the Spirit. He faces temptation when he comes to it, indeed faces it down, parrying the thrusts of the devil with the right words of Scripture, the right spirit of faith and faithfulness.

There is much that is frightening and genuinely dangerous also for the followers of Jesus, for us ordinary folk who sometimes wander frightened and exposed in desert places. We may feel ourselves in shadowed valleys and lonely wastes. We may be exhausted or famished and feel no reserve of strength. At such times it may seem an irrelevant metaphor to speak of ourselves being reconsecrated by this wilderness. What we need then is simply more courage and hope to resist temptation. What we need is a quality of faith we can carry into the domain of demons so that it becomes a territory of the Spirit after all. That is what Luke is describing for us, The wilderness does not consecrate; it gets consecrated. It proves the place not of lost wandering but of the Spirit's leading. It is like that alien place where the fleeing Jacob lay down only to discover that this was Beth-El after all: his Lord was at home there.

We who witness Jesus vanquish his tempter may likewise dare imagine the fearful landscapes of our own lives transfigured. Even the exhausted and weak among us may be brave enough to take his example, to resist evil and choose right, to speak our no and our yes. For the desert is not God-forsaken nor does it belong to the devil. It is God's home. The Holy Spirit is there, within us and beside us. And if we cannot feel that spirit inside of us or at our side, perhaps we can at least imagine Jesus there, not too far away, with enough in him to sustain us, enough to make us brave.

SECOND SUNDAY IN LENT

MARCH 11, 2001

REVISED COMMON	EPISCOPAL (BCP)	ROMAN CATHOLIC
Gen. 15:1-12, 17-18	Gen. 15:1-12, 17-18	Gen. 15:5-12, 17-18
Ps. 27	Ps. 27 or 27:10-18	Ps. 27:1, 7-9, 13-14
Phil. 3:17—4:1	Phil. 3:17—4:1	Phil. 2:17—4:1 or 3:20—4:1
Luke 13:31-35	Luke 13:(22-30) 31-35	Luke 9:28b-36

WE ARE A LITTLE FURTHER INTO LENT NOW, not weary yet but perhaps no longer as sure or energetic as at the outset. On our way still, but wondering, doubting, a little afraid of just what does lie ahead, or maybe still more that nothing awaits us, just a nothingness and no future. Or maybe we haven't felt any of that yet, but now these lessons, bidding reassurance and courage, invite us to think about the needs that they address.

FIRST READING

GENESIS 15:1-12, 17-18 (RCL/BCP); 15:5-12, 17-18 (RC)

Interpreting the Text

God's covenant with Abram is revealed in encounter and promise more than once. We may think of it spoken forth in the call to leave his homeland at the beginning of Genesis 12, or in the LORD's renaming and commanding pledges found in chapter 17, or in the words of the divine guest at Mamre in chapter 18. In today's passage also is God's covenant made with Abram, and the mode of its making, the verb itself in Hebrew, is a cutting (v. 18: "YHWH cut a covenant with Abram"). God carves this pact, but it is also sealed with the blade that Abram himself wields and with the mysterious vision of Abram's own seeing.

God's verbal promises here answer in turn both Abram's childlessness and his landlessness; they pledge both a future and a place for his seed. In v. 6—in words that Paul and countless subsequent Christians have read, literally or typologically, as descriptive of "justification by faith"—Abram righteously turns from doubt to trust. Just two verses later, however, he seeks something more, some further sign and greater assurance. Thus the killing and cutting that follows is a sacrifice not as negotiation, expiation, or appeal, but rather one that consecrates a time and space for revelation. It creates the context for the sign of presence and promise which God will grant. Abram lays out the sacrifice and drives away the carrion birds that threaten to dismantle the scene. The stage is set, and he waits for the vision to come.

This vision is described for us: deep sleep with terror and darkness and then words and then fire coming down in the midst of the offering. The visual imagery could be intentional prefiguring of the fire and cloud by which God would later guide Israel's children from slavery back to the land of promise. It might also more simply be a sign of the dualities of God's presence: not only the smoking heat of the kiln but the light-giving flame. The fundamental and primary point is however the one that the text gives. Abram's desire to know (v. 8) receives an answer. Through this vision God not only reveals but makes—cuts—the covenant with Abram. One of the classic views of Abram in Jewish tradition is of a seer, a visionary; here, when Abram questions and doubts, God speaks not only to the ears of his servant but to his eyes, or to the imagination of his heart.

Responding to the Text

If Lent puts before us themes of wandering and wilderness, alienation and home, then certainly Abram will be there. He became Abraham, the father of us all, the first whom God called from the familiar to an alien home. Though already old enough to be past any reasonable hope of reaching this future, he lit out from Ur to find it. So he is for us also the model of faith. He trusts enough to go toward what is not yet there. He believes. That is his righteousness.

Yet Abram is not just this classic example of one who is able to move forward on nothing but trust, able as it seems even to stand on nothing, or nothing but a remembered word, a past promise. He does believe, but he also wants more. He asks, "How am I to know?" A sign, a vision, something more than only words to remember. This might not mean full certainty, there might still be some doubt, but yet he asks for something further to carry him over into that realm of believing which feels like knowledge.

Note that God does not mock Abram's yearning or insist on faith's purity of trust. We might be tempted to point our father Abraham to his task as exemplar of faith, not knowledge. Paul might chide him with the observation that "hope that is seen is not hope; who hopes for what is seen?" (Rom. 8:24) God, however, turns not aside Abram's desire for something more to go on. The covenant is signed here with sacrifice and vision. It is cut. If the form of this covenant-making appears weird and bloodily primitive to us, perhaps we will remember how strange and messy our own language of covenant appears. (It may indeed be remarked that Christianity keeps alive and central a language of sacrifice and blood that has had no equivalent significance for Jews at least since the destruction of the Temple.) Yet the point here for us may not be so much the particular form and seal of the covenant as the simple fact that it is given. As much as Abram walks by faith rather than by sight, there is also this vision. He ventures in hope, but there is also this event: not the promised future itself but rather that promise enacted and seen and thus become a memory, a work of remembrance.

The final verse of this reading is of course politically problematic. Are these literally the God-decreed boundaries of the land for all time? Is such a "Greater Israel" today the form and substance for God's promise to Israel as a nation? What of Ishmael and of Esau, the displaced firstborns, and what of all the other peoples, from Canaanites to Palestinians, who have contended for this sacred bloodied land? The theme of supersessionism is not exclusively a problem for Christianity, and we can hardly read these words without cognizance that the borders of Israel are still in dispute. A tragic history continues to attach itself to the extravagant geography of God's remembered promise. We who would lay hold of this story for our own blessing must therefore handle its application with great care.

Thus it might be easier just to avoid the whole messy business of this version of the Abrahamic covenant, or to pass it by quickly with a friendly nod of the head or tip of the cap. Moreover, our more "protestant" sensibilities are apt to recoil from these cruder tokens of covenant, eschewing the overt symbols that others might eagerly treasure. They can seem to us as superstitious devices, invitations to misplaced hope, religion rather than faith. Aspiring to a purer, more athletic faith than Abram's, we may hope to know and trust without further sign. God's sharp word within our memory should be altogether sufficient, no further cutting needed.

The time can in fact come when worn and insubstantial words seem to be all that we have to keep hope alive, to keep on keeping on. May it then be sufficient, and may God provide us faith enough. But if we fear and wonder like Abram, "How am I to know?" perhaps it will not be counted to us as shame. Perhaps a sign or liturgy—some sacrament performed on the alien ground to which we have come or a mark of the cross on our flesh—will help us. Maybe we'll see something that brings our hoping closer to knowing.

RESPONSIVE READING

PSALM 27 (RCL/BCP); 27:10-18 (BCP alt); 27:1, 7-9, 13-14 (RC)

This Sunday's psalmody joins its ancient song to the texts of courage before us. "Wait for the LORD; be strong, and let your heart take courage."

Here is confidence: with God on our side, whom need we fear? Should father and mother fail us, he will take their place. Though enemies plot and threaten, there is safety with the Lord. Yet, as so often in the psalms, this confidence is not itself easy and sure. It is prayed for and argued. In some verses the protection and vindication of God seems already a possession, while in others it is still future, a gift both sought and hoped. In this psalm we pray as in a place of peril, yet claiming courage and blessed assurance

SECOND READING

PHILIPPIANS 3:17—4:1; 3:20—4:1 (RC alt.)

Interpreting the Text

First and last here are words of exhortation. Its encouragement is spoken not from a detached distance but in the language of connection and warmth. Even if imprisoned and cut off from them, Paul is present to his beloved Philippians, in their midst by his example and then further through the examples of those who emulate him. Thus woven into their lives, he can exhort them from afar with a lover's words.

Between these words of affectionate solidarity, however, come sharp-edged warnings, a bitter characterization of those who live by another rule than this example, whose way of life is enmity to the cross of Christ. Paul's description of these people—"their god is the belly, and their glory is in their shame"—may suggest to us the libertine indulgence of appetite and libido often thought characteristic of pagan society, and perhaps Paul's urgency does concern the perils of Christian antinomianism or moral indifference. On the other hand, Paul may rather be aiming these words in a markedly different direction, against a party of "Judaizers." It would then be an insistence on dietary laws that he describes as idolatry of the belly and pride in circumcision that he condemns as glorying in an object of "shame." Yet whether these damned people (I use the ugly colloquial adjective to convey the combination of meaning and feeling in the first clause of verse 19) are impious libertines or pious Judaizers, the underlying issue would be for Paul the same. They have set their minds on earthly things.

Against the deadly example of such "enemies of the cross," Paul offers the exhorting reminder of a different hope. It is from heaven, our true commonwealth (politeuma), that both our identity and our salvation come. It is there that we look to see our coming savior, there that the power and glory reside for us. This is a different kind of glory, not the one of earthly pride; it is that of a body that can transform the body of our humiliation. It has the energy (energeia) that conquers all.

Responding to the Text

If we understand Paul's animus here as directed against a Judaizing faction, it is a frighteningly short step to hearing his words as an attack on Jewish religious practice itself. Circumcision and keeping kosher would thus be presented as forms of swindling worldliness, false faith. Such anti-Judaic reading of the text is misuse and distortion of Paul both in these verses and in the larger sweep of his writing, but full exposition of Paul's relationship to his own Pharisaic tradition is probably not on the preacher's agenda.

It may seem too large a task for us to sort this out in the day's preaching. Here again, it may seem easier to nod a quick greeting and move along. Let us be careful, however, how we are heard here, lest we seek to speak a truth and instead achieve a slander, false witness against our neighbor.

One gift we do have in this passage is the intensity and urgency of Paul's love. He speaks as a lover to his beloved here, and he is like a lover also in warning against his rivals. He looks for the reciprocation of his love as in a kind of mirroring, that his example would be also their way of life. It may be partly the self as seen in the eyes of the other but also something aspired to, a future or truer self revealed to the eyes of love. That vision—and we are here again, as with Abram, in a realm of vision—is transformative. It is not idolatrous, neither self-satisfied nor self-satisfying, in the manner of those other suitors. It looks up to a heavenly belonging and a future glory.

Yet note that this love is not about going to heaven. Its feet, its bodies, remain solidly on earth, standing firm, as Paul says. It is here on earth that the beloved is loved and exhorted, in the lowly body, not as an ethereal ideal abstracted from the world. The Savior will come from heaven to transform and conform us. We look to that future, and it is our lives on earth that take on its meaning. Our citizenship is in heaven, but it is here, on this alien ground, that love has claimed us.

THE GOSPEL

LUKE 13:31-35 (RCL); 13:(22-30) 31-35 (BCP); LUKE 9:28b-36 (RC)

Interpreting the Text

The Roman Catholic Gospel for this Sunday is Luke's account of the Transfiguration, the epiphany that offers to Jesus a heavenly reassurance before he begins his journey to Jerusalem. This shining forth of Jesus' identity, a preview of his resurrected glory, is for his sake, not for the disciples' benefit. It would be easy to portray this mountaintop experience as a kind of destination for the Christian life, the vision afforded Jesus' inner circle of followers, the gnosis of his glory for the blessed few. The Synoptic Gospels put the story to a very different use, however, subordinating it to the narrative of Jesus' journey toward his death. Jesus goes up the mountain to pray, not to show off. His bringing along his dearest disciples (as also later to Gethsemane) suggests his desire for the comfort of friends before a time of trial, and in fact God vouchsafes him the heavenly friends who, Luke's version makes explicit, talk with him about what will happen in Jerusalem. Thus a story that could have been about glory and power is located poignantly in the narrative of Jesus' faithful vulnerability. The "gnostic" reading of the mountaintop experience is forcefully repudiated in the divine rebuke to Peter's enthusiastic desire to build shrines. Listening to Jesus will mean discipleship, going with him to Jerusalem.

For those who marked the Transfiguration event on the Sunday before Lent, the Episcopal and Roman Catholic Gospel reading this week reminds us more intently of the danger surrounding Jesus. Jesus has been at work in Galilee, Herod's jurisdiction. Luke has already made it clear that all this will lead to Jerusalem, toward which Jesus has "set his face" (Luke 9:51). There is foreboding here, a quality of all four Gospels as Jesus' ministry seems so inexorably to entail his suffering and death, as indeed he himself begins to speak of it. In the second half of this reading, we hear the poignant lament over Jerusalem that locates Jesus in the tradition of rejected and martyred prophets. Jesus knows where he is going; he is going to die. Tenderly, with a maternal image, he grieves over Jerusalem and her people. He sorrowfully speaks both yearning and judgment. He speaks of what in fact happened, the house—house of David, house of the temple, holy city—forsaken, "left."

JESUS' COURAGE DERIVES NOT FROM A SENSE OF INVULNERABILITY BUT FROM THE DEEP CERTAINTY OF THE CROSS.

The prophecy of judgment ends with a richly ambiguous reference to Jesus' entry into the city. Do these words exclusively refer to his historical arrival some short time later (Luke 19:38) or do they also more hopefully suggest a future that is still open for Luke's audience, when the Lord who left will return and when the word of messianic welcome will prove a more faithful joy?

Before these Synoptic words of lament and warning, however, we have this uniquely Lukan and curious story of Pharisees warning Jesus away from danger. Are they enemies of Jesus themselves as eager as Herod to be rid of Jesus, their warning just a tactic of opposition? Or is this a rare sympathetic depiction of the Pharisees within the Gospel narrative? Just what, moreover, was the role of Herod, or of "the Herodians," in the politics that sought Jesus' destruction?

There is much to speculate on here. The point, however, is more simply the threat and the response. Jesus *is* in danger, but he is defiantly unafraid. In fact, he says, he isn't in danger at all. He has his mission, he will fulfill it, and Herod will not have him. For all the craftiness of Herod Antipas—"that old fox"—Jesus' fate lies elsewhere. It is in fact impossible for him to perish in Galilee; his death is scheduled for Jerusalem. Antipas' murderous intent here is as thwarted as Herod the Great's and Pharaoh's in the second chapters of Matthew and Exodus, respectively.

Responding to the Text

In Galilee, one might think, Jesus is on home territory. Judea is the danger zone. (Of late there has indeed been the proposal that hoi Ioudaioi in John's Gospel should be translated as not "Jews" but "Judeans," a problematic notion overall but certainly plausible in the case of John 7:1.) In this passage, however, we are reminded to begin with that, even in his own region, Jesus has been making enemies in high places. He has been, after all, waging war against the dominant powers. The warning he receives from these Pharisees bids him leave, but his words and actions have already put him at odds with his own land, made him alien among his own people. His inaugural sermon in Nazareth set that theme.

There is something a bit perverse and comical in Jesus' defiant message to Herod here. The reason Jesus' safety is assured against this murderous tyrant is that his death must come in another venue. He will survive in order to die under Pontius Pilate. His courage derives not from a sense of invulnerability but from the deep certainty of the cross. Headed toward that death, he will fulfill the pattern of faithfulness. Undeterred by apparent danger, he carries out his mission, ministering and healing in the land until the time comes to be gone.

In one sense, Jesus probably was in danger here. His enemies were out to destroy him, and certainly Herod had proved himself able to silence troublemakers. Jesus was walking treacherous ground. What this reading does, first with humor and then with pathos, is to subordinate the danger to the pattern of God's plan. Jesus knows what needs to happen. He will be relentless in his work of compassion and healing, turning not back for any tyrant whose pretensions do not fit God's purposes. When the time comes he will move on, but that also will be by faithfulness, not by fear.

We hardly see ourselves possessing such clarity as this about God's plan. We would hardly claim immunity from danger in one place because we are certain to reach another fate. Yet there seems in Jesus' brave resolution here still something for us to emulate—an example, as Paul might say. To defy fear and peril because we do know the deeper pattern of God's will, to refuse the threats of tyrants because we have a work of faithfulness to do, to move ahead as servants of God today and tomorrow and the next day: maybe these things we can do with Jesus. They may not be entirely safe, and the ground under our feet may no longer feel like home, but we'll be where we are meant to be and so need not fear.

When Jesus described his resolve to continue his ministry he used that expression about the third day when he would finish his work. In this context it reads as simple reference to the job still to be completed in Galilee, but of course it resonates for us with further meaning and hope. The real safety, the covenant that engenders our courage, is not in knowledge of our particular fates—it is in that work which Jesus goes to Jerusalem to do, which he completes on the third day. That is the sign and the pattern, the promise and the vision.

THIRD SUNDAY IN LENT

MARCH 18, 2001

REVISED COMMON	EPISCOPAL (BCP)	ROMAN CATHOLIC
Isa. 55:1-9	Exod. 3:1-15	Exod. 3:1-8a, 13-15
Ps. 63:1-8	Ps. 103 or 103:1-11	Ps. 103:1-4, 6-8, 11
1 Cor. 10:1-13	1 Cor. 10:1-13	1 Cor. 10:1-6, 10-12
Luke 13:1-9	Luke 13:1-9	Luke 13:1-9

LAST SUNDAY'S GOSPEL READING dealt with Jesus in danger. This week it seems more explicitly *our* lives that hang in the balance. The lessons bid us see the peril of our existence, the fatal or saving difference our choices can make. Their challenge and blessing is that they call us to wake up and watch out, to see the landscape around us and the road before us.

FIRST READING

ISAIAH 55:1-9 (RCL); EXODUS 3:1-15 (BCP); EXODUS 3:1-8a 13-15 (RC)

Interpreting the Text

The Roman Catholic and Episcopal lectionaries both look to the theophany in Exodus 3 as the first lesson for today. The story of the burning bush at Horeb strikingly calls Moses to an identity and a mission of frightening holiness. A fugitive in a strange land, orphaned from both Israel and Egypt, he discovers himself standing in God's space and time. Here he is called and sent to go first back to Egypt and eventually forward to the ancestral land, both homeward journeys in some sense but both passages to alien and dangerous ground. The words of divine solidarity and deliverance here are majestic, but what they entail for Moses is a frightening calling, one he understandably seeks to decline. This fiery bush, burning without burning up, is an image of eternity within time; what it brings is not timeless serenity but a time for decision.

The RCL for this day draws on Isaiah 55:1-9. These words introduce the powerful conclusion of Deutero-Isaiah's Book of Comfort. We may hear in this poetry both priestly exhortation and the imagery of Wisdom's house, rhetoric woven to announce God's salvation as joyous hope and invitation.

The invitation comes first, calling to all who hunger. The spring of plentiful clean waters is a powerful image of refreshment by itself, but then comes also language about wine and milk and bread, rich and delightful nourishment for a table. Here is a feast for the hungry, and it is not objects to be striven for but rather gifts to be received from the generosity of God. God gives not only water and manna for the desert journey, refreshment for the new exodus from exile; given also are bread and milk and wine, gifts of the promised land, feast of the people come home.

This call to a feast without price is followed by the challenge to the people: "Why do you spend your money for what is not bread, and your labor for that which does not satisfy?" The prophet addresses those who labor for objects of no abiding value. This people appears to have no higher or common purpose. To them the prophetic word is now offered for their recollection and hope. Here is the food and drink they really need. "Incline your ear, and come to me; listen, so that you may live."

Isaiah speaks of God's covenant with David. It was not just God's particular love for his servant in that prior time: it is an everlasting relationship, still in effect now for the people, still binding them to God's desire and design. As David was favored in the days of greatness, so it shall be now; as he was a witness to the nations, so shall this nation, glorified by the Lord, call and draw the gentiles. The Davidic covenant is made with Israel now. They are called to its glory, and all the nations will see it.

Called to such identity with David and relationship with God, the people of Isaiah are bidden also to repent. To live in this covenant means seeking the Lord, forsaking wickedness and unrighteousness, accepting the gift of forgiveness and restoration while there is still time. For the time is not infinite. It is urgent.

The selection ends with affirmation of the profound distinction between God's ways and those of the people. God does not think as they do. The implications here may be several. The distance between God's thinking and the people's thought underlies the compassion and forgiveness being described, for such grace is unexpected and unnatural for humankind. The covenant redeemed and restored, the shamed vindicated and made glorious—this too violates human expectations. The people could well have despaired of God's plan in history, but its mysteries are here grounds for hope.

To the point further is also this: that to live faithfully with God in this covenant means to act and think in ways that will not come naturally to us. That is one reason that repentance is hard work, not automatic and instinctive. It is God's way, not the drift and drive of selfishness or fear. To share in the glory of David, to be a witness to the gentiles, will demand more than the operation of habit and desire. In this context, though, the distance between earth and heaven describes not despair and judgment, for the prophet has sounded an invitation into the realm of God's thought and action. The Lord is now near. The door stands open, the homeward highway awaits, and the table is spread. Yet hurry, he says, while there is still time.

Responding to the Text

We in our own time probably know something about life and work dedicated to the purchase of worthless stuff. We inhabit a consumer culture devoted to buying and getting. The drive is not so much to amassing many objects as it is to the addition of new ones, each acquisition serving as a temporary fix, a passing satisfaction soon forgotten. Many go shopping as an answer to feelings of depression, a solution that only feeds the problem. We may also spend our time and attention on the entertainment and diversions so plentifully available to us today. We call the captives of these various addictions "junkies" because their lives are given over to junk, to stuff of no real value or substance. Yet it seems often that the objects of addiction—food, culture, information, relationships—are of themselves good and delightful. Thus, for example, such wonderful media of communication as television and the Internet have become draining and isolating compulsions for millions. There is food that does not nourish, drink that leaves us all the more thirsty.

To people adrift in a culture of appetite and consumption, Isaiah's words speak of the pricelessly nourishing and satisfying. An aspect of the health in these words is their urgency. It is not just that we are called to lives of greater purpose and connection, but that we are called now. "Seek the LORD while he may be found." Isaiah challenges the deadly sense in us that there will always be more time, always time enough to begin our lives later, to grow up or take care or attend to God's purposes tomorrow or on some other morrow in an infinite succession of days. This is the kairos, now is the acceptable time. (This was probably the import of the first line of James Russell Lowell's famous hymn, "Once to every man and nation, comes the moment to decide." It wasn't of course that God gave no second chances, but rather that such forgiveness was not to serve for the evasion of God's critical now.)

It is also striking in this text that the distance of the divine from the human does not at all entail renunciation of our human sense of longing. The prophetic critique is of *misdirected* hunger and thirst, of obsession and appetite for that which does not bless or save, but the invitation which calls us appeals directly to our desire and need. All who hunger, all who thirst, come. For all the difference between God and us, there is something instinctive here as well. It isn't just that the food and drink are convenient metaphors. What is aimed at is also that we should more fully hunger and thirst as God does, that is for justice and mercy. Jesus suggested something along those lines, after all.

Responsive Reading

PSALM 63:1-8 (RCL); 103 or 103:1-11 (BCP); 103:1-4, 6-8, 11 (RC)

The psalmody carries on the themes of thirst and refreshment found in the first lesson. Our song is of a parched land but also of God's answer to our yearning. Psalms often oscillate internally in their mood and circumstance: in this case, the thirst with which we begin dissolves in joy, gladness at the presence of the Lord in the sanctuary, delight at his faithfulness and mercy. The pleasure of a banquet is evoked and then rather deliciously the sweet restlessness of thought that can keep us awake in the night hours. Such strong satisfaction sits right by the cry of thirst. God is so absent from us here, and yet then, joy of joys, he has come, or does come, or surely shall come for us. In song and imagination we are invited to recognize both kinds of experience as our own. Each indeed deepens and informs the other, and both speak truth.

Psalm 103, the Episcopal and Roman Catholic selection for this day, is a more consistently glad doxology, one whose joy ascends to what may seem hyperbolic affirmation—God saves us from death and heals all our diseases. The song is not, however, one of bold defiance of danger such as we voiced with Psalm 91 two weeks ago. It is rather a praise of God's tender compassion for us, as a father for his children, in our vulnerability and finitude, his anger melting because he understands our weakness.

Second Reading

1 CORINTHIANS 10:1-13 (RCL/BCP); 10:1-6, 10-12 (RC)

Interpreting the Text

Paul has been offering his counsel to the Corinthians on matters of moral conduct. The problem is not only a point of division and discord but a source of profound danger for the Corinthians. A dispute over law and grace here becomes an argument about behavior, one in which it appears some have used Paul's theological affirmations about grace and freedom as warrant for rejection of all law and external constraint. Paul has argued on the contrary for a number of ways and instances in which responsibilities to Christ and to others—and others' "rightful claims" on us—must temper our use of the freedom he has proclaimed. Now he goes on to attack the moral smugness that a sense of election might have helped engender or protect.

Paul makes use of the Exodus narrative to make his point. The typological reading of the wilderness experience is powerful in this context. Who, after all was more surely in the covenant of God than those who were led through the wilderness, whom God accompanied there, who received the great signs of grace? Yet thousands of them perished because of their unfaithfulness. (Apparently, however, one thousand fewer in Paul's version compared to the 24,000 dead in Numbers 25:1-9; the discrepancy is obviously not intended to offer any comfort or hope for sinners.) There is no true hope in overconfidence or Christian presumption: "If you think you are standing, watch out that you do not fall."

Paul's typological understanding of the wilderness experience is of course striking. The stories of these ancestors in Exodus and Numbers are read as both parallel to and fulfilled in the present. For those Israelites too there was revelation and promise; for them as for the Corinthians there had been a baptism, and they too were fed with spiritual food and drink (pneumatikon does not mean that the food was not physical but rather that its source and purpose was spiritual). Paul draws on an extra-scriptural tradition of Numbers 21:17 to provide an especially striking connection with Christian experience. The rock of life-giving waters had not been left behind, but had traveled with the people. That rock was of course Christ. He had been there with them, and nonetheless so many had perished.

This midrashic fragment may catch our attention most of all since we have been so freshly engaged with the imagery of Isaiah 55:1, yet let the wonderful details of this typology not obscure what Paul is doing here. It isn't only that he is taking the imagery and narrative of Scripture (what Christians later come to call the Old Testament) as a basis for talking about what God has done in Christ. The conviction about an underlying connection or pattern of God's working there finds dogmatic expression in the Nicene Creed: Christ rose *in* accordance with the Scriptures. But here is an interpretive principle that seems to a modern reader even stranger: these events weren't really about our ancestors, but rather about us. "These things happened to them to serve as an example, and they were written down to instruct us, on whom the ends of the ages have come" (v. 11). Scripture and history come down to this place and time. Here they speak their warning against smugness and false confidence. The section then concludes with Paul's reassurance that God will provide the way, that whatsoever trials are faced will prove surmountable.

Responding to the Text

Paul's hermeneutic here, using scripture as intended for the present—for this "end of the ages"—is of course both flawed and risky. It is good that we have learned to attend to scripture's earliest meanings and original settings, and that we should maintain our humility and a human sense as we eavesdrop respectfully on the utterances of the Spirit to the men and women who went before us. We may need to make distinctions between what a text meant and what it seems to mean in our ears, and, God knows, we should have enough sense not to think that everything God has said was said to us.

Nevertheless, there is also something quite wonderful, and even sensible, in Paul's bold use of scripture here. It needs to be part of our repertoire, our available discourse. I would suggest that it is also the approach that underlies the familiar words about scripture in 2 Timothy 3:14-17. That passage has been anachronistically used to defend certain modern concepts of inspiration but seems to me rather to argue the usefulness of scripture. Thus the ancient writings were inspired "to instruct you" and to be used "for teaching, for reproof, for correction, and for training in righteousness."

A related concept may moreover inform Jesus' reported words about the least in the Kingdom being greater than John the Baptist (Matt. 11:11 and Luke 7:28): however great the saints and heroes of the past, their lives were but prologue to the present age. While such an idea seems peculiar and somewhat arrogant to us, it has about it also an empowering sense of value for the present. Even if we can give the concept only a partial endorsement, we may recognize in it a corrective to an opposite and all too common notion. Here is a challenge to the sorry thought that all real greatness and glory and sanctity lies past and we are at best the lesser beneficiaries of a better age. Isaiah's words about David and Paul's invocation of the Exodus join in pointing the past to the now, the dramatic and critical kairos of the living. This is a matter of life and death. Here, to use a phrase of outmoded but pertinent slang, is where it's happening.

The Gospel
LUKE 13:1-9

Interpreting the Text

We step back to the beginning of the chapter that ends with last Sunday's Gospel. There Herod's power breathed its threats and here we glimpse of Pilate's cruelty; both remind us of where Jesus is headed. While Luke no doubt wants us aware of the power and violence to which Jesus will be vulnerable, however, such is not the principal point here. Jesus connects the massacre of the Galileans (apparently pilgrims come to offer sacrifice in the temple; we have no other reference to this particular Roman atrocity) to the deadly collapse of a tower in Siloam, human violence and accidental catastrophe each

WE ARE NOT IN THE REALM OF PHILOSOPHY HERE, AND JESUS IS NOT SPEAKING *ABOUT* THE MATTER OF THEODICY. INSTEAD HE IS SPEAKING TO US.

taking a toll of lives. They who reported this killing might be imagined as seeking Jesus' comment on the political realities and dangers of the time. We might also hear them as drawn to speculate about the slain, about their status as martyrs of Israel or as sinners condemned by some unknown guilt.

In either case, Jesus quickly moves away from such implicit questioning, both by recalling the disaster in Siloam and by his assertion that such fate is visited on people who are no worse sinners than their neighbors, indeed no worse than Jesus' audience. The point is to take warning: judgment hangs over all, and death may come suddenly. The logic of Jesus' words here may presuppose a view of death as punishment—"Unless you repent, you will all perish as they did"—but the edge of his argument might be found in the adverbial "as they did." These words raise the specter of sudden and unprepared death, life ended without amendment of evil, without repentance. These bloody and crushed corpses can of course be seen as warnings of the judgment to come upon Jerusalem, but Jesus uses the horror more pointedly to call his hearers to repentance.

And there is still time to repent. That is clear also from the parable Jesus tells about the unfruitful fig tree whose gardener intervened against the owner and bought it a year's reprieve. There is grace, and no excuse for despair. The time, however, is limited, without room for complacency.

Responding to the Text

At first this reading may sound as if it will give us a theodicy, some explanation for suffering or justification, as Milton essayed, "of God's ways to Man." But that's not where Jesus is going with the news of the dead Galileans. What develops is almost an anti-theodicy. Do you really think these were more deserving of death than those who were spared? Than you? Jesus does not allow us the satisfaction of some imagined justice. He bids us be frightened and to change our thoughts.

Jesus is here doing something quite similar to what Paul did with the ancestors in the wilderness. The point is not in the story itself but in its working on the hearers. It has been told for our sake, and it happened as an example to us. A philosophical argument that the suffering and death of others occurs in order that we might be moved seems not only dubious but obscene. Yet we are not in the realm of philosophy here, and Jesus is not speaking about the matter of theodicy. Instead he is speaking to us. And we are again, quite simply, exposed, out in the open. There is danger and there is hope and there is still time.

Thus the concluding parable is not just a story of grace but a reminder of judgment. It is forgiveness, but as reprieve rather than as removal of danger. The spared fig tree calls to mind another, the one that Jesus cursed and destroyed for its fruitlessness (Mark 11:12-14 and Matt. 21:18-19). There was no gentle gardener to intercede for it. It was not even granted the excuse that this was still just early springtime. (I think of this when I remember the old argument that of course we wanted racial justice but our country just wasn't ready yet.) When the time came, when Jesus wanted some fruit and found none, there was no reprieve from his disappointment and wrath. Both these trees, the reprieved and the withered, stand on the same landscape. And so do we.

FOURTH SUNDAY IN LENT

MARCH 25, 2001

REVISED COMMON	EPISCOPAL (BCP)	ROMAN CATHOLIC
Josh. 5:9-12	Josh. (4:19-24) 5:9-12	Josh. 5:9a, 10-12
Ps. 32	Ps. 34 or 34:1-8	Ps. 34:2-7, 9
2 Cor. 5:16-21	2 Cor. 5:17-21	2 Cor. 5:17-21
Luke 15:1-3, 11b-32	Luke 15:11-32	Luke 15:1-3, 11-32

THIS SUNDAY WAS KNOWN OF OLD AS LAETARE, an oasis of gladness along the Lenten journey. As customary for the designation of Sundays, the name was taken from the first word of the Latin introit of the day, in this case a command to rejoice. In some places, it was even given (along with the third Sunday in Advent) a shift of liturgical color, the seasonal purple lightening to a rosy hue. That sense of the day, albeit usually without any extra fussing at the sacristy cabinet, is not altogether lost. We have descended from the epiphanic heights into this shadowed valley, but here it seems as if we come to a rise in the road, a spot midway through Lent from which we can glimpse the glow of Easter behind the dark horizon. We can imagine there the home toward which we go, and the prodigality of its welcome.

FIRST READING

JOSHUA 5:9-12 (RCL); (4:19-24) 5:9-12 (BCP); 5:9a, 10-12 (RC)

Interpreting the Text

The forty years of wandering is done. The days of Moses are past. The people have crossed from Shittim to Gilgal. As the sea had opened to free their parents from Egypt, so the waters of the Jordan have parted for them. There remains a struggle to reclaim the land, but already now they are standing upon it; they are home at last.

When Israel has crossed into the land of Canaan, Joshua circumcises all the men, the "warriors" who had been born on the journey from Egypt. During their long wilderness sojourn the sign of circumcision had not mattered. They had not been settled among the nations, and the wandering itself had defined them. Now, however, about to dwell again in the land, this new generation of Israel's sons is consecrated by the covenant of Abraham.

It is after this mass circumcision that God declares to Joshua, "Today I have rolled away from you the disgrace of Egypt." This somewhat cryptic announcement may be referring to the uncircumcised state, symbolically the foreskin itself, as a reproach. The term "disgrace" (cherepah) is used also in Genesis 34:14, where Dinah's brothers explain that her marriage to a man with a foreskin would be a reproach for them. The disgrace of Egypt—uncircumcision but, represented therein, also slavery and dishonor in an alien land—has been overturned now and the covenant sign of Israel has been restored.

As is often the case with biblical etymologies, the derivation of Gilgal from galloti, "I have rolled away," is more likely a creative gloss of the narrator than an actual etiology. As such, however, it draws suggestive power from the connection between the place name and the Hebrew for a wheel or a rotation. Gilgal is a place where the past was rolled away, and there Israel also turned toward a new future.

At the outset of that future is not just the circumcising remembrance of their father Abraham. Newly arrived in the land, they celebrate as well the more recent heritage of their liberation from Egypt. The Passover, no less than the old patriarchal covenant, is to mark their identity in the place to which they have come. Now for the first time, however, they celebrate that remembrance with the actual produce of Canaan's fair and long-sought land.

Most likely, much of the composition and redaction of Joshua dates to the seventh century, the era of Josiah. The entire deuteronomic work carries with it an agenda of shaping and reformation for the nation, a new sense of peoplehood grounded in a canonical history of exodus and covenant. The joy of entry into Canaan is strong in this Gilgal story, but the gladness itself involves a turning toward responsibility and remembrance. They must now reconsecrate the land.

Responding to the Text

Our Lenten imagination may still be making some kind of wilderness journey but on this Sunday we are invited to Israel's homecoming. The days of slavery and wandering are over, and there is real food now, the yield of the soil rather than the barely substantial manna from heaven that had sustained them in the desert. That they have arrived is intense joy; it is literally on their tongues and they can taste it.

Yet the fulfillment here is not the end of the story but more a pause and turning from one striving to another. The newfound home is also in many ways foreign to them; it is not theirs. A struggle lies ahead, not just the hard and bloody work of settlement described in Joshua but the abiding challenge of the deuteronomic agenda, faithfulness and justice in the land. Discomfort and apprehension may well have tugged at the edges of their homecoming's feast. This Passover is celebrated on the plain beneath the alien city of Jericho, and their ritual consecration is still a recent wound for the warriors of Israel. They are not entirely at ease.

This is all pertinent for us who read the text in the already-but-not-quite-yet of our Christian worship, not least on a Sunday's resurrection celebration in the middle of Lent. What might most catch our attention, however, is the verb galal with which the Lord describes what has happened: "I have rolled away from you the disgrace of Egypt." Apart from the narrative's etymological adornment here, we might have expected a straightforward verb such as "remove," or perhaps a more crudely metaphorical "cut away," but instead we have this rolling away, as of a great stone. For the Christian assembly, this word of God resonates in the opening of a tomb. These words seem for us to be about another Passover when our disgrace and bondage were rolled away. For the moment, Laetare's oasis is not just a stop for refreshment. Transfigured, it has become the garden of Easter's sweet dawning.

Responsive Reading

PSALM 32 (RCL); 34 or 34:1-8 (BCP); 34:2-7, 9 (RC)

"Be glad in the LORD and rejoice!" "Happy are those who take refuge in him." The psalmody here preserves the old theme of Laetare Sunday. It is again striking how the joy involved is not exclusively presented in the language of happiness. To speak of it the psalmists must describe also groaning and affliction, repentance and fear. These psalms are about joy but also about sin and righteousness; they are hortatory and instructive, not just elated. Sometimes joy is sheer doxology and eucharist, pure and instinctive response to an experience of goodness, but sometimes also it is more like this, a gratitude that both remembers the yearning for forgiveness and acknowledges the ongoing need for faithfulness and wisdom. Thus rejoicing and praise here have the form of a commandment: it is a choice and discipline, not just a feeling. The call to rejoice as a moral and spiritual imperative may be a particular gift to the many of us who think we are but passive wanderers in the realm of our emotions.

SECOND READING

2 CORINTHIANS 5:16-21 (RCL); 5:17-21 (BCP/RC)

Interpreting the Text

We are back again in the section of 2 Corinthians that was visited on Ash Wednesday, a wonderful exposition on reconciliation and embodiment. The lesson that day began at 5:20b and carried Paul's entreaty for reconciliation further in terms of both urgency and authority. This reading begins earlier, in the effect that Christ has had on the perception of the world. Paul has been commending himself and his ministry on the basis not of himself nor of outward appearance but of the love of Christ that urges him on (5:14). The transfiguring force of that love has come upon the world, according to Paul, and now he no longer sees anyone in the same way as before (5:16). Note that Paul speaks of this change in perception as something that happened in looking at Christ. We first saw him in just a fleshly way, but then we saw him altogether differently. That transfiguration in our eyes now applies to the world. In Christ, people are created anew, their old sins and guilt no longer counted against them.

This new creation thus involves not just a changed vision of the world but God's act of reconciliation: "in Christ God was reconciling (katallassōn) the world to himself" (5:19). This reconciliation has already been effected—it is the reality that is now visible—yet it is also still unachieved, requiring the entreaty of ambassadors on God's behalf. The call goes out: you have been reconciled, now live reconciled. God's work in Christ is a challenge and appeal. In a particularly bold image of the incarnation, Paul describes the grounding of this reconciling work in a strange divine action, that the sinless one was "made sin" in order that we might "become righteousness" in him.

Responding to the Text

The strong formulation with which this reading ends suggests the force of Paul's conviction about the difference that Christ has made. The world looks different to us now, he says; people, including we ourselves, are not the same old selves. In order to express this it appears insufficient to say that Jesus has known our sinful nature or that we have come to share in his righteousness. It is not enough for Paul to picture Jesus dipping into the messy and nasty streams of human existence, nor does it say enough to affirm that human beings have had righteousness imputed to them. Such descriptions are tellings of the story, but the effect of the story is a more radically altered sense of the world than they convey. Jesus was made sin. He didn't just redeem from it or understand it or visit in its realm. He entered into its core reality and bore its profoundest meaning in himself. It somehow got all mixed into him so that now we cannot look at sin and not see him. Conversely, when we look at him we cannot help but see the reality of our human sin.

There are a number of ways in which we may define this concept of sin in Paul, but its face and meaning now belong to Jesus. It is him that we now see whenever we think of our weakness or guilt or judgment. It is he who embodies—who is—what sin has become. And if our eyes can look on that absurd incarnation, can imagine the reality of Christ in the place of sin, then a corollary absurdity rises up. If Jesus actually becomes sin for our sake, then it is possible to think that we also become something quite different from our accustomed nature as well. In Paul's rhetoric, we become righteousness. We don't just know it and practice it; it becomes part of us and even becomes what we are. What does God now mean by righteousness? The answer is written on our flesh and in our lives. It is us God means.

Or at least this is what God intends and desires. We still have far to go, and Paul has to plead that those who are reconciled be reconciled, that is to act on, to trust and live out, their reconciliation. Nonetheless, it has come and it can be seen, not as some religious abstraction but in flesh and blood. The righteousness of God plants the righteousness of God's beloved in us, even as this beloved one puts our sin onto himself.

Where this leads is more than a theological word-game. It points to, and indeed demands, a radical reassessment of the world. It has to do with what we see, or what we imagine and name, when we look at our world and ourselves. If Christ becomes our sin and we become his righteousness, the world begins to shine in a different light. It has of course been a traditional trope in Christian teaching to say that God is savingly won over when he looks at us and sees his beloved Son. This wonderful text invites us also to look and see, as with God's eyes, the glory of Christ in the face of humanity. Then all our landscape changes.

The Gospel

LUKE 15:1-3, 11-32

Interpreting the Text

This is among the most recognized and loved of all Jesus' teaching stories. Its familiarity could make a freshness of hearing difficult but might also dispose us to attend all the more to the text, eager not only to return to a familiar place but to find there something new. We come back to beloved words not only to hear them again but to hear them as they will now sound to us. Though the words have not changed, their meaning may be different, for we are not the same as before.

The story known in our tradition as The Prodigal Son is the third of three parabolic responses to the voices in Luke 15:2: "This fellow welcomes sinners and eats with them." Jesus answers these grumblers with the parallel stories of the lost sheep, the lost coin, and the lost son. Each story ends with an image of rejoicing at the recovery of the lost, a challenge to those who would not join in the divine logic of such elation.

This third of these stories is of course the longest and richest of them. The other two have already established the pattern—we could foresee, even if we hadn't heard it countless times before, where this story will come out—but there's also a sense in which we have been "set up" for a much more difficult lesson. There are interesting ways, we might argue, that the sheep and coin stories are counter-intuitive and challenging, but after we have grasped and endorsed their point we do have a sense of what to expect in regard to the lost son.

What happens, however, is that the unfolding parable snares us with a more complex humanity. There are two sons in this story, and we may identify intensely with either of them, or perhaps with both in different ways. The story of the younger son may tell of our folly and forgiveness, while that of his brother may help us feel in ourselves the discomfort of those who grumbled at Jesus' eating with sinners. We may also be drawn into identification with the waiting father, rejected and helpless in love for his child. Given the people whom Jesus is addressing in this Lukan context, it might be said that the parable is finally "about" the elder son and his resentment, but all three characters are important actors in this drama and none exists as just a foil for the others.

REJOICING . . . AS A MORAL AND SPIRITUAL IMPERATIVE MAY BE A PARTICULAR GIFT TO THE MANY OF US WHO THINK WE ARE BUT PASSIVE WANDERERS IN THE REALM OF OUR EMOTIONS.

The story begins with the younger son's claiming his inheritance and leaving for a distant country. A youth leaving home to make his way in the world does not of itself seem objectionable or unnatural. An act of such leaving could be the start of an adventure story or possibly the first chapter of a Bildungsroman. Yet clearly this younger son's journey away from home is pictured as more selfish than heroic, evidence of both cruelty and folly. By demanding his inheritance from his living father and then moving out, he effectively declares his father dead. Although the sexual detail offered later on (v. 30) is supplied by his brother's imagination, he does squander his inheritance, his share of his father's living. (The shockingly spendthrift lifestyle here is what caused prudent Englishmen to call this parable "The Prodigal Son.") Even when the young man finally "comes to himself," there is no indication that the repentance is anything deeper than a cool calculation of selfish interests. Resurrecting the image of his father, he rehearses the speech he will use to get back into the household. We cannot tell if the emotion in that speech is genuine or merely manipulative, though we may guess what his brother would think.

The father, however, rushes out to embrace his boy. He interrupts the well-crafted speech of repentance with an effusion of welcome. The son isn't just given a cot in the bunkhouse, a place with the servants. He is the guest of honor and gets the fatted calf. Did he expect this all along, that his father would welcome him so uncritically?

The father doesn't seem to care about the motivation or sincerity of his son here. He is just thrilled to have him home. Though he will describe this as the son's resurrection (v. 32), it is in a sense his own that he is celebrating. The death inflicted when his son took the inheritance and went away is now reversed. The joy of the father is for himself.

The third actor in the story, the elder son, cannot share in that joy. The resentment he feels is probably understandable to us, especially if we have noticed the absence of reason to credit his brother with sincerity of contrition. It is his father who is now a prodigal, and probably a sucker as well. The arithmetic, moreover, seems clear: what is being squandered now is the remaining estate. The generosity of the father comes out of the elder son's share.

Such thought interestingly puts the elder son where his brother was at in the story's beginning, thinking into the death of the father. But now that father comes out to him. He is alive with the joy of the feast taking place inside. His words do not logically answer the unfairness resented by this "good" son. Rather, they invite him to see differently what has happened. They bid him see his brother in "this son of yours." They call him to feel his father's joy, to experience his brother's return as a resurrection.

Responding to the Text

The younger son literally alienates himself, traveling to a distant country. He goes afar off, in a place that first drew him by its freedom and pleasure and then cast him down into bondage and disgrace. That alienation begins its ending only as he recognizes it, as he "comes to himself." Then he heads homeward, drawn now perhaps by nothing nobler than his continuing selfishness or nothing more complex than his hunger. Yet what draws him will not be the issue for his father; simply coming home is enough. And so it is that often we worry about purity of motive and depth of feeling when the critical thing is simply what we do or where we go or remain.

The father's prodigal joy may be naive, perhaps even gullible, but Jesus' parable does not counsel wariness or prudence. Elsewhere, when Jesus was challenged about his eating and drinking with sinners he responded by talking about the need of the sick for a physician. Unfortunately, that excellent riposte could be taken to mean that it was only for therapeutic reasons that Jesus was hanging around with folks like these: the Great Physician was making house calls, but he was still on the clock. He loved them with a condescending grace; he didn't necessarily like them. Yet no, by telling this story Jesus describes instead a giddy welcoming joy in God's heart. Thus he tells us something also about his own heart, his own joy in the fellowship of sinners. He is our elder brother and he delights to be at our party.

Not so the elder brother in this story, however. At the parable's close he is the alien one, refusing to go into the house, the home that seems alien now that his brother is there. Even if only a few steps outside the door, resentment drives him as far away as his brother once was. Still, his father has come out to ask him in. Maybe Laetare's glad noise is coming from inside that house. Perhaps we are being invited to come in.

FIFTH SUNDAY IN LENT

APRIL 1, 2001

REVISED COMMON	EPISCOPAL (BCP)	ROMAN CATHOLIC
Isa. 43:16-21	Isa. 43:16-21	Isa. 43:16-21
Ps. 126	Ps. 126	Ps. 126: 1-6
Phil. 3:4b-14	Phil. 3:8-14	Phil. 3:8-14
John 12:1-8	Luke 20:9-19	John 8:1-11

IT IS TWO WEEKS BEFORE EASTER, just a week to Palm Sunday: we are in an approach, as on the verge of an edge. An anticipation is building now, but with it also another, more static sense of waiting, both a soon and a not yet. God says, "I am about to do a new thing." Jesus is but a few days away from his great and terrible Passover. But stay now, just a little while longer. Hold on to this moment and savor its goodness. It will pass soon enough, but while it is here it is a gift indeed

FIRST READING
ISAIAH 43:16-21

Interpreting the Text

Our text is Deutero-Isaiah again, the so-called Book of Comfort, offering hope and promise of redemption. The imagery here is of a new exodus. The Hebrew gives a parallel emphasis to the word derek, "way," in vv. 16 and 19. God had once made a way through the sea but now he will make the way for his people through the desert. The might of Babylon will be vanquished as were the armies of Pharaoh. Remembrance of Passover, the recollection of that first exodus, has consoled the people through the years of their exile, but now the Lord will make for them a new work, a different memory. The dry wilderness will be watered for the refreshment of God's people on their journey. God gives water to his people as a sign of his special relationship to them: they are those whom he formed that they might praise him.

Thus God's new work of liberation for Israel carries with it an agenda beyond just hitting the homeward highway. Their side of the covenant is an honoring and praising work. God's love for Israel has this honest emotional selfishness to it. God wants their praise, cares about their worship and devotion. (That such praise has a vital ethical dimension is also important—and should be self-evident—but that strong prophetic theme is not the immediate one here.) The election of Israel is understood here as more than an act of disinterested charity. God desires relationship from this people, people who will be witnesses to his work and proclaim his name before the nations.

Responding to the Text

We who are people of memory, who return repeatedly to ancient stories and who receive grace by an act of remembrance, may nonetheless find it natural and right to be told that we are not to "remember the former things, or consider the things of old." It is not only that there are certain and many things in the past that we need to forget or stop dwelling on, that God has already forgotten much of what we worry about. Our work in the gospel often has to do with surrendering such resentments and regrets as keep us in domains of exile, but there is beyond that also a sense in which the nature of the gospel is itself repeatedly a newness. What was constituted in God's covenant and is remembered in Passover and Eucharist is a fresh and present reality rather than simply a work of history. What is remembered is not so much a thing of the past as gift of the present, put in our hands to be opened now.

The Christian description of the Sinai covenant as old, in contrast with the new one of which Jesus spoke at the Last Supper, is often used in forgetfulness of Exodus 33–34, the story of Moses' intercession for and God's forgiving grace toward Israel. The covenant had been smashed like the tablets on which it was written, and thus the "old covenant" itself had to become a new one, a gracious restoration and forgiveness, already there. The saving work and presence of God, full of mercy but also bearing justice, must from its beginning and repeatedly come anew. When we remember rightly, it is that newness which we enter. It is the future that we savor.

Responsive Reading
PSALM 126

There are few passages of scripture that capture so well the dazed wonder that can be felt in a day of blessing. The image may here recall the people's return from exile, walking back to Zion. They walk as if dreaming, somnambulent yet also giddy with uncontrollable mirth. This trance of joy is recalled in such a way that we could almost enter it anew. Its moment in history had of course not lasted. The vindication of Zion was followed by the hard tasks of community and justice. Faithfulness and covenant would not remain so easy a walk of grace and gift. Thus the psalm is not only a recollection but a prayer. Recalling the great things that God did for us—so great that the nations exclaimed in wonder—we bid in our remembering that the pattern will again hold true, water in the desert and sweet reward for all our tears.

Second Reading
PHILIPPIANS 3:4-14

Interpreting the Text

This is an earlier portion of the section we visited three weeks ago. Here Paul is explicitly contending with opponents who make much of circumcision. After warning against those who "mutilate the flesh," Paul goes on to argue that true circumcision is the possession of spiritual believers, they who do not trust in the flesh. It is typical of this apostle that he both rejects pride in circumcision and makes clear that he could boast in it himself. Paul was a frequent practitioner of this rhetorical device, the non-boast boast, making sure that his readers remembered that he had the authority or gifts. He could brag but he wouldn't. He could speak in tongues with the best of them even though he wouldn't make too much of that charism. It wasn't out of envy that he argued; he had the credentials too. Thus Paul one-ups his opponents even as he deftly steps away from the competitive game.

In this particular passage, Paul slips in an especially telling touch: in regard to zeal, his excellence had been shown in persecution of the church. A polemicist of strong convictions and robust ego, Paul seems at times powerfully drawn to the heady pleasures of zealotry. Then the memory of his career as a persecutor of Christ serves him painfully and well, for he knows firsthand the harm such righteous certainty can do. The dangers of confidence have become a recurrent theme for him.

Turning away from the false and swindling assurances of the flesh, the apostle speaks of his true hope and joy, the one that makes the old satisfactions seem garbage by comparison. Paul has found a righteousness—not his own but one given in Christ—that satisfies and makes all the old striving and comparing a foolish waste. Even though this relationship to Christ is a fulfillment and satisfaction, however, it also awakens immense longing and striving, a "pressing on" to be closer to Christ, to enter more deeply into the mystery of this gift. This passion—to be near Christ and like Christ—drives upward and onward to glory and also, with the same breath, into suffering and death with Christ. The straining eagerness of this passage drives on into the exhortation we heard in our reading on the second Sunday of Lent, Paul calling others to join him as his imitators in the pursuit of this strange upward call.

Responding to the Text

Within the Pauline corpus, 1 Corinthians 13 is the section most commonly associated with love. To the fractious community of Corinth, however, Paul was writing about love as a principle and force, that is, about the greater gift that those gifted folk so sorely needed. The Epistle to the Philippians, on the other hand, is truly what we would call a love letter. It breathes Paul's affection and his yearning. It is passionate, the words of one who has fallen in love.

But with whom? Certainly his love is strong for those to whom he writes, a community that he seems particularly to cherish and for which he gives such ready and glad thanksgiving. The epistle is a love letter addressed to them, its longing directed at those real people. They are long gone now, as dead as the man who loved them, yet in this letter both he and they are near at hand. Not that they are alive, of course, but that somehow the love is.

Yet it is not simply, or most passionately, Paul's love for his friends in Philippi that pulses still in these ancient words. The one with whom he has fallen so wondrously in love is not this community. That is a simpler affection. It is Jesus who has made him his own, Jesus for whom he would give all. The drive in this passage is not really a passion to achieve and accomplish. It is like a race to win a prize, but the prize and goal and glory of it all is in "gaining Christ," being with him through his death and so in his resurrection.

This straining forward may be felt to point us on toward Holy Week and Easter, or onward into our own futures and discipleship. Yet there is also something in this ardor of Paul's that touches on the other quality in this day, the love that wishes to linger with Jesus when he is here, to be intensely present with him as he tarries a while at our meal. It is not hard to imagine Paul joining Mary, and us, on this day to anoint our Jesus with love here and now.

The Gospel
JOHN 12:1-8 (RCL)

Interpreting the Text

Somewhat as Capernaum functioned for Jesus' earlier ministry in the north, Bethany appears as a base from which his final work in Jerusalem is carried out. As must have been the case for most pilgrims to the city, Jesus and his disciples must find lodging outside the city walls. That circumstance reinforces the nearly military sense we have of this time in the narrative. Without arms or any real army, Jesus is preparing an assault on the capital city. The political theater of his temple action—described in John as on an earlier visit but in the Synoptics connected with these final days—was only one part of his campaign. He will carry his mission for his Father into the city, and there the terrible confrontation will unfold at last.

Here in Bethany, however, he is with his friends. In John it is the home of Lazarus and his sisters, especially beloved. He is safe with them. In the morning Jesus will go on to Jerusalem, where the crowds will cheer him. Passover is now just six days off. But now he is here. During supper, while her sister and brother fulfill their given roles—Martha serving and Lazarus at table with Jesus and his companions—Mary takes precious nard and anoints the feet of Jesus, wiping them with her hair.

This anointing is, of course, an honoring. Just a chapter after Jesus' raising of her brother from his tomb, it makes particular sense in John that Mary should thus mark Jesus not just as honored guest but as the Anointed One, the Christ. She might simply have been moved to this extravagance by esteem and gratitude; how conscious she is to be thought of a messianic recognition in her own action John does not tell. Even less does John tell us whether she understood the meaning Jesus then gives to her action, that the anointing was an anticipation of his burial, a beautiful act of love in the face of death. The intimate identity of exaltation and crucifixion that is so strong in John here shows forth once more. The Christ is anointed for death, his glory is assumption of mortality.

THERE IS ALSO SOMETHING IN THIS ARDOR OF PAUL'S THAT TOUCHES ON THE OTHER QUALITY IN THIS DAY, THE LOVE THAT WISHES TO LINGER WITH JESUS WHEN HE IS HERE, TO BE INTENSELY PRESENT WITH HIM AS HE TARRIES A WHILE AT OUR MEAL.

In Mark and Matthew there is a chorus exclaiming the waste represented by this anointing. The ointment was expensive and could have been sold and given to the poor. In John, this argument is put forward by Judas, who is depicted as insincere and himself a greedy embezzler. The response of Jesus in each of these versions includes the same elements: a defense of the woman as having done something beautiful for him, a note that the poor will remain with them but that he will not, and the characterization of her anointing as a preparation for burial. After Jesus' words, the narrative moves on to the larger course of events, moving inexorably toward his arrest and death.

This is a sensuous scene. John tells that the ointment's fragrance filled the room. Jesus may be pictured as seated, though more likely he was lying by a low table. The woman is touching him, rubbing the ointment on his feet, using her own hair to take back the excess. This motif, a woman at the feet of Jesus, a woman anointing him or washing him and making so physical a display of devotion, recurs differently in all four Gospels. In Matthew and Mark, it is striking—especially given Jesus' words about her—that this anonymous woman at Bethany remains nameless. Luke locates the story earlier in his narrative and tells it, rather typically, as Jesus' compassionate acceptance of an anonymous outcast and sinner. In John's telling, however, she is a friend and she has a name.

We may rightly wonder about the sexual and political dynamics in this icon of love, about the ways in which these stories, along with that of Mary Magdalene in the garden, have been culturally used and misused. Even before and beyond that consciousness, however, some readers and listeners may have felt an embarrassment here, as if witnessing something more personal than is seemly for us. Perhaps we would rather not have these women and their emotionality making such a scene. Or perhaps it is the indulgence that troubles us in this, the sense that this is not really what the gospel is about, this kind of individual and personal relationship to Jesus. There are bigger issues, a whole hurting world to be healed and redeemed. Jesus must be about the larger work of community and justice, and little me and little you shouldn't be trying to claim him with our infatuated and greedy attentions.

Even though John wants us to know that wicked old Judas spoke without sincerity, our minds may still endorse his objection. Would it not have been better to have turned this luxury into something useful? Surely the real needs of the poor are what matter more to God and any true Messiah. Mary and all of us need to get with the program. But surprisingly, even shockingly, Jesus says, "You always have the poor with you, but you do not always have me." It hardly seems a moral answer.

Mary Gordon's 1978 novel Final Payments includes the peculiar feature that a passage of scripture is actually described as functioning the way we hope and claim that such words do. At a critical point in the novel, the memory of this passage is triggered for the protagonist. Suddenly she understands it differently than she had before, however, and the meaning that it takes on illumines the sad waste she has been making of her life. The story awakens her to herself. Jesus' words about the permanence of the poor and his own transience had "seemed to justify to me the excesses of centuries of fat, tyrannical bankers. But now I understood. What Christ was saying, what he meant, was that the pleasures of that hair, that ointment, must be taken. Because the accidents of death would deprive us soon enough. We must not deprive ourselves, our loved ones, of the luxury of our extravagant affections. We must not try to second-guess death by refusing to love the ones we loved in favor of the anonymous poor."[1]

Gordon's reading of the Bethany story will not remove our discomfort with the moral and political issues we discern in both the scripture and in her novel. We may still be, indeed should be, uneasy. But we can also understand, I hope, Mary's devotion and Jesus' acceptance of it. When we come to church, or when we spend time in that transfigured space which is sabbath, it is not just for the sake of the mission and agenda that lies ahead of us. It is also to be there, to have some time like this in Bethany, to cherish the gift of Christ in the now, and to anoint him already while he is our guest.

JOHN 8:1-11 (RC); LUKE 20:9-19 (BCP)

The Roman Catholic and Episcopal lectionaries each take the day's anticipation in a somewhat different direction:

The Roman Catholic selection is the familiar story of the woman caught in adultery and Jesus' majestic answer to her accusers. Absent from all our earlier manuscripts, once it began appearing in the canon this old story was variously placed in Luke and John. Combining traits of both those Gospels, its pedigree may be uncertain but its authority is clear. Jesus is not so much the recipient as the giver of forbearance and compassion here. The mysterious quality of his tracings in the dust should humble the pretensions of both our knowledge and our secrecy. His wisdom proves stronger than the arrogant knowledge that presumes to judge. Turning an open-and-shut case of human judgment into an occasion for humility, he stops the flow of time and consequence. A closed future opens to something not yet determined.

The Roman Catholic reading describes a rejection of judgment but the Episcopal selection gives us dominical words of harsh warning. The story of the wicked tenants and their obsessively persistent landlord seems most obviously presented as an allegory for God's relationship with Israel. On that level, it could so easily be just a gentile political cartoon with a supersessionist punch line. Both within its narrative context and in its liturgical use, however, the text bears more helpful possibilities.

First, the supersessionist threat is itself a profoundly Jewish theme; Jesus' warning serves narratively as a prophetic appeal from within the nation rather than as a coldly external statement of heilsgeschichtlich fact. This appeal, secondly, is now heard liturgically as a word to us. Our stewardship is now what is at stake. As a parable, finally, this word of condemnation can suggest something quite different. The parable may indeed have begun as an allegory for Israel's displacement, but we can hardly hear it and not recall the similar story we are approaching in Lent. In that story there is a God also so desperate for acknowledgment and relationship that he sends his beloved one on what appears a suicide mission. What we Christians describe in our narratives of atonement is the suggestion that the son's fatal mission, and the besotted passion behind it, can or will work for us murderous tenants after all. Imagining such a surprise ending—the blood of guilt become our expiation—wrenches our vision to a newness like that of which Isaiah wrote.

Notes

1. Mary Gordon, *Final Payments* (New York: Random House, 1978), 289.

HOLY WEEK

SAMUEL E. BALENTINE

HOLY WEEK IS A JOURNEY. It is *Jesus' journey* through the last week of his life on earth. The journey begins in Jerusalem, when Jesus took his place at the table and invited his disciples to share communion with him. The journey continues as Mary anoints Jesus' feet in preparation for his burial, and Jesus in turn prepares his disciples to understand what the events of this week require of him and of them. The journey includes the ominous announcement that one of the disciples will betray Jesus. Jesus washes the disciples' feet in preparation for the journey. They profess to love him to the end and to keep faith with his journey, wherever it leads. The journey winds its way to Gethsemane, to the courtyard of the high priest, to Golgotha, to a cross, and finally to a tomb without a body. From Jerusalem to the tomb, Jesus follows the journey God has prepared for him. Disciples and friends follow and falter. They love and believe, fear and betray. At the end of the journey, before the empty tomb, the last word spoken about Jesus is, "He is not here, but has risen" (Luke 24:5). The last word spoken about the disciple named Peter is that "he went home, amazed at what had happened" (Luke 24:12).

Holy Week is also the *journey of the God of Jesus*. The collection of Old Testament readings follows God's journey from the creation of a world full of divine hopes and expectations that are "very good" to God's judgment of a world that has yielded to the subversion of human sin. It is a journey of God's mercy in the face of that sin, a journey in which God recreates what human sin destroys, makes a covenant with a people who cannot be obedient, and responds to plaintive cries for help when covenant promises seem lost and impossible. It is a journey that leads God into exile, there to vouchsafe new revelations through prophets who announce that the "everlasting covenant" (Isa. 55:3) will not fail. Ezekiel prophesies that dry bones will live. Isaiah announces that a Suffering Servant bears our sin and makes us whole. From creation to exile and beyond, the God of Jesus journeys with a fragile people, whose hope can be sustained by nothing other than God's relentless commitment to love, forgive, renew, and restore the world that is and will be "very good."

As a witness to this commitment God commissions a servant to "sustain the weary with a word" (Isa. 50:4). As a witness to this commitment God summons a prophet to proclaim that a weary people will be gathered, restored, and empowered with praise that reverberates "among all the peoples of the earth" (Zeph. 3:14-20). As a witness to this commitment God journeys with Jesus to a cross, descends with him into a grave, and rolls away a stone. From first to last the God of Jesus is the one who will not relinquish one single, inviolable commitment: "You shall be my people, and I will be your God" (Ezek. 36:28).

Holy Week is also *our journey*. We are invited to go with Jesus to Jerusalem. We take our seat at the table where bread is broken and a cup is poured. We see Jesus wash our feet. We listen as he explains the journey we are to follow. We profess our love for him. We hear him speak of betrayal. We wonder and worry and hope that he is not addressing us. We go to Gethsemane, we see him arrested, tried, convicted, crucified.

When Jesus steps into the world of his forebears' lament—"My God, my God, why have you forsaken me?"—he takes us with him. We remember this God who created the world, called a people, made a covenant, delivered a people from exile, promised to be present, to forgive, to be merciful. We remember that God, those promises, and we look at this Son, dead, buried, sealed in a tomb. From outside the tomb the journey of Holy Week seems a dead end. How can this be a "very good" world? How can this be the last truth about an "everlasting covenant"? What has become of the promise that God would always be our God, that we would always be God's people?

Our journey into Holy Week leaves us with all these questions about God and Jesus. At the end of the journey there is darkness, and there is the first faint trace of an early dawn. There is silence, and there is a strange voice summoning us to remember all that we have seen and heard. There is a tomb, there are mourners, and there is a report that he has risen. On the eve of Easter, while we are still vexed by unequal measures of faith and doubt, Holy Week leaves us to consider where the journey goes from here.

Holy Week's journey brings us face-to-face with the gospel of resurrection. It leaves us before an empty tomb, a promise that he has risen, and an invitation to believe that if "we have been united with him in a death like his, we will certainly be united with him in a resurrection like his" (Rom. 6:5).

SUNDAY OF THE PASSION PALM SUNDAY

APRIL 8, 2001

REVISED COMMON	EPISCOPAL (BCP)	ROMAN CATHOLIC
Isa. 50:4-9a	Isa. 45:21-25 or Isa. 52:13—53:12	Isa. 50:4-7
Ps. 31:9-16	Ps. 22:1-21 or 22:1-11	Ps. 22:8-9, 17-20, 23-24
Phil. 2:5-11	Phil. 2:5-11	Phil. 2:6-11
Luke 22:14—23:56 or Luke 23:1-49	Luke (22:39-71) 23:1-49 (50-56)	Luke 22:14—23:56 or Luke 23:1-49

WHAT LINKS THESE READINGS IS THE THEME of learning how to be God's disciple. Whether the teacher is the anonymous servant in Isaiah or the servant named Jesus in Philippians, we are summoned to listen "as those who are taught" (Isa. 50:4). If we learn our lessons well, we will know that the road to discipleship leads necessarily through risky obedience, suffering and abuse, promised vindication, and ultimately to exaltation. Whether we tune our hearts to the psalmist or to Luke we will learn that when our times are in God's hands (Ps. 31:15), then even our failures are part of the journey toward living into the new covenant that Holy Week remembers and celebrates.

FIRST READING

ISAIAH 50:4-9a (RCL); 45:21-25 or 52:13—53:12 (BCP); 50:4-7 (RC)

Interpreting the Text

This is the third of four "Servant Songs" in Deutero-Isaiah (42:1-4; 49:1-6; 50:4-9; and 52:13—53:12). Lectionary readings for Holy Week typically include all four of these passages, which is the case for this year as well. Both the RCL and the Roman Catholic lectionary, however, alter the sequence in Isaiah by selecting 50:4-9 as the first reading. The modified sequence invites us to encounter the one who is identified as "servant" in all the other passages (42:1; 49:3; 52:13) as one who must first learn to be a "disciple" (cf. NJPSV, REB). The Hebrew word in v. 4, *limmûd*, refers to one who is taught, like a student in school, and *then*, having learned the lessons well, is prepared to become the teacher of others (see the marginal note in NRSV). Our first clue, then, about what it means to enter into the journey of Holy Week is that we must listen and learn before we can serve.

The teacher of the one who would be a servant is "the Lord God," an emphasis made clear by the fourfold repetition of this phrase in these verses (vv. 4, 5, 7, 9). By taking our cue from this phrase, we may discern four lessons that the "Lord God" offers for the disciple's instruction. First, it is "the Lord God" who "opens" the disciple's ears and empowers the disciple to articulate the lessons that God imparts (vv. 4-5). The disciple neither initiates the instruction nor controls the empowerment. God gives what is needed, not grudgingly but "morning by morning" as each new day presents new possibilities and challenges.

Second, the objective of the instruction is to teach the disciple how "to sustain the weary with a word" (v. 4a). We may suspect that disciples must learn some literal words of consolation to speak, but the text of v. 5 curiously shifts the emphasis from what may be *spoken* to what must be *experienced.* The ability to encourage and to console comes not so much from learning what to say as from knowing firsthand what it means to be numbered among those targeted for abuse and shame. To speak to those who are smitten, one must be willing to learn what it means to be struck. To minister to those who are victims, one must be vulnerable to the indignity of being treated as an object of contempt.

Third, the disciple must trust that the same "Lord God" who commissions such a hard task will also "help" bring it to successful completion (v. 7). The disciple may be confident that vindication is "near." He may even challenge all adversaries to a confrontation in court, assured that the one who pleads his case is also the judge who will hand down a final verdict of "innocent" (v. 8). The disciple must also learn, however, that in the interim between "now" and "then" he must "set his face like flint" (v. 7) in order to withstand the hostility and abuse that is certain to test every hope of vindication and every promise of help.

The final use of the phrase "the Lord God" (v. 9) amplifies this last lesson. Because God's "help" is certain, the disciple may be confident that no one who condemns him as guilty will be proved right. Here, however, as in the preceding verse, the disciple's confidence in God's ultimate help is framed as a question rather than a simple assertion: "Who will contend with me?" The question anticipates contenders, even though they will not be successful. "Who are my adversaries?" The question recognizes that there will be opponents, even though they will be overmatched in the contest. "Who will declare me guilty?" The question does not fear the challenge, but it anticipates that guilt will be assigned. The lesson to be learned is how to yield to the shame of being labeled guilty in the public's eye without being "disgraced" and "put to shame" (v. 7). Isaiah 45:21-25, the

Episcopal lection (on the alternate reading Isa. 52:13—53:12, see Good Friday), provides a different perspective on this last point. Those whose fidelity to God makes them vulnerable to challenge and defeat by the powers of the world may take comfort in the truth that the God they serve is the sovereign Lord of history. The God of "righteousness and strength" (v. 24) has already won the victory that secures the redemption of the faithful. In the strength of this promise, "all the ends of the earth" (v. 22) are invited to participate in God's redemptive purpose. All who fear they are not equal to the task may know that "in the Lord, all the offspring of Israel shall triumph and glory" (v. 25).

Responding to the Text

In his commentary on Deutero-Isaiah, C. R. North has provocatively entitled this passage "The Gethsemane of the Servant."[1] The allusion to Gethsemane anticipates the linkage the readings for this day will make between the anonymous disciple's preparation for servanthood in Isaiah and Jesus' preparation on the Mount of Olives for the suffering and death he knew was imminent (Luke 22:39-53). We do not have to believe that the author of Isaiah's text intended this linkage. It is enough to recognize that Holy Week invites us to consider that everyone who would be God's disciple, including Jesus, must learn the lessons of Gethsemane.

Gethsemane is the place where God prepares disciples for ministry to the weary. In Isaiah's world it was the exile that represented the Gethsemane of Israel's journey with God. Exile was for Israel a time of great loss. Lost was the temple, the central symbol of the presence of God on earth. Lost was the security of the homeland that sustained a people's peace and prosperity. Lost was the freedom to shape one's own destiny in accordance with God's directives. Most importantly, exile represented the loss of all the conventional assurances about who God is and who God's people are called to be. In the vacuum of exile, other powers and circumstances threatened to squeeze the life out of faith in God. In the place of Jerusalem's glory and promise, there was Babylon's coercive political sovereignty over a conquered people. In the place of freedom, there was the shame and abuse of slavery that threatened to cancel the future once and for all. In the place of God, there was a heavy, inexplicable absence that exhausted faith and fueled despair. In such a world as this, the words "the Lord God" summon people of faith to believe Gethsemane is not their final destination.

Gethsemane is not just a place on a map. It is every place where the weary hunger for a word that will sustain them when they are the target for abuse and shame. If they are to "set their face like flint" for the journey that lies ahead, there must be someone, some disciple, who can teach them the hard lesson about what it means to listen "morning by morning" for a new word from the one who remains "the Lord God" of every situation. It is in risky obedience to such powerfully promised vindication that disciples learn how to be servants.

Responsive Reading
PSALM 31:9-16 (RCL)

For Psalm 22 (BCP and RC), see Good Friday.

From a similar vantage point as Deutero-Isaiah, the psalmist gives voice to what is required of those who enter into the tensive world shaped by trouble and trust. The trouble is real and undeniable, and in today's reading it stands at the center of what compels the psalmist to cry out to God (vv. 9b-13). First (vv. 9-10), the psalmist articulates the personal distress of a life wasted by "grief," "sorrow," and strength-sapping "misery." Then (vv. 11-13) the psalmist enlarges upon this picture by describing the "scorn" heaped upon him by others, here variously described as "adversaries," "neighbors," "acquaintances," "those who see me in the street," and those who "scheme together" and "plot to take my life." For all these reasons the psalmist feels like one who is more dead than alive. By any normal assessment these are the words of someone who has been labeled by the world as completely useless. Like a broken piece of pottery (v. 12; cf. Jer. 22:28), this person feels unwanted and utterly expendable.

Trouble, however, does not have the final say in life, for the psalmist frames the lament with an expression of trust (vv. 9a, 14-16) in a different reality that no trouble can thwart. The petitions for mercy (v. 9; cf. NIV: "Be merciful"), deliverance (v. 15), and love that will not let go (v. 16: *ḥesed*; the same word occurs in vv. 7, 21) rest securely in the God who can be trusted to act like God. When one can say with the psalmist, "My times are in your hand" (v. 15), then hope is redeemable in both the present and the future.

> "Hope" is the thing with feathers—
> That perches in the soul—
> And sings the tune without the words—
> And never stops—at all—
>
> (Emily Dickinson, #254)

Second Reading

PHILIPPIANS 2:5-11 (RCL and BCP); 2:6-11 (RC)

Interpreting the Text

This early Christian hymn evokes the same somber notes of suffering, obedience, and promise that we hear in Deutero-Isaiah and Psalm 31. In this case, however, Paul urges the Philippian church to celebrate, indeed to *sing* the doxology of Christ's discipleship and lordship. Christ Jesus exemplifies discipleship by submitting his life to God (vv. 6-8). He chooses not to cling to his equality with God but instead enters fully into the human predicament. He knows what it means to be a slave, to be humbled by suffering and shame, to be obedient to God's will, even to the point of death. Here, as in the passage from Isaiah 50:4-9, the community of faith is encouraged to remember that those who would be disciples must first know what it means to live fully in the world of brokenness and loss, where life may be cut tragically short by powers that seem too overwhelming to resist.

The second half of the hymn (vv. 9-11) shifts from the decision Christ makes to be a disciple to God's exaltation of Christ. God bestows upon Jesus the name "Lord," thereby affirming that the confession of his lordship brings glory and honor to the "Father" in whom he placed his trust. In the exaltation of Christ, the Philippians may know that there is no place in the universe, no power in heaven or on earth, no suffering, servitude, or humiliation, that is beyond God's redemption.

The key to this doxology lies not in the complex scholarly debate concerning its origins, authenticity, or hymnic form—as important as these matters are. Nor does it lie primarily in any christological debate about Jesus' place in the Trinity. Instead, the key is in the introduction to the hymn: "Let the same mind be in you that was in Christ Jesus" (v. 5). The implication is clear. If the church at Philippi is to act in accord with the discipleship of Christ, it must conform itself, for the sake of the world, to his model of relationship with God.

Human beings can only approximate what Christ exemplified. Perhaps this explains in part why this great hymn about Christ occurs in the middle of two other very practically focused admonitions for the human community: "Do nothing from selfish ambition or conceit, but in humility regard others as better than yourself" (v. 3); "work out your own salvation in fear and trembling" (v. 12). In sum, the church is to actualize Christ's model of discipleship in very concrete ways. It is to build community and enhance life that gives glory to God. When this mission is undertaken with humility and resolve, the community of faith may know with assurance that the same God who was at work in exalting Christ is also at work in them, enabling them "both to will and to work for his good pleasure" (v. 13).

Responding to the Text

We may think of this doxology as a hymn with two verses and a repeating refrain. The first verse (vv. 6-8), the place where the singing begins, celebrates the requirements of discipleship that Christ modeled: "emptied," "humbled," "obedient," "death." The second verse (vv. 9-11), the place where the singing ends, celebrates the promise of following Christ's example: "exalted," "name that is above every name," "every knee should bend," "the glory of God the Father." We may be tempted to sing only part of this great hymn—to lend our voices enthusiastically to the promise of exaltation but to skip the summons to be emptied of the identity we have constructed for ourselves. We may eagerly affirm that in Christ we are at the top of the list of those whom God and the world will profess as exemplary models of disciples. But we may be inclined to forget or ignore that this list will be composed only of persons who have learned humility and obedience. We may welcome the opportunity to give glory to God by the words we sing but flinch when we realize that our song commits us to a life that requires obedience, even "to the point of death."

Given the temptation to want to share in Christ's exaltation without following his model for discipleship, the refrain of this hymn (v. 5) becomes all the more important for us: "Let the same mind be in you that was in Christ Jesus." It is this refrain that makes the song complete. Without it, we may be making noise, but we will not be singing (or living) the notes that are "worthy of the gospel of Christ" (1:27). To take Christ's example of discipleship seriously means that our song must celebrate both his woe and his joy. We must sing ourselves into trusting that to be in "in Christ Jesus," in both his suffering and his exaltation, is the key to giving glory to God on earth and in heaven.

The Gospel

LUKE 22:14—23:56 or 23:1-49 (RCL); (22:39-71) 23:1-49 (50-56) (BCP); 22:14—23:56 or 23:1-49 (RC)

Interpreting the Text

The two lengthy readings from Luke offer numerous themes for reflection and preaching. Both texts include the accounts of Jesus' trial before Pilate (23:1-25) and his subsequent crucifixion, death, and burial (23:26-56). The longer of the two passages adds to these accounts the report of Jesus' last supper with the disciples (22:14-38), the scene at the Mount of Olives (22:39-53), and an introduction to Peter's denial of Jesus in the courtyard (22:54-56). The full sweep of Jesus' journey with his disciples from the "hour" of Passover (22:14) to the noon when "darkness came over the whole land" (23:44) informs the whole of the church's liturgy for Holy Week. So important is this story for what we do this week that various parts of it will be repeated—especially the details of Jesus' arrest, trial, and crucifixion—in subsequent lectionary readings from the Gospel of John.

On this first Sunday of the journey, however, it is helpful to focus our thoughts on Luke's account of Jesus' conversation with the disciples at their last meal together (22:14-38). By attending to this passage, which Luke seems to regard as singularly important for understanding all that will follow, we keep ourselves mindful of one of the emphases of the first reading for this day: we listen to the one who comes among us to "serve" (22:27) "as those who are taught" (Isa. 50:4).

According to Luke's account, *after* Jesus took the cup and the bread, *after* he blessed and gave thanks for the new covenant that he was announcing, *after* he pledged to give his body and blood for his disciples, *after* he commanded them to eat and drink in remembrance of what he had taught them (vv. 14-21), a dispute arose among them over who was to be the greatest in the kingdom of God (vv. 24-30). Jesus had announced that one of them would betray him, and they had fallen into disbelieving discussion among themselves about who this might be (vv. 22-23). That discussion seems to have slid almost simultaneously into a debate concerning their presumed status and greatness. They could no more fathom the possibility of betraying Jesus than they could the possibility that they had miscalculated their own place in the kingdom.

To take Christ's example of discipleship seriously means that our song must celebrate both his woe and his joy. We must sing ourselves into trusting that to be "in Christ Jesus," in both his suffering and his exultation, is the key to giving glory to God on earth and in heaven.

Jesus responded by instructing them that they still had much to learn on both accounts. Their relationship to one another and their identity in the kingdom needed to conform to the new reality he had come to show them. If they were to eat at his table and share in his kingdom (vv. 28-30), they must not think of themselves as kings who exercise authority over their subjects but as servants whose singular commitment is to enrich and enhance the lives of those in their community. In God's kingdom the conventional standards of power and authority are turned upside down. Those who are the greatest should think of themselves as the youngest; those who would be leaders must first learn what it means to become followers of the teacher who sat among them as "one who serves"

(vv. 25-27). As they dispute among themselves about who could possibly betray him, the disciples already tilt toward the betrayal they cannot imagine by forgetting the true meaning of the bread and the cup they have just shared with Jesus.

Simon Peter was among the disciples sitting at table with Jesus. Presumably he had shared in the discussion about who could possibly betray the teacher. Now Jesus singles him out by name to tell him that Satan has demanded God's permission to test whether he will be the one to betray his Lord (vv. 31-34). Like flour sifted for impurities, Peter will be shaken by the events that are coming, and the true quality of his fidelity will be exposed. Jesus has prayed that Peter's faith will not fail him, but then, as if looking past the failure that he knows is inevitable, Jesus assures him that once he has "turned back," Peter will "strengthen" others as Jesus has strengthened him. The hint that he may turn away and need to turn back prompts Peter to declare his readiness to follow Jesus, even if the journey leads to prison and death (cf. Acts 4:3; 5:18; 12:3-5). Peter, like the other disciples, overestimates his ability to live out the promises of his commitment. Jesus does not ignore Peter's frailties. He knows that before the sun dawns again Peter will deny three times even knowing him. But Jesus has already seen beyond the failure to the faith that survives failure and draws upon its honed resources to strengthen others who will be no less frail and no less empowered by his investment in them. This too is part of the lesson Peter must learn before he can "do this," in word and deed, "in remembrance" of the one who has come to teach his followers the true meaning of discipleship.

Jesus' final instruction to the disciples before they embark together on the crucial journey to the Mount of Olives (vv. 35-38) is the most difficult of all for them to understand. He reminds them that he has provided for their every need. He had sent them on their mission carrying no purse, no bag, no sandals (9:3; cf.10:4). "But now" the situation is about to change radically. When Jesus is no longer with them, they must learn to provide for themselves by drawing upon their own resources, including the sword (v. 36). By including the sword as a necessary provision, along with the purse and the bag, Jesus warns them that the persecution that lies ahead will be severe. Jesus is not instructing them to take up arms against their opponents. He wants them to remember that he has come to fulfill scripture as a *suffering servant*, not as an armed warrior. Citing Isaiah 53:12, he teaches them that the true servant of whom Isaiah spoke is the one who "poured out himself to death, and *was numbered among the transgressors*" (v. 37).

Once again the disciples indicate that they have not really understood what Jesus is saying. They report that they already have two swords, which to their way of thinking confirms their readiness for the journey. Jesus dismisses their response with the words "It is enough" (v. 38). Perhaps he does so with a sigh of anticipation concerning what is to come: when one of the disciples takes up his sword against his enemies, Jesus will rebuke him and his model of servanthood by saying "No more of this!" (22:50-51).

Responding to the Text

The failure of faith takes many forms. It may come when we are sharing the most intimate fellowship with Christ and with one another that we can imagine, when thoughts of betrayal are so unthinkable as to seem impossible. On such occasions we may be tempted to assume that engaging in the rituals of faith is the same thing as actualizing the discipleship these rituals require. Upon hearing the challenge to "*do* this" in body and blood in remembrance of the one who gives his life for the sake of the kingdom, we may be inclined to believe that the summons requires little more than partaking of the symbols of the cup and the bread. Christ warns all those who are content with mere symbols that the ones who share his table may be the first to betray him when the *ceremony of faith* ends and the time for the *sacrament of obedience* begins.

The failure of faith may come when we are tempted to believe that the status we seek for ourselves is identical with what Christ intends for us. When we seek our advantage at the expense of others, when we pride ourselves in benevolences that patronize the needy but do nothing to change the world that denies them justice and freedom, when we assume that our rightful place in the kingdom is among the strongest, not the weakest, then we should not be surprised to have our aspirations turned upside down. Holy Week is the time for remembering that we are summoned to the high calling of being the servants of others, not their masters. When we choose the latter instead of the former, we betray the one who has come to teach us that the kingdom of God requires fidelity to a new vision of community and a new understanding of greatness.

Faith may fail when we are exposed to trials that make it more convenient to deny our commitments than to exemplify them. We may declare our resolve in the presence of God and others. But when the powers that confront us seem greater than the principles we profess, we may find that we have overestimated our capacity to stand firm against all odds. Many are the times when silence, if not denial, seem the better course of wisdom. It is for such times as these that we sit at table with Christ, there to ponder again and again the assurance that comforts us even as it puts us on notice about what lies ahead: "I have prayed for you that your own faith may not fail."

Faith may fail when we discover that we must take responsibility for ourselves rather than rely on God to do everything for us. It is easier to be given exactly what we need for every situation without having to share in the work of finding it for ourselves. It is less exacting to have a clear blueprint for everything we do than to wrestle with different options that make us vulnerable to wrong choices and flawed decisions. It requires far less courage to believe that we are called to be warriors than to choose the way of suffering and self-sacrifice. Sometimes, even when we know that being "numbered among the transgressors" is the true measure of servanthood, it is exceedingly difficult to believe that this is enough for the dangers we face.

The disciples bring all these capacities for betrayal, and more, with them into the fellowship they share with Jesus. Jesus knows them and their frailties well; indeed, he has called each and every one of them by name and invited them to follow him. They have committed to do so, but from this point on that commitment will require more of them than they can possibly imagine. Peter is the most confident and determined of them all, and so we pay particular attention when Jesus charts the future of this one who will deny him three times before the night is over. Because we are so much like Peter, we may also take note that his failures do not disqualify him from being the disciple Jesus has called him to be. Jesus has prayed that Peter's faith will not fail. Curiously, what Jesus predicts is not Peter's failure of faith, for that seems to be inevitable. He predicts instead that Peter's faith will survive failure, that he will turn back after he has fallen away. He will learn to strengthen others who are similarly weak and unable.

As we head down the path to Gethsemane and the cross and the betrayals that we all must own along the way, we prove ourselves faithful not by never failing, but by turning back to God when we do. That is the true answer to Jesus' prayer for those who will be his "model" disciples.

MONDAY IN HOLY WEEK

APRIL 9, 2001

REVISED COMMON	EPISCOPAL (BCP)	ROMAN CATHOLIC
Isa. 42:1-9	Isa. 42:1-9	Isa. 42:1-7
Ps. 36:5-11	Ps. 36:5-10	Ps. 27:1-3,13-14
Heb. 9:11-15	Heb. 11:39—12:3	
John 12:1-11	John 12:1-11 or Mark 14:3-9	John 12:1-11

GOD IS ALWAYS DOING "NEW THINGS." This is the affirmation of both Isaiah (42:9) and of Hebrews (9:11). These new outpourings of God's presence often come in unexpected ways. They may be manifest in a servant who works for justice in ways that challenge conventional understandings of power. They may come in a woman named Mary (John 12) who demonstrates love and devotion in ways that subvert conventional models for discipleship. However God chooses to be present, the psalmist reminds us that God's love for us is both precious and extravagant. It is such love that Christ embodies in the promise of a new covenant, which summons us to a similar extravagant devotion.

FIRST READING

ISAIAH 42:1-9 (RCL/BCP); 42:1-7 (RC)

Interpreting the Text

Today's text consists of two parts, which were probably originally independent units before they were joined in the present context. In the first (vv. 1-4) God calls the servant to be an agent for justice, a theme repeated three times (vv. 1, 3, 4). The second (vv. 5-9) focuses on the characteristics of the God who calls and commissions the servant to be a "covenant to the people, a light to the nations" (v. 6). When these two units are read together, they effectively interpret each other: the summons to "bring forth justice" can only be fulfilled when the whole world is liberated and redeemed.

In vv. 1-4 the Lord presents the servant for public recognition: "Here is my servant" (v. 1). Such a designation recalls the way God appointed Israel's leaders, especially those who rule as kings (e.g., Saul in 1 Sam. 9:15-17 and David in 1 Sam. 16:6-13). But whereas kings are typically empowered to issue edicts and command compliance with political and military force, the servant is equipped with nothing more powerful than the spirit of God. The servant has no special qualities or qualifications for the appointment, and none are needed. God has chosen this one because to do so gives God pleasure. This is all that is necessary for the journey toward discipleship to begin.

After God calls and empowers the servant, God identifies the mission that lies ahead. The servant's task, specified no less than three times (vv. 1, 3, 4), is to be an agent of God's "justice" (*mišpṭ*). Paul Hanson succinctly comments on what justice means: "*Mišpṭ* is the order of compassionate justice that God has created and upon which the wholeness of the universe depends."[2] When Israel was in Babylonian exile the moral order of the world seemed to be turned upside down. This horrifying experience was all the more difficult because of Israel's abiding despair that God either could not or would not intervene to help. Thus Israel complained "My right (*mišpṭî*) is disregarded by my God" (Isa. 40:27). That same God, who from Israel's perspective has too long been absent and silent, now declares that the cry for help has been heard. A servant has been summoned to embody and actualize God's answer.

With a string of seven negatives (vv. 2-4) God declares that the way the servant will carry out this task stands in sharp contrast to conventional expectations. The servant will not cry out when abused. He will not make a public declaration of his power. He will not break those who are already broken nor extinguish those whose light is already flickering dimly. Instead, with the broken he will be broken, but he will not succumb to defeat. With those whose faith is nearly extinguished he will yield his light to the forces that swirl around them, but his faith in God and in God's justice will not falter before the mission is accomplished.

The second part (vv. 5-9) is also a direct address from God. It is not clear whether the subject of God's address is the servant of vv. 1-4 or collective "Israel" (Isa. 49:6). It is likely that the identity of the servant is intentionally ambiguous and that the summons to be an agent of God's justice includes not only specifically designated individuals but also communities and even nations who will yield themselves to God's call. In this unit that call is strategically prefaced by a hymnic affirmation of God as the Creator and sustainer of the universe (v. 5). The One who creates heaven and earth and gives the breath of life to everything in creation is the One who "calls," "takes by the hand," and gives the commission to become "a covenant to the people" and "a light to the nations" (v. 6).

These last two phrases have occasioned enormous scholarly discussion, not least because they seem to envision a servanthood that so outdistances anything that God's people have done in the past or may do in the future as to be both unimaginable and impossible. And yet, such a vision is consistent with what we read elsewhere in the Servant Songs. The summons to the servant is a summons to bring forth justice "*to the nations*" (42:2) and to establish it "*in the earth*" (42:4). The commission to become "a light to the nations" is repeated in Isa. 49:6, where it is amplified by the statement "that my salvation may reach to the *ends of the earth.*" Indeed, the Isaianic corpus envisions the work of God's servants as nothing less than becoming part of a divine promise of salvation that ultimately creates "new heavens and a new earth" (Isa. 65:16). In the continuum of this ever-expanding and seemingly unobtainable promise, God declares in 42:9 that even now, before the vision becomes reality, the "new things" that will come to pass are already being spoken into existence.

In the interim, between the injustice that exists and the justice that must be, God's servants have specific tasks. They are to attend to personal suffering by opening the eyes that are blind to what God is up to. They are to attend to the social and political structures that enslave people by setting the prisoners free (vv. 7-8).

Responding to the Text

The mission of all who would be God's servants is to be agents for justice. God teaches, promises, calls, and empowers persons, communities, even nations for the task. Justice is to be declared and embodied. It is to be envisioned as the hope for the future, and it is to be actualized in the present through concrete deeds of compassion and righteousness. Justice is to triumph not because its servants have the raw power to defeat the forces of evil but because they are empowered by the spirit of God, who will not allow the mission to fail.

Justice is such a noble idea. It is so compelling and seductive, so urgent and necessary. *And* it is so elusive and seemingly impossible that we are tempted to concede it is nothing more than religious fiction. Those who know the heavy truth about life in exile, where injustice makes brokenness and despair the norm not the exception, cannot be faulted for responding to the servant's mission by saying "Uh-huh. In your dreams sucker."[3] Michael Dorris articulates the skepticism that many of us will bring to our Holy Week journey:

> Religion is not the opiate of the people, the conception of justice is. It's our last bastion of rationality, our logical lighthouse on a stormy sea, our anchor. We extend its parameters beyond death—if we haven't found equity in this life, all the great belief systems assure us, just wait till the next. Or the next. Someday our prince will come.
>
> That may be true, but the paradigm is based on faith, not fact. We can believe in the tooth fairy until the alarm goes off, but unless there's a benevolent parent to value our loss as worth a quarter, we wake up with used calcium, not negotiable currency, under our pillow.[4]

If the hope for justice is to be more than a myth, there must be Someone who values our yearning as worth the investment of our lives. The word from Isaiah invites us to believe that there is. "Thus says . . . the LORD, who created the heavens and . . . the earth . . . , Here is my servant, whom I uphold. . . . He will bring forth justice."

Dorris is surely right about one thing. The promise requires our faith. This is the currency with which we negotiate the purchase of the new things God is already bringing into existence, even before our journey is complete.

RESPONSIVE READING

PSALM 36:5-11 (RCL); 36:5-10 (BCP); 27:1-3, 13-14 (RC)

Psalm 36 focuses on God's unending love (*ḥesed*: vv. 5, 7, 10), which is the basis for both genuine praise (vv. 5-9) and confident petition (vv. 10-11). God's love is built into the very structure of the universe and extends as far as the "heavens" above and the "great deep" below the earth. It is manifest by God's faithfulness, righteousness, and justice—the very attributes that God marshals for the salvation of "humans and animals alike" (vv. 5-6). "All people" may confidently take refuge in their absolute dependence on God's love, for there they receive shelter, food, drink, and light sufficient for their journey (vv. 7-9). In sum, God liberally provides for every need, hence the response of praise that is both exuberant—"How precious is your steadfast love, O Lord!" (v. 7)—and resilient, even in the midst of trouble and opposition (see vv. 1-4). The same theme is present in the reading from Psalm 27: "The Lord is my light and my salvation; whom shall I fear? The Lord is the stronghold of my life; of whom shall I be afraid?" (v. 1).

God's love is not only a summons to praise. It is also the reason one may confidently appeal to God for help in the midst of trouble (vv. 10-11). The appeal is not for God to *begin* to be compassionate. It is instead for God to "*continue*" the gracious provisions for life, especially when the power of the wicked overwhelms our capacity to believe in the love that will not let us go.

On Monday of Holy Week, when the journey from darkness to light is just beginning, the psalmists remind us that a love greater than our faith or our doubt summons us onward. This love is incarnate in Christ, whose resurrection testifies to the truth about God's *ḥesed*. For the light that shines in the darkness and will not, cannot, be extinguished (cf. John 1:5), we praise and pray and wait with confident expectation. Both our words and our actions bear public witness to the journey of faith on which we have embarked. With the concluding words of Psalm 27 we may extend to others the very summons that shapes us as a community of hope and courage: "Wait for the Lord; be strong, and let your heart take courage; wait for the Lord!" (v. 14).

Second Reading

HEBREWS 9:11-15 (RCL); 11:39—12:3 (BCP)

Interpreting the Text

Hebrews 9 echoes God's announcement in Isaiah 42:9 of the "new things" already set in motion by the servant. The promise that has sustained God's hope for the world now shifts to focus on Christ, who embodies the "good things that have come" (v. 11). Christ is the exemplary high priest whose mediation of God's presence enacts and extends the ministry of Israel's priests. By juxtaposing these two models of priestly ministry, the writer invokes the witness of Israel in order to make clear that these ancient exemplars of faith have paved the way for the work Christ has come to do. In the words of the Episcopal lesson, they are part of the "great cloud of witnesses" (Heb. 12:1) that surround and support Christ's entrance into the presence of God on our behalf (on Heb. 12:1-3, see Wednesday in Holy Week).

Christ's high priestly ministry comprises three features, each of which is rooted in and flowers from the seeds of the levitical priests (vv. 12-14). First, like his predecessors Christ enters into the "Holy Place," the innermost sanctum of the tabernacle, where the high priest makes atonement for the sins of the people that defile the sanctuary and pollute the world that God has designed (for the rituals on the Day of Atonement, see Leviticus 16). Whereas Aaron entered the Holy Place once a year (Lev. 16:29-34), Christ enters "once for all." Second, Christ offers his own blood to make atonement for the sins of the world, not the blood of goats and bulls. The blood of goats and bulls, along "with the sprinkling of the ashes of the heifer" (v. 13; cf. Numbers 19), is understood to be capable of purifying the flesh. Christ's blood purifies the conscience (v. 14); it atones not only for external sins but also for the inner sense of guilt that corrupts the mind and soul long after the sin has been committed. Third, Christ's ministry secures eternal redemption. The key word is "eternal," which signifies that Christ's redemption is not limited by time and space, as were animal sacrifices. Christ works through the "eternal Spirit" (v. 14) to secure freedom that endures forever. The purpose of Christ's high priestly ministry is to enable worship of the living God.

For all these reasons, Christ is the mediator of a "new covenant" (v. 15). The covenant of which the writer speaks is not the Mosaic covenant, which God's people broke, but the "new" covenant announced by Jeremiah (Jer. 31:31-34).

By his death Christ redeems not only the human failure that subverted the first covenant but also God's abiding commitment to stay in covenant relationship with a sinful people. Hebrews 12:1-3 effectively builds on this assertion. Because of Christ's work, and because of the great "cloud of witnesses" that surround and sustain his ministry on our behalf, we may "lay aside every weight and the sin that clings so closely" in order to "run with perseverance the race that is set before us."

Responding to the Text

The witness of Hebrews 9, like that of Isaiah 42, is that God is always doing a new thing. Two metaphors, both deeply rooted in God's relationship with Israel, help us to understand what this means. The first is the metaphor of atonement, which signifies God's relentless intention to be "at one with," that is, to be "at home with" the world God has created. In Israel atonement revolves around purifying people of sin (Lev. 16:17, 24, 30, 34) and cleansing the sanctuary (Lev. 16:16, 20, 33) and—by extension—the world of sin's defilement. The purpose of atonement is to prepare a people and a world for the indwelling of a holy God. Christ's atonement is part of this same purpose. Its goal is the eternal redemption of humankind and the world, redemption that issues forth in the new and ever-renewing summon to love God absolutely and to live in such a way that this devotion is manifest in both word and deed.

The second is the metaphor of covenant, which signifies God's relentless intention to stay in partnership with humankind and the world, even when sin and disobedience threaten to break that partnership and deny its transforming power. Through Jeremiah, and again through Jesus, scripture affirms that God refuses to settle for broken covenants. Neither human sin nor failure has the power to thwart God's ultimate goal of covenant partnership. God is restlessly at work in the world, ever renewing the "promised eternal inheritance" that continues to summon and shape people for receiving the new covenant.

The problem is that we are inclined to settle for old atonements and former covenants. We are tempted to believe that God is already at home in our midst, hence that sin and defilement no longer exercise any claim on us. We tend to be possessive of the relationship we have carved out with God, hence we fail to see that God continues to invite us into new and deeper covenants than those that we have molded to conform to our failures. Old atonements and former covenants are constantly in need of review and repair, because worship of the living God is an unending summons to deepened devotion and more radical obedience. The good news is that even when we do not or cannot see what God is doing, God is always doing a new thing in the hope of moving us toward "greater" and "more perfect" (Heb. 9:11) understandings of what we may yet become.

JOHN 12:1-11 (RCL/RC); 12:1-11 or MARK 14:3-9 (BCP)

Interpreting the Text

Each of the Gospels records the story of Jesus' anointing (Matt. 26:6-11; Mark 14:3-9; Luke 7:36-50). Matthew and Mark locate the event at the home of Simon the leper in Bethany, where an unnamed woman anoints Jesus' head as preparation for his burial. Luke sets the story earlier in Jesus' ministry, in Galilee, in the home of Simon the Pharisee, where a sinful woman anoints Jesus' feet. Luke uses this anointing to show how the woman's love and respect for Jesus leads to the forgiveness of her sins. John also sets the scene in Bethany and portrays the anointing as a Passover event, which prepares Jesus for burial. In John's account, however, the anointing takes place in the home of Mary and Martha, and the immediate occasion for the act is their gratitude for the raising of Lazarus. More importantly, John understands Mary's act not only as preparation for Jesus' burial (12:7) but also as a foreshadowing of Jesus' washing of the disciples' feet at the last supper (John 13:5).

John recounts Mary's anointing with a single verse (v. 3). She does not speak a word to Jesus. She responds to what Jesus has done in raising Lazarus simply by acting out her love and gratitude. She takes a pound of costly perfume, pours it upon Jesus' feet, and wipes them with her hair. The verb "wipe" (*ekmasō*) is the same verb John will use to describe Jesus' wiping of the disciples' feet in 13:5. Mary models for the disciples, and in a provocative way also for Jesus, what it means to love God without consideration of cost or consequence. The extravagance of her deed is symbolized by the fragrance of the perfume that pervades the house. Where once before there had been the stench of death (11:39), now there is the smell of life, love, and devotion.

> HOLY WEEK IS THE TIME FOR REMEMBERING THAT DISCIPLESHIP IS ALWAYS A CALL TO THE UNCONVENTIONAL, THE UNEXPECTED, THE STARTLING COMMISSION TO BE UTTERLY EXTRAVAGANT STEWARDS OF BOTH JUSTICE AND LOVE.

The rest of the story invites us to reflect on the different responses this scene at Bethany evokes. First, there is the response of Judas (vv. 4-6). He equates Mary's extravagant love with wasteful management of limited resources. What she lavishes upon Jesus would be worth a year's wages on the open market ("three hundred dinarii"), and at least theoretically a greater good could be achieved if this were invested in caring for the poor. John undercuts the sincerity of Judas' protest by informing us that (1) Judas is about to betray Jesus, and (2) Judas is a "thief." It is interesting that Jesus does not rebuke Judas for either of the reasons John has suggested. Instead Jesus admonishes Judas for being stingy with his love (vv. 7-8). The poor will always be present (cf. Deut. 15:11), Jesus says, and they will always require generosity and justice. But Jesus will not always be present. His impending death and burial will be unrepeatable events that provide singularly important opportunities for people to express their love and devotion in the fullest measure possible. Mary has apparently been saving up her best for just this moment. When the time comes to prepare Jesus for burial, she is eager to be as extravagant as her resources will allow. Jesus says, "Leave her alone," a subtle reminder to Judas that deeds of love no less than acts of justice can never be wasteful.

A second response is registered by the "great crowd of Jews," including the "chief priests" (vv. 9-11), who have presumably been standing in the background while these events at Bethany took place. Jesus' healing of Lazarus has occurred in the middle of their fear (cf. 11:48) and plotting (cf. 11:53). The fear is that what Jesus is saying and doing will create such a fervent belief that the Roman authorities will counter with repressive measures. The plotting behind the scene results in a determination to kill both Jesus and Lazarus. By including vv. 9-11 at this point, just before Jesus' climactic entry into Jerusalem (12:12-19), John suggests that there is a concerted, last-ditch effort to eliminate Jesus and to silence all those who might bear public witness to his deeds.

This fear and plotting is formative for all those who were in Bethany six days before the Passover (12:1). Judas essentially trims his response to that of the crowd, perhaps hoping that he will not be targeted as one of those who have foolishly gotten caught up in the furor surrounding Jesus. By his pretense of caring more for the poor than for Jesus, he already tilts toward the betrayal that will confirm his alignment with the fear and plotting of the crowd. Mary essentially ignores the pressures swirling around her. By caring so much for Jesus, she demonstrates in advance the truth that a later Johannine traditionist will declare: "There is no fear in love, but perfect love casts out fear" (1 John 4:18). John indicates that "the next day" Jesus entered into Jerusalem, surrounded once more by "the great crowd" who would now have to decide what to do with him (12:12). There will be fear and plotting and death. There will be love, sometimes silent and from a distance, other times bold and public. All who would be disciples may reflect on this small transition scene from Bethany in order to get their bearings on whether they should be excessive in fear or in love.

Responding to the Text

The most pregnant line in John's account of the event at Bethany is spoken by Jesus in v. 8: "You do not always have me." As he prepares to enter into the last week of his life on earth, Jesus wants his followers to understand that his presence is not a permanent possession. We cannot respond to the gift he offers on our own time and in the way that is most convenient for us.

John gives us two models to consider, Judas and Mary. Judas is one of Jesus' handpicked disciples. He has enjoyed intimate fellowship with Jesus from the beginning of his public ministry. He has heard Jesus' teachings, and he has witnessed his miracles. He has been entrusted with responsibility for managing the "common purse" (cf. 13:29) and dispensing financial resources in a way that sustains and advances Jesus' ministry. In the last days of Jesus' life Judas remains very much a part of Jesus' inner circle. He continues to see, to be responsible, and to manage, but for all his attentiveness to the things that have been entrusted to him, he does not understand that discipleship must be more than calculated fidelity.

He knows that the poor deserve generosity, but he does not understand that helping others does not substitute for loving Christ as if there were no tomorrow. He knows that one's resources for doing good are always limited, that these resources must always be carefully managed. But he does not understand that one can never postpone the full expenditure of love until such time as it is convenient and the costs can be counted. He knows that the events swirling about Jesus have evoked public fear and loathing. He knows that every step he takes with Jesus just now is precarious. If he makes the wrong move now he may not survive to do the good he might do later. But he does not understand that a disciple's love for Jesus is not measured by public opinion, long range planning, or prudence.

Judas is a disciple of Jesus—and he is a thief. He steals from justice while being stingy with love. He steals from the future the excuse for not living fully in the present. He steals from public opinion the justification for being safe rather than sorry. Judas will go into the garden with Jesus as one of his intimates but, when the last line of the story is written, he will not be found among the disciples who have seen and understood and been commissioned to spread the gospel.

Mary was not one of Jesus' twelve disciples, but she was a friend who offered intimate hospitality when Jesus needed a place to retreat from the powers that plotted against him. She was not present when Jesus instructed his disciples to love others as he had loved them (John 13:34-35), but she did not have to be taught to demonstrate that love when the opportunity was present. She had not been entrusted with responsibility to manage available resources, but she knew how to expend the fullness of what she had when she was in the presence of the one who meant more to her than life itself. She did not know that in anointing Jesus' feet she was imaging his peculiar model for the disciples' ministry to others (John 13:14-15). She only knew that Jesus' presence in her home was a precious gift, and she wanted to respond with a preciousness that conveyed her gratitude for the moment.

We do not know if Mary entered the garden with Jesus, or if she was present at his cross or his empty tomb. If she ever said or did anything further to witness to what she had experienced with Jesus, there is no record of it in scripture. We do learn from the other Gospel writers, however, that wherever the gospel is preached, Mary will be remembered for "what she has done" (Matt. 26:13; Mark 14:9).

The models for authentic discipleship sometimes come from the least expected sources. They come from servants, empowered by nothing more than the Spirit of God, who act in unconventional ways "to establish justice in the earth" (Isa. 42:4). They come from the Marys of the world, compelled by nothing so great as their love for God, who simply act out their discipleship without speaking a word.

TUESDAY IN HOLY WEEK

April 10, 2001

Revised Common	Episcopal (BCP)	Roman Catholic
Isa. 49:1-7	Isa. 49:1-6	Isa. 49:1-6
Ps. 71:1-14	Ps. 71:1-12	Ps. 71:1-6, 15, 17
1 Cor. 1:18-31	1 Cor. 1:18-31	
John 12:20-36	John 12:37-38, 42-50 or Mark 11:15-19	John 13:21-33, 36-38

The summons to be God's servant is a summons to look despair and discouragement, failure and disappointment square in the eye. Isaiah's servant is persuaded that he has "labored in vain" (Isa. 49:4). The psalmist fears that God will forsake him when his "strength is spent" (Ps. 71:9). Paul reminds the Corinthians that foolishness and weakness are the very means by which God works in the world (1 Cor. 1:25, 28). Because the challenge is so great, the costs so high, and the resources we bring so meager, we will be tempted to believe that we are not ready to make the decision to follow where Jesus is leading. John's Gospel reminds us that "the hour has come" (12:23) to step out in faith in the assurance that God is intimately involved in our struggle to act on what we have seen and heard.

First Reading

ISAIAH 49:1-7 (RCL); 49:1-6 (BCP/RC)

Interpreting the Text

This Servant Song builds on those cited for Sunday and Monday. In Isaiah 50:4-9 the speaker is the one who learns how to be a disciple. In Isaiah 42:1-9 the speaker is God, and the servant commissioned to be "a light to the nations" listens in respectful silence as God spells out what it means, *from God's perspective*, to be called and equipped for such a task. In today's reading the servant speaks again, this time allowing the reader to gain some insight into what it means, *from the servant's perspective*, to be called (vv. 1-3), to despair of failure (v. 4), and to be reassured by God (vv. 5-6). The concluding verse (v. 7) affirms that the One who chooses such a feeble and despondent person for such a high and noble task is none other than the "Lord, who is faithful."

The servant announces that the message he has received from God concerns not only Israel but the whole world. He summons the "peoples from far away" (v. 1) to know that God's plan is eternal. God's plan neither begins nor ends with this servant. It was conceived long before he or any other servant of God was born (v. 2; cf. Jer. 1:5; Gal. 1:15), and it is restlessly at work in the world until the salvation that is its ultimate goal extends to the "end of the earth" (v. 6).

Verse 3 identifies the servant with collective Israel. This identification is problematic, for the attributes mentioned elsewhere in the song (vv. 1, 2, 4, 5) appear to refer to an individual. Further, it is somewhat awkward to think of the *servant Israel* as being given a mission *to* Israel (vv. 5-6). As was noted in the comments on Isaiah 42:1-9 (see Monday in Holy Week), it is likely that the author did not draw a sharp contrast between the individual and communal aspects of servanthood. More important than the identity of the servant is the purpose of the One who calls and commissions the servant. Whoever would be God's servant will honor and glorify God by becoming faithful stewards of God's redemptive work in the world (cf. Isa. 44:23).

From God's perspective the servant's mission is clear and realizable. *From the servant's perspective*, however, the mission is overwhelming. When he reviews the success of his efforts thus far he is tempted to believe that he has "labored in vain" and has spent himself "for nothing" (v. 4). Out of this despair he leans hard into the hope that even in failure there yet remains a "cause" and a "reward" that is secure "with God" against all odds. The Hebrew word translated "cause" is *mišpāṭ*, the same word rendered in 42:1, 3, 4 as "justice." In that context as in this one, we may understand that the cause of compassionate justice upon which the world depends and to which God is relentlessly committed cannot be thwarted, not even when those who are called to be its enablers yield to doubt and discouragement.

From the servant's perspective we might assume that God would respond to despair by reducing the commission to something that more modestly conforms to human limitations. *God's perspective*, however, is again quite different. God honors the servant not by conforming the divine plan to human weakness but by empowering human weakness for a still greater and more demanding ministry (vv. 5-6). From God's perspective, the redemption and restoration of Israel is imperative and urgent, but that alone is "too light a thing." Nothing short of servanthood that becomes "a light to the nations" and nothing short of salvation that reaches "to the end of the earth" can quench the hopes and expectations of the God who created the world, blessed it, and declared its possibilities to be "very good" (cf. Genesis 1).

Verse 7 introduces a new and originally independent announcement concerning God's chosen servant (vv. 7-13). The servant will not only despair of failure but will also be "despised" and "abhorred" by those who cannot or will not accept his ministry. And yet this servant, so weak and so contemptible in the world's eyes, will be the very one before whom kings and princes will one day bow in respect and adoration. They will do so not because of the servant's intrinsic merit or worth but because the God who has chosen him is "faithful" in watching over both the limitations and the possibilities of the work to which he has been called.

Responding to the Text

What does it mean to be called and commissioned as God's servant? At the center of this song there is a hard truth that enables us to sustain the perilous and promising journey of Holy Week. To be a servant is to look full into the face of failure and rejection. The failure is in a real sense inevitable, because the mission is so great, and we are so frail and limited. The rejection is also predictable, because the world would rather conform to status quo limitations than become vulnerable to redemption that extends God's subversive grace "to the end of the earth." The one who would be God's servant will grow weary with the failure and be humiliated by the rejection. The temptation will be to give up the commission or at least to scale it down to more reasonable objectives. Second Isaiah reminds us that it is precisely in living honestly inside this tension between giving up and scaling down that God is at work calling, equipping, reassuring, and enlarging our vision of servanthood. Like Isaiah's servant and like Jesus who embodies the truth of the servant's commission, we are most receptive to this vision when our faith is stretched between the two poles of impossibility and promise. As Elie Wiesel observes of his compulsion to write about the Holocaust, even though he knows no words can ever adequately convey the full truth of what must be said, "If the violin is to sing, its strings must be stretched so tight as to risk breaking; slack, they are merely threads."[5]

Responsive Reading

PSALM 71:1-14 (RCL); 71:1-12 (BCP); 71:1-6, 15, 17 (RC)

The themes of despair and discouragement that are present in Second Isaiah's portrait of the servant are echoed in the psalmist's fear of being shamed (v. 1b), forsaken (vv. 9, 11b), and abused (vv. 4, 10, 11a, 13). Interlaced with these fears are repeated petitions for God's deliverance (vv. 2-4, 9, 12). Despite the fear, anxiety, and needfulness, the psalmist speaks as one who trusts in the care and salvation of God, his "refuge" (vv. 1, 3), "fortress" (v. 3), and "hope" (v. 5).

The discouragement of Isaiah's servant is countered by a reaffirming word from God (Isa. 49:7). For the psalmist there is no direct word from God. Instead, it is in the very act of hoping and trusting in God that the psalmist discovers the faith he seeks. In the midst of trouble and uncertainty the psalmist speaks into reality the truth about God that already sustains him, even though he cannot as yet discern its full and immediate presence. He declares that God is "my hope, my trust" (v. 5), and in the process he is empowered to "hope continually" (v. 14a). He resolves to praise God "continually" (vv. 6, 8), and in the act of praising he discovers that he is praising God "yet more and more" (v. 14b).

The psalmist asserts that he has been "like a portent (*môpēt*) to many" (v. 7). The expression may convey different meanings. To be a portent may indicate that someone has become a sign or symbol of God's punishment (cf. Deut. 28:46). The psalmist's adversaries seem to take this view, for when they look upon him all they can see is a person "whom God has forsaken" (v. 11). Portents, however, are often persons or events that demonstrate God's unparalleled, unimaginable power to accomplish divine objectives in the face of seemingly insurmountable obstacles. For example, God's miraculous deliverance of the Israelite slaves from Egypt is frequently described as a "portent" or "wonder" (cf. Exod. 7:3; 11:9; Deut. 6:22; 7:19; 26:8). It is tempting to conclude that the psalmist understands himself as a portent in just this way, that he bears public witness, despite how others may view him, to God's power to do the impossible in extraordinary ways.

It may be prudent, however, given our temptation to reach too quickly for comforting affirmations, to linger within the psalmist's uncertainty about what he is and how he will fare in this tense world of trouble and hope. Marvin Tate has captured this uncertainty with his evocative translation of v. 7: "I have been a *mystery* for many."[6] The psalmist's trust and praise, like Jesus' obedience unto death, is a "mystery for many." Our response to this mystery will bear public witness, for good or for ill, to God's miraculous power to save, even when the world insists "there is no one to deliver" (v. 11).

Second Reading
1 CORINTHIANS 1:18-31

Interpreting the Text

What God disclosed to the "one deeply despised, abhorred by the nations" (Isa. 49:7), what the psalmist whose "strength is spent" (Ps. 71:9) learned from leaning on God, Paul affirms by proclaiming the "message about the cross"

(v. 18). The cross is a scandalous reminder that God's way in the world subverts conventional expectations about weakness and power. Whereas Jews look for signs that demonstrate God's power on earth and gentiles look for wisdom that conforms to what reason can verify (v. 22), the message of the cross is that God has chosen surprising new ways of being present and known in the world. The power of God is manifest in weakness that is "stronger than human strength" (v. 25b). The wisdom of God is revealed in foolishness that is "wiser than human wisdom" (v. 25a).

Paul's discernment is new, and yet it conveys a truth about God that has been available to all from the very beginning. To make his case Paul appeals to two pieces of evidence. First, he quotes from Isaiah 29:14 to show how God has always done "shocking and amazing" things that result in deliverance when none is expected or deserved. Even as the "wisdom of their [Judah's] wise" (v. 19) withered in the face of Assyrian opposition, God was at work protecting Jerusalem in ways that enabled the deaf to hear, the blind to see, and the meek to obtain fresh joy (Isa. 29:18).

Second, Paul appeals to what the Corinthians may observe about God's work in their own community (vv. 26-31). Not many of them are "wise by human standards." They are not distinguished by their education, skill, or philosophical sophistication. Not many are "powerful" in the ways that society normally defines those who occupy influential positions in government or religion. Not many are of "noble birth," hence they have no recognizable claims on prestige and privilege. And yet God has chosen them, flawed as they are by ignorance, weakness, and ignominy, to participate in the "righteousness and sanctification and redemption" (v. 30) for which the whole world yearns. God's purpose in choosing "what is low and despised in the world" is that "no one might boast in the presence of God" (v. 28).

Toward this end Paul summons all who are called into partnership with God, "both Jews and Greeks" (v. 24), to boast not of their own power but of their empowerment by the One who works in mysterious ways through the very weakness that the world holds in contempt. To buttress his exposition of this long-standing truth about God, Paul concludes this part of his address with a second citation from Hebrew scripture. Echoing the words of the prophet Jeremiah (see Jer. 9:23-24), Paul reminds his audience of an ancient admonition: "Let the one who boasts, boast in the Lord" (v. 31). In sum, the God who is the source of the Corinthians' "life in Christ Jesus" (v. 30), the God who empowers lowly Israel to be "a light to the nations" (Isa. 49:6), is a God who always chooses "what is foolish in the world to shame the wise" (v. 27).

God's way of being present in the world is scandalous. Who could believe that servanthood is the route to salvation, that suffering is the way to redemption, that weakness is the truest measure of power, that death does not have the final say about life? By any rational estimation of what the world values as right and good, the summons to commit ourselves to God's way must be judged foolish in the extreme. It is not only the ancient Jews and Greeks who found it nearly impossible to yield themselves to God's foolishness. We only need examine our own aspirations and fears to recognize that we are similarly seduced by the world's models for success and failure. If we are to win, we are convinced that we must display superior power. If we are to succeed, we believe that we must be wiser than our nearest competitor. If we are to have the status and recognition that secures our place in the world, we think we must not rest until we have climbed to the top rung of the ladder. For all of us who set our compass by the world's lights, Holy Week seems to offer a one-way ticket on a train going in the wrong direction.

To follow the God of Jesus into Jerusalem is to own the world's shame as the cost of discipleship. It is to risk being regarded as a failure in order to be faithful to a victory that is often both so incomprehensible and so intangible as to seem more illusory than real. It is to believe that a cross is a crown, that a grave is a gateway, that death is not the end of life's journey. At every step along Holy Week's journey we will be tempted to turn back, for the closer we come to the final destination the more we will be tempted to believe that the mystery is too great and our faith is too little.

The promise of Holy Week is that by attending to these ancient and difficult words of scripture we may find ourselves numbered among those "who are being saved" (v. 18) by the foolishness of God. We may discover that when the wisdom of the world discounts our "lame hands of faith," God surprisingly empowers these same hands to do marvelous things. We may learn that when the world mocks our "faint trust" in a God it glibly reckons to be a non-factor in its calculations, God miraculously sustains that same trust with a "larger hope" that changes the calculus of everything.

I falter where I firmly trod,
    And falling with my weight of cares
    Upon the great world's altar-stairs
That slope thro' darkness up to God,

I stretch lame hands of faith, and grope,
    And gather dust and chaff, and call
    To what I feel is Lord of all,
And faintly trust the larger hope.[7]

The Gospel

JOHN 12:20-36 (RCL); 12:37-38, 42-50 or MARK 11:15-19 (BCP); JOHN 13:21-33, 36-38 (RC)

Interpreting the Text

In today's Gospel, Jesus announces that "the hour has come" (v. 23; cf. v. 27). This announcement marks a moment of dramatic pause in John's story of Jesus' journey to Jerusalem. Inside this tensive hour between what has been and what will be all the major participants in this story—gentiles, Jews, Jesus, God—will be called upon to consider their level of participation in the momentous events that have been set in motion.

The first ones to appear in this hour are the Greeks (vv. 20-21). They are the representatives of the gentile world, and as such they bear witness to the universal reach of God's salvific work in Christ. They have come to Jerusalem to observe the Passover festival, and they announce that they "wish to see Jesus." Their request is couched in the conventional rhetoric (cf. Luke 8:20; 9:9) that indicates they seek a personal meeting with this one who, in the aftermath of the raising of Lazarus, has stirred the imagination of the whole world (cf. John 12:19). Perhaps they have already made their decision to follow Jesus. Perhaps they desire further information that will help them decide whether they should become disciples. In any event they are numbered among the "crowd" (vv. 29, 34) that wants to know more about the "Messiah" and the "Son of Man" the scriptures have promised.

The second group gathered in this hour are the disciples of Jesus, here represented by Philip and Andrew (vv. 21-22). In the alternate reading from John 13, which relates a subsequent scene in the story, Simon Peter, Andrew's brother, is the primary disciple who gathers around Jesus to ask, "Where are you going?" (v. 36). In John's Gospel, Andrew is among the first of the disciples to whom Jesus gave the invitation, "Come and see" (1:39). Andrew in turn found his brother Peter and brought him to Jesus (1:41-42). On the next day, according to John, Jesus called Philip to follow him (1:43), and Philip in turn called Nathaniel with the same invitation to "Come and see" that Jesus had given to Andrew (1:46). Now Andrew and Philip may be understood as extending the invitation to discipleship still further, beyond the ranks of the Jewish

> GOD'S WAY OF BEING PRESENT IN THE WORLD IS SCANDALOUS. WHO COULD BELIEVE THAT SERVANTHOOD IS THE ROUTE TO SALVATION, THAT SUFFERING IS THE WAY TO REDEMPTION, THAT WEAKNESS IS THE TRUEST MEASURE OF POWER, THAT DEATH DOES NOT HAVE THE FINAL SAY ABOUT LIFE? BY ANY RATIONAL ESTIMATION OF WHAT THE WORLD VALUES AS RIGHT AND GOOD, THE SUMMONS TO COMMIT OURSELVES TO GOD'S WAY MUST BE JUDGED FOOLISH IN THE EXTREME.

disciples, to the gentiles who have come requesting to "see" Jesus. When the hour comes for deciding who will be numbered among Jesus' disciples, John would have us know that the invitation is inclusive; it summons all who seek relationship with God and Jesus to "come and see" what this journey to Jerusalem means.

The third participant in this story is Jesus. When the hour comes for "the Son of Man to be glorified" (v. 23), Jesus begins a series of teachings about the meaning of his impending death (vv. 24-26, 32-33), which underscores the urgency of the moment for him and all those gathered around him (vv. 35-36). Jesus frequently uses the metaphor of sowing to teach that seeds properly planted have the capacity to produce an exceedingly abundant harvest (Matt. 13:3-32; Mark 4:3-20, 26-29; Luke 8:5-15). Paul uses the same metaphor in 1 Cor. 15:35-41 to illustrate Jesus' death and resurrection. John's appropriation of the sowing imagery contains a reference to Jesus' death (v. 24), but his emphasis, as elsewhere in the Synoptics, is on the miracle of life. "Just a single grain" planted in the soil and nurtured toward its full capacity can "bear much fruit"; in the words of Matthew and Mark, the harvest may reach thirty, sixty, even a hundredfold (Matt. 13:23; Mark 4:20). For the crowd who listens to Jesus' teaching, the parable of the seed is an invitation to ponder the vast potential they have to bear fruit that creates a community of faith beyond anything they can reasonably expect from their own meager resources. If they are willing to follow him, to go where he goes, to serve others in the manner he has taught them, to risk being planted in the earth and being lifted up from the earth, then the seeds of their discipleship, like the seeds of life Jesus has scattered among them, will "draw all people" to the God to whom he bears witness (cf. v. 32).

In between Jesus' announcement that "the hour has come" and his anticipation of the future time when he will be "lifted up," he pauses in the interim of his own "now" to disclose that his "soul is troubled" (v. 27). His words echo those of the psalmist in Psalm 42:5, 11 and thus recall the shifting emotions of one who is at once disquieted and comforted by his relationship to God. What should Jesus say and do in his own hour of decision? Should he pray for God to save him "from this hour" (v. 27b; cf. Mark 14:34)? Should he pray that God will be glorified by his obedience to what this hour holds for him? Jesus chooses the latter, and by so doing he models for those he teaches the very faith they have come to see and ponder for themselves.

The fourth participant in this drama is God (v. 28b). John would have us know that when the hour comes for Jesus to make his definitive turn toward Golgotha, God is intimately involved in what is taking place. In a publicly audible response to Jesus' prayer, God affirms that God has indeed glorified the moment and will "glorify it again" when the events set in motion by Jesus' decision come to pass.

After v. 28, two of the participants in these events have clearly declared their commitment to what the hour at hand means for them. Jesus has resolved to live fully into the mission that God has set before him. God has publicly committed to honor, sustain, and direct every step Jesus takes toward the ultimate fulfillment of God's hopes and expectations for the world. All that remains is for those who have come to see—the crowd of Jewish and non-Jewish disciples—to decide how they will respond to the moment. Some have heard the voice from heaven and thought it to be thunder (v. 29a). Others have taken it to be the voice of an angel, although they seem yet uncertain that it is the word of God for them (vv. 29b-30). Still others discern that what they have seen and heard connects them in some way to the sacred traditions about the Messiah and the Son of Man, but at this juncture they have more questions than clarity. What does Jesus mean when he says that the "Son of Man must be lifted up"? "Who is this Son of Man?" (v. 34). Like those who gather around Jesus in the alternate reading from John 13, this crowd of persons may now be looking at one another with bewilderment, wondering in the aftershock of Jesus' words what he is speaking about (see 13:21).

John concludes this scene by reporting Jesus' response to those who ponder such questions (vv. 35-36). He tells them that they have just "a little longer" to make their decisions. The time is urgent. Like travelers who seek to complete their journey before darkness sets in, they must quicken their pace while they still have the light to guide them. The metaphor of light and darkness is double-edged, for while light symbolizes the promise of salvation, the impending darkness warns that the time of judgment draws near (cf. v. 31). When Jesus had said these things to them, John reports, he "departed and hid from them" (v. 36b). It is a sign that the decisions yet to be made are ones these who have to come to see and listen can only make for themselves.

Responding to the Text

The ritual of Holy Week is not a nostalgic journey down memory lane. To be sure, the ritual of reading sacred texts refreshes our memory of these momentous events in the last week of Jesus' life. But, as Leon Wieseltier learned from reciting the traditional Jewish kaddish in the year after his father died, "a ritual life is not an unexamined life." As he puts it in one of the entries to his spiritual journal, "ritual is a conversion of essences into acts."[8] Jesus' words "The hour has come" serve notice that when we engage in the ritual of reading this Gospel text, we must do more than simply remember an old story. We remember in order that we might live and act in a different way. We enact the ritual so that we may convert our memories of Jesus into living testimony that we have become "children of light" (v. 36).

The high holy days of Easter are marked on virtually every calendar in this country. No matter our religious orientation—whether we are devout or lukewarm, interested or apathetic—few of us will go through this season completely unaware of the ritual significance of these days. In fact, during this one week of the year the numbers of those who will "come and see" the great pageantry of Easter will swell to such extent that we may be tempted to think the whole "world has gone after him." Some, like the Greeks, may come because they are curious about this one who has been rumored to have extraordinary powers to raise the dead. Some, like Philip and Andrew, may come because they are certain they belong to the select group of "insiders" who represent Christ and extend his invitation to discipleship to others. Others may be part of the large crowd who come because they have heard about the Messiah but are not yet certain what it all means for them. At this auspicious hour when the diverse crowd gathers to remember the old story, they learn that they must do more than simply listen. The time has come for them to turn curiosity, faith, and wonderment into action.

When the hour comes for the Son of Man to be glorified, each of us in the crowd gathered around Jesus must find the "single grain" that we can plant in the kingdom of God. If that grain is curiosity, we can sow it and nurture it until it blossoms forth into a restless search for truth. If it is faith, we can exercise it by following where Jesus leads and serving like Jesus serves. If it is wonderment, we can act on the possibility that the Messiah we have heard about is speaking directly to us. In the judgment of the world, curiosity and faith and wonderment are often regarded as reasons to think without deciding, to believe without acting. But at this hour in Holy Week's journey Jesus reminds us that unless we plant the grains we have, the opportunity to bear "much fruit" will come and go without our knowing. Like Jesus we have choices to make. We can decide to avoid the hour of decision in the hope that we will be spared the pain and disappointment of risking too much on certainties too costly. We can decide to risk everything on truths too important to relinquish to fear, doubt, and uncertainty. Those willing to see and act upon the model of faith Jesus images in his hour of decision may be assured that God is intimately involved in our struggle to convert essences into acts.

When he began the year-long ritual of saying the kaddish, Wieseltier worried that his religious commitments would interfere with his life. Gradually he recognized that he had embarked on a season of "soul renovation," and as a result he began to worry that the ordinary affairs of his life were interfering with the imperatives of his ritual. He describes the moment of his conversion as follows: "I study the old texts because I hope to be infected by their dimensions, to attain the size of what I read."[9]

At this juncture in Holy Week we have reached a critical pause when we must decide whether reading this old story may be more than a mere ritual. The invitation to remember the journey Jesus made is an opportunity to attain the size of what we read.

WEDNESDAY IN HOLY WEEK

April 11, 2001

Revised Common	Episcopal (BCP)	Roman Catholic
Isa. 50:4-9a	Isa. 50:4-9a	Isa. 50:4-9
Psalm 70	Ps. 69:7-15, 22-23	Ps. 69:8-10, 14, 21-22, 31, 33-34
Heb. 12:1-3	Heb. 9:11-15, 24-28	
John 13:21-32	John 13:21-35 or Matt. 26:1-5, 14-25	Matt. 26:14-25

The readings for this day bring us to the midpoint of Holy Week's journey. Isaiah's disciple reminds us that the course ahead will be difficult (Isa. 50:5, 8-9). The psalmist reminds us of our need for God to come swiftly to our aid (Ps. 70:1, 5). The writer of Hebrews admonishes us to run the race set before us with endurance (Heb. 12:1). And yet in the midst of our journey we hear Jesus say "one of you will betray me" (John 13:21). When we remember that our journey towards Jerusalem is a vexed blend of difficulty, need, endurance, and betrayal, we stay mindful of the importance of lingering in this tensive interim between how far we have come thus far and where we have yet to go.

First Reading

ISAIAH 50:4-9a

The first reading is the same as the one assigned for Passion Sunday. Readers may consult the discussion there for the commentary on the passage.

Responsive Reading

PSALM 70 (RCL); 69:7-15, 22-23 (BCP); 69:8-10, 14, 21-22, 31, 33-34 (RC)

Psalm 70 is an individual prayer for help that repeats almost verbatim Psalm 40:13-17. It is difficult to determine whether Psalm 70 is an independent poem or a fragment of Psalm 40. In either case, these verses display a literary coherence that invites reflecting on them as they stand.

The psalm begins and ends with an urgent petition for God to help: "O Lord, make haste to help me!" (v. 1); "hasten to me, O God!" (v. 5). The psalmist underscores the urgency of the moment with a series of petitions establishing what is at stake for both those who trust in God and those who assault them for trusting in God. Those who oppose the psalmist seek to "take life" and "hurt." The psalmist petitions God to shame and dishonor them (vv. 2-3). Those who seek the Lord and love the Lord's salvation are helpless before their enemies. Like the "poor and needy" who know their meager resources cannot protect them, they are utterly dependent on God's help. The psalmist petitions God to act so that those who know the truth about God may reclaim their witness: "God is great!" (v. 4). In anticipation of the help that is expected but is not yet a reality, the psalmist affirms God as "deliverer," even as he repeats the petition that God act now (v. 5).

Psalm 69 includes portions of a similar prayer for help, although it provides more detail concerning the psalmist's plight (vv. 7-15). The psalmist is shunned by family (v. 8), ridiculed for observing the rituals of faith (vv. 10-11), mocked by those who administer justice in the gate (v. 12a), and joked about in the songs of drunkards (v. 12b). The ignominy of the situation is all the harder to bear because it is precisely the psalmist's faith in God that targets him for attack (vv. 7, 9). The psalmist despairs because wherever he looks there is no pity, and there is no one to comfort (v. 20). When he expected to be invited to a good meal he was given "poison for food" and "vinegar to drink" (v. 21), a menu designed to sicken the famished and hasten their demise. For all these reasons the psalmist looks to the one constant that can be counted on when all else fails: the "steadfast love" and "faithfulness" of the God on whom he depends for deliverance (vv. 13-15).

Second Reading

HEBREWS 12:1-3 (RCL); 9:11-15, 24-28 (BCP)

Interpreting the Text

The exhortation in Hebrews 12 begins by commending to second-generation believers (cf. Heb. 2:3-4) the "cloud of witnesses" who have modeled for them what it means to have "perseverance" (v. 1) in the face of suffering. The witnesses of faith are listed in chapter 11 and include the legacy bequeathed to the church by Israel's forebears Abraham, Isaac, and Jacob. The writer indicates that these and other heroes of faith, male and female, named and unnamed, have run their race and have now assembled to cheer on those for whom the journey has just begun.

New Testament writers frequently use the metaphor of a race to describe faith as a moral contest in which one competes against all contenders for victory (cf. 1 Cor. 9:24-27; Phil. 1:27-30; 3:14; 1 Tim. 6:12; 2 Tim. 4:7-8; Jude 3). Like runners who train rigorously to build up their strength and endurance, those who compete in the race of faith must prepare themselves to finish the course "that is set before us." Toward that end the writer encourages the audience to lay aside every encumbrance (NRSV: "weight") and every sin that may hinder their competition. The writer does not identify specifically what should be discarded but given the emphasis on faith in the preceding chapter, it is plausible to consider that the fatigue of despair and unbelief are among the principal concerns (see further v. 3).

For the race "that is set *before* us" we should model our preparation on the way Jesus resolved to complete the journey "that was set *before* him." Jesus is the "pioneer" (*archegos*) of our faith, because he creates the path upon which his followers are to walk. And he is the "perfecter" (*teleiōtēs*) of our faith, because he completes the path he prepares with perfect obedience (cf. Heb. 2:10). Between the beginning and the end of his journey with God on earth, Jesus "became like his brothers and sisters in every respect" (cf. Heb. 2:17-18). He knows completely and from our vantage point what it means to have his faith in God tested, to suffer for his obedience, to be shamed by those who could not accept his trust in and commitment to God, and to die for that which he believes. Because Jesus endured and overcame everything the world could place between him and the completion of his journey with God, because he created the path of obedience and walked in its every step without yielding to the temptation to choose another way, he now sits "at the right hand of the throne of God."

The alternate reading, Hebrews 9:24-28, supplements this image by affirming that Christ's ministry in heaven is "on our behalf" (v. 24). Although Hebrews 9 uses a different metaphor (high priest) to illustrate Jesus' work, the combination of the two texts offers a most suggestive image for us. When we set out to run the race that is set before us, the crowd of witnesses who surround and sustain us with encouragement and support includes not only the great heroes of Israel's faith but also Jesus, who is the perfect example of the promise of victory that lies ahead.

The final verse of today's reading provides an effective conclusion to the "therefore" of v. 1 that introduces this exhortation. *Therefore*, because we have such a cloud of witnesses to cheer us on, we should run the race set before us with perseverance. When we look into the faces of our ancestors Abraham, Isaac, and Jacob, when we see the face of Jesus himself, we should take heart that we can complete the course. When we grow weary with the journey or lose faith in its ultimate outcome, we should remember those who have gone ahead and secured our place at the finish line. It is not the suffering or hostility that makes the journey worthwhile. These are but the obstacles that test our mettle for the journey. It is the victory, for waiting at the end is the prize of knowing that we have been faithful to the task of becoming the people God has called us to be. In the words of Paul, we run because we have been summoned to "press on toward the goal for the prize of the heavenly call of God in Christ Jesus" (Phil. 3:14).

The remainder of the alternate reading from Hebrews 9 (vv. 11-15) is the same as that for Monday in Holy Week. Readers should consult the discussion there for further commentary.

Responding to the Text

In Henry Fielding's *The History of Tom Jones,* the narrator observes of Jenny's patience that it is "a virtue apt to be fatigued by exercise."[10] This wearied conclusion about the so-called virtue of patience speaks for many of us who have discovered that suffering often seems to outlast our resolve to stand firm in the face of its withering assault. The writer of Hebrews uses a word—*hypomonē*—that invites a larger understanding of "patience." The summons to "run with *perseverance*" (12:1) and to "*endure*" (12:2, 3) past the shame and hostility that come from following Jesus carries a more active sense than the passivity conveyed by the conventional understanding of patience. To run is to move forward with a vigorous and disciplined pace; to endure or persevere is to go past weariness and despair toward something still more real and compelling. Two aspects of the endurance the writer commends merit further reflection.

First, we are invited to reflect on the support made available to us by the great cloud of witnesses who cheer us on in the journey of faith. The crowd gathered on our behalf is large, and their experience is a compelling witness to the promise that drives us forward. Numbered among those who lend their strength to our journey are Abel, Enoch, Noah, Abraham, Isaac, Jacob, Joseph, Moses, Rahab, Gideon, Barak, Samson, Jephthah, David, Samuel, and the prophets (cf. 11:1-40). By any conventional assessment they are an unlikely source of strength, because their frailties and weaknesses are so similar to our own. When challenged to believe the incredible promises of God, Abraham laughed (Gen. 17:17), Jacob wrestled (Gen. 32:22-32), Moses despaired and protested (Num. 11:11-15), Gideon questioned (Judg. 6:13), Samuel was afraid (1 Sam. 3:15). And yet the writer of Hebrews commends their witness to us because by their indefatigable faith they "conquered kingdoms, administered justice, obtained promises, shut the mouths of lions, quenched raging fire, escaped the edge of the sword, won strength out of weakness, became mighty in war, put armies to flight" (11:33-34). In the middle of this crowd stands one whose voice is louder than all the rest, and yet his words of encouragement may be the most difficult for us to hear. Jesus endured the cross and endured the hostility that led others to nail him to it with such conviction. No one knows better than he where the race begins and where it ends. It is he who tells us to believe that we can finish the course, that our fatigue and despair, our frailty and failure, will not keep us from the finish line if we will but place our feet in the path he has run.

Second, this great crowd of witnesses supports us not only because of *their faith in God* but more importantly because of *God's faith in them*. Their endurance bears witness to God's reliability. From God's creation of the world (11:3) to God's presence to the prophets of Israel (11:32), from God's inscrutable approval of Abel's sacrifice (11:4) to God's wondrous work in the sacrifice of Jesus (12:2), God has been at work securing the "race that is set before us" (12:1). Like our forbears in faith, we will falter and stumble on the journey with God. At times we will succumb to the temptation to laugh with incredulity. Often we will feel too uncertain or too frightened to believe. On more than one occasion we will pray that God will spare us the journey. At each and every point where fatigue and failure threaten to end our journey before its appointed end, God's relentless faith in us proves greater than our weakness.

When we listen carefully to all those in *heaven* and on *earth* who are cheering us on, the most important word we hear may be the first word spoken in today's Epistle: "Therefore." On the other side of this transforming word, our understanding of patience may be enlarged beyond anything Fielding's Jenny could discern. We may discover, in the evocative words of Longfellow, that " Sorrow and silence are strong," but "patient endurance is godlike."[11]

THE GOSPEL

JOHN 13:21-32 (RCL); JOHN 13:21-35 or MATTHEW 26:1-5, 14-25 (BCP); MATTHEW 26:14-25 (RC)

Interpreting the Text

Both readings, from John and from Matthew, focus on Jesus' announcement of his imminent betrayal, but they do so in different ways. Matthew reports that Judas had already accepted payment in return for handing Jesus over to his enemies (26:14-16; cf. vv. 3-5) when he shared in the intimacy of the Passover meal with Jesus and his fellow disciples. Given this sequence of events, Judas' denial of his deeds—"Surely not I" (v. 25)—signals that betrayal may be act of an hypocrisy masquerading as intimacy. John does not include the scene of Judas' payment for conspiracy, although he does report that the thought of betrayal had already entered his mind (13:2). Thus when Judas gathers with the disciples to share in their farewell meal with Jesus, he does so as an intimate follower and friend who is deeply conflicted by the tension between what he is doing and thinking. When Jesus announces that one of the disciples will betray him (13:21), Judas does not say a word. When Jesus singles him out by offering him a piece of the common bread, Judas knows that he must decide whether he will exercise his fidelity for or against Jesus. When he takes what Jesus offers, he departs into the darkness of the night he has chosen (v. 30). In John's sequence of these events, Judas' actions signal that the temptation to betrayal may be most seductive when Jesus invites his followers into intimate communion with him. Whether we read Matthew or John, betrayal is a seductive reality that we cannot afford to ignore.

John reports that after Jesus had washed the disciples' feet, thus preparing them for the ministry of service to others, he was "troubled" (*tarasō*; v. 21). John's use of this expression recalls two similar moments of anguish in Jesus' journey to Jerusalem. In 11:33 Jesus was "deeply moved" by the grief surrounding the death of Lazarus, and he added his own tears to those who mourned the loss of their dear friend. In 12:27 Jesus was "troubled" at the coming of his hour of decision. Now, as he looks at his beloved disciples in their own hour of decision, Jesus' anguish is compounded by the betrayal he foresees. He has given himself in love to those who surround him. Their rejection of that love is a source of grief no less wrenching for him than the death of a treasured friend.

"VERY TRULY, I TELL YOU, ONE OF YOU WILL BETRAY ME." AT THIS MIDPOINT IN THE JOURNEY OF HOLY WEEK, JESUS SPEAKS A CHILLING WORD INTO THE MIDST OF OUR PREPARATIONS. STILL MORE UNSETTLING IS THE FACT THAT JESUS IS SPEAKING TO HIS DISCIPLES, THE VERY PERSONS WHO HAVE LEFT EVERYTHING TO FOLLOW HIM.

When Jesus announces that one of them will betray him, the disciples cannot comprehend what he means. Matthew (26:22) and Mark (14:19) report that each one of the disciples asked if he could be the one who would be the betrayer. In John's account the lone questioner is the disciple "whom Jesus loved" (v. 23). The name of the disciple is not given. Although tradition identifies him with the author of this Gospel, he is consistently described simply as the one Jesus loves (19:26; 20:2; 21:7, 20). This scene emphasizes the disciple's special relationship to Jesus by reporting that he was "reclining next to Jesus," that is, he was resting on Jesus' bosom. The suggestion is that he enjoys an intimacy with Jesus that mirrors Jesus' intimacy with God (cf. 1:18). His question—"Lord, who is it?" (v. 25)—brings into sharp relief the contrast between the intimacy of the occasion and the impending estrangement of betrayal.

The counterpart to this disciple is Judas (vv. 26-27). He too is one of Jesus' intimate associates, a fact Jesus underscores when he singles him out by offering him a piece of bread from their common plate. For Judas as for the rest of the disciples, receiving what Jesus offers marks a moment of truth in their fellowship. They may share intimately in his suffering or they may share intimately in his betrayal. Jesus knows that Judas is wrestling with the choices before him. He knows that the devil has already put the prospect of betrayal into Judas' heart (13:2). When Jesus offers him the bread, Judas must decide whether by taking it he will choose for Jesus or against him. At the moment he receives the bread "Satan entered into him" (cf. the same language in Mark 5:12 and Luke 8:30), and he yields to a different lord and another journey. Knowing that Judas has reached the point of no return, Jesus instructs him to do what he is going to do "quickly." Satan may control Judas, but Jesus remains in control of the journey God has set before them all.

The other disciples still do not comprehend what has happened. From the vantage point of their intimacy with Jesus, they suspect that Jesus has simply sent their colleague on a routine mission (vv. 28-30). Perhaps Judas himself thinks that by leaving as instructed his betrayal may somehow be an act of obedience. And yet by departing into the night, Judas embarks on a journey into the darkness that seeks to bring Jesus' light on earth to an end (cf. 8:12; 9:4-5). Jesus reminds all his intimates, however, that even "now" (v. 31), as darkness envelops their journey, the hour of glory is imminent. The fivefold repetition of the verb "glorify" (*doxazō*) in vv. 31-32 echoes the inviolable truth with which John introduced his Gospel: "The light shines in the darkness, and the darkness did not overcome it" (1:5).

Responding to the Text

"Very truly, I tell you, one of you will betray me" (John 13:21; cf. Matt. 26:21). At this midpoint in the journey of Holy Week, Jesus speaks a chilling word into the midst of our preparations. Still more unsettling is the fact that Jesus is speaking to his disciples, the very persons who have left everything to follow him. They, like we, have journeyed faithfully with him to this point, and they, like us, are preparing to share with him the intimacy of the meal that joins them in fellowship and fidelity to a common cause. They cannot believe their fellowship and fidelity are vulnerable to betrayal.

Both Gospel readings for today record that the disciples do not comprehend the gravity of the moment. John reports that the disciples are uncertain about what Jesus is saying (13:22). When the beloved disciple asks "Lord, who is it?" (v. 25), he hints that they all suspect Jesus must be referring to someone outside their inner circle. When Jesus responds by singling out Judas, they still cannot fathom the possibility that one of their intimate associates is capable of anything other than the commitment they all hold in common (v. 28). Matthew reports that the disciples "became greatly distressed" at Jesus' words. They are tempted to wonder that Jesus may be referring to one of them, but the thought is so unsettling that they strain to reject it with an anxious confidence: "Surely, not I, Lord? (26:21). John and Matthew remind us that those who are most confident of their discipleship may be the last ones to realize that they may be the first to succumb to betrayal.

We also may be tempted to take comfort in the prospect that Jesus' warning applies to someone other than us. In the history of Christian tradition Judas has become a convenient scapegoat for all believers who want to be confident that they would never be as guilty as he of deserting the cause of Christ. Judas is such a tortured, pathetic figure that we glibly dismiss his infidelity as wholly atypical of the faith we profess. The Judases we know are always outsiders; they are always easily identified by their evil deeds; they are always someone other than us. We cannot imagine that Jesus might give us the piece of bread designated for Judas. We cannot imagine that once we have shared fellowship with Jesus we may depart into our own dark night of subterfuge and deceit. We cannot fathom the possibility that when we ask "Lord, who is it?" the answer may be that we are the ones. Perhaps this is why the rituals of Holy Week are so important: they bring us face to face with the realization that Judas dwells in our midst.

Like the disciples in Matthew's Gospel, we may respond to the possibility of betrayal by fearing the worst and hoping for the best. When we anxiously ask, "Lord, is it I?" we may cling to the desperate hope that our fears are unfounded. We may believe that once we have dipped our hand into Jesus' bowl we could never lend that same hand to those who would fill it with the payoff for betrayal. Because we cannot entertain the possibility of falling away, we will not hear the hypocrisy in our words, "Surely not I, Rabbi?" (Matt. 26:25). It will not occur to us that more is required than simply knowing the words of direct address, the words of popular recognition, the words of carefully crafted respect and acknowledgment. When Jesus turns to us and says, "You have said so," we will be tempted to believe that he is unaware of the duplicity we try to camouflage as faith. Perhaps this too is why the rituals of Holy Week are so important: they confront us with the huge gap between what we say and what we do.

In "All That Glisters Isn't Gold," Doris Betts tells the story of a young girl whose faith is disturbed by the blasphemous words of Granville. Granville had gone off to university and learned that the great chunks of comforting catechism he had parroted in his youth were vulnerable to critique and dismissal. The little girl knew she should be able to counter Granville's arguments, but she could not ignore the possibility that he knew something about the faith she professed that she had not been willing to see. Betts describes her ruminations:

> Each of his words was like a splinter and each slid invisibly inside me. There was a sore spot wherever one had penetrated; soon there were bruises all over my religion it was not safe to touch. I preferred the soreness of those splinters to the painful operation of having them removed.[12]

When we gather round Jesus at this point in our Holy Week journey, we must pay close attention to those splintering words "one of you will betray me." Unlike Granville, who took some pleasure in unsettling another's faith, Jesus is "troubled in spirit" when he calls his disciples to reexamine their commitments. Both his anguish and the truth that compels him to speak invite us to ponder what is perhaps the most important question of the entire week's ritual: Is it I, Lord? It is up to us to decide if we will allow this painful question to bruise our veneered certainty that we are not Judas.

MAUNDY THURSDAY HOLY THURSDAY

APRIL 12, 2001

REVISED COMMON	EPISCOPAL (BCP)	ROMAN CATHOLIC
Exod. 12:1-4 (5-10) 11-14	Exod. 12:1-14a	Exod. 12:1-8, 11-14
Ps. 116:1-2, 12-19	Ps. 78:14-20, 23-25	Ps. 116:12-13, 15-18
1 Cor. 11:23-26	1 Cor. 11:23-26 (27-32)	1 Cor. 11:23-26
John 13:1-17, 31b-35	John 13:1-15 or Luke 22:14-30	John 13:1-15

MAUNDY THURSDAY IS A TIME FOR REMEMBERING and reenacting some of faith's most important rituals. We remember the Jewish Passover (Exod. 12:1-14), and with Jesus we step into its abiding promise of freedom and salvation. We remember the psalmist's thanksgiving for having been delivered, and with Jesus we take anew the ancient "cup of salvation" that celebrates his resurrection victory over death (Psalm 116). We remember Paul's instructions concerning the Lord's Supper, and we commit ourselves to do this as a means of proclaiming the gospel (1 Cor. 11:23-26). We remember John's account of Jesus' foot washing, and we are cautioned against believing that any ritual—Passover, thanksgiving, or communion—can be uncoupled from the commandment to love God not only in word but in deed (John 13:1-17, 31b-35). In their respective ways, each of today's readings is a reminder that Maundy Thursday is not only about observing ceremonies. It is, in keeping with the derivation of its name (Latin *mandatum,* "commandment"), a mandate for radical obedience that transforms our relationship to God, the world, and each other.

FIRST READING

EXODUS 12:1-4 (5-10) 11-14 (RCL); 12:1-14a (BCP); 12:1-8, 11-14 (RC)

Interpreting the Text

The Gospel readings for Holy Week have prepared us to know that the last week of Jesus' life coincides with the celebration of Passover (Luke 22:15;

John 12:1; cf.13:1). Today's reading from Exodus draws us more deeply into the sacred memory of Passover by inviting us into the old story that provides the context for understanding Jesus' last meal with his disciples.

Exodus locates the instructions concerning Passover at the penultimate point before Israel's departure from Egypt (12:29-39). Nine plagues against Egypt have been enacted (7:14—10:29). The tenth has been announced (11:1-10) but not yet enacted (12:29-39). In the tense interim before God's final demonstration of liberating power, the narrative pauses to focus on the ritual of Passover that precedes and prepares for the climactic moment when the bonds of slavery and oppression are finally broken. The narrative sequencing suggests that the ritual of Passover is a crucially important part of Israel's preparation for freedom; in its own way Passover has power and import equivalent to the ten plagues.

The instructions are unevenly divided between matters of ritual procedure (vv. 1-11) and theological interpretation (vv. 12-14). We may prefer to rush past the former to get to the latter, but Exodus insists that we linger over the details of the ritual. Apart from these details, our theological *reflection* may become disconnected from *acts* that are meant to be more than mental exercises.

The pertinent details of the ritual of Passover are these. The celebration takes place during the first month of the year (vv. 1-2), thus it marks a beginning point, a place on life's calendar when the past is released and the future is greeted with fresh anticipation. It is a celebration that includes "the whole congregation" (vv. 3, 6). All are invited, none are to be excluded. The instructions focus on blood and food. The food consists of a one-year-old lamb, unleavened bread, and bitter herbs (vv. 4-5, 8). The lamb represents a costly and unblemished gift from the flock; the unleavened bread represents a grain offering that is uncorrupted by yeast; the bitter herbs recall the bitterness of Egyptian oppression (cf. Exod. 1:14). The blood is spread over the doorposts and lintels of the houses, a sign of the life that is being celebrated on the inside and the life force that is stirring for freedom on the outside. The meal is to be eaten "at twilight" (v. 6), literally, "between the two evenings," and those who share in the moment are to be dressed for travel: with loins girded, feet sandaled, staff in hand, they are to be ready to depart on the journey that begins when the Lord "passes over" (v. 11).

The theological interpretation of these instructions follows in vv. 12-14. In and of themselves, the time, the blood, and the food are no more than ordinary components of an ordinary occasion. Woven into the story of God's redemptive purposes they becomes "signs" of an extraordinary truth. God will pass through the land of Egypt, and nothing will be the same again. God will "execute judgments" (v. 12) that strike down oppression and abuse in Egypt. Those same judgments will open the door of freedom to a people who yearn for a new beginning they are powerless to effect without God's help. Both the ritual they have observed and the act they will witness become from this day forward a "perpetual ordinance" for God's people in all generations (v. 14). Each time they reenact the ritual they *celebrate* and *activate* the transforming power of the One who speaks into the midst of oppression the promise of abiding presence: "I am the Lord" (v. 12).

Responding to the Text

Passover marks the intersection between past and future. In the unsettled interim of the present, between the oppression and enslavement that constricts and denies life and a future still too uncertainly discerned to promise salvation, Passover invites us to live inside a memory. The memory of bondage keeps us sober about the capacity of the world to use us up and spit us out like persons who do not matter. The memory of salvation keeps us poised to respond to the One who refuses to allow the afflicted and the abused to go unnoticed. Without the memory of oppression we may be tempted to forget not only our own affliction but also the affliction of others who know that the world too often offers more death than life. Without the memory of salvation we may be tempted to believe that the future promises no more than a repetition of the sorrow we have already experienced. When we celebrate Passover we refuse to forget either the reality of affliction or the promise of salvation.

But Passover is about more than just memories of what has been or what might be. Passover is a liturgical act. It invites us to gesture into reality the truth of a memory that refuses to lie dormant. Part of that truth concerns *what God is prepared to do on our behalf.* Part of that truth concerns *what we do to prepare ourselves to participate in God's redemption.* The detailed instructions of the Passover narrative insist that we must not forsake the ritual of preparation. Each time we linger in the twilight of that last meal, each time we eat the bread and the bitter herbs, each time we mark our journey with that sacrificial blood, we act *as if* the salvation we anticipate is a present reality. In one sense, of course, what we do is *mere* ritual; we may even be tempted to regard it as fiction, a construction of reality that has no basis in fact. In another sense, however, ritual's fiction, like all good fiction, aspires to move us toward belief. When we live *as if* the ritual is true, we enter into the story we tell, we become one of the characters of whom we speak, we act out our quest to verify the promise of the One who generated the story in the first place.

In the Jewish liturgy for Passover the celebrants step into the old story of Israel and make it their own. When they say "*We* were slaves of Pharaoh in Egypt and the Eternal God brought *us* out from there. . . ," they say words the world might view as mere fiction. The contemporary celebrants were not in Egypt. They did not experience the exodus. And yet they enact a drama that turns the world's fiction into God's truth. After Jesus stepped into this sacred memory of Passover, after he enacted its truth and invited his disciples to participate in its claim, he said to them "Do this in remembrance of me" (Luke 22:19; cf. 1 Cor. 11:24). It is that invitation, with all of its "fiction," that promises these days have the potential to be a *Holy* Week for us, not just another ordinary time on the calendar.

Responsive Reading

PSALM 116:1-2, 12-19 (RCL); 78:14-20, 23-25 (BCP); 116:12-13, 15-18 (RC)

Psalm 116 is an individual song of thanksgiving. The portions selected for today tie together its beginning and ending. The psalmist gives thanks because God has heard a cry for help and has responded with deliverance (vv. 1-2). The concern of the psalmist then is how to find an appropriate way to show gratitude for what God has done (vv. 12-19). That gratitude is expressed with a ritual act, which in turn offers public witness. The ritual consists of lifting up the "cup of salvation" (v. 13) and of offering a "thanksgiving sacrifice" (v. 17). Both offerings suggest a worship setting involving a meal of fellowship (on the "consumption" of the "thanksgiving sacrifice," see Lev. 7:11-15; 22:29-30). The public witness is the proclamation "in the presence of all his people" (vv. 14, 18) that God has "loosed the bonds" (v. 16) of distress and anguish. Both the ritual and the proclamation validate the truth of the psalmist's opening words: "I love the Lord" (v. 1).

Psalm 78 offers a contrasting perspective on Israel's response to God's wondrous deeds of deliverance. Like other "historical psalms" (cf. Psalms 105, 106, 136), this psalm traces God's *ongoing fidelity* to Israel (vv. 14-16) and Israel's *ongoing infidelity* to God (vv. 17-22), which provokes God's wrath. The last word in the psalm, however, is not about wrath and judgment but about grace and forgiveness (vv. 23-25). In its own way then, Psalm 78 tells a history that seeks to move Israel to the same commitment and thankfulness that Psalm 116 affirms. When we "give ear" to this teaching (cf. 78:1), our response should be the same as the psalmist in Psalm 116:1: "I love the Lord."

Like the blood and food and marked doorposts that focused our attention in Exodus 12, the "cup of salvation" and the "thanksgiving sacrifice" of Psalm 116 may be viewed as merely ordinary elements of an ordinarily ancient ceremony. Two facts about the history of this psalm's use serve to remind us that ancient liturgies offer new opportunities to actualize old truths.

First, although composed for an individual, Psalm 116 came to be used by the wider community in association with the collective memory of Passover. As the fourth in the sequence of the *Hallel* psalms (Psalms 113–118), Psalm 116 was recited in association with the offering of the fourth cup of wine that was drunk in celebration of the Passover liturgy. In this context lifting up the "cup of salvation" was a ritual accompaniment to the verbal thanksgiving for God's deliverance from Egypt. As the Mishnah puts it, "Therefore are we bound to give thanks, to praise, to glorify, to honor, to exalt, to extol, and to bless him who wrought all these wonders for our fathers *and for us*" (*Pesahim* 10.5; emphasis added).

Second, Psalm 116 has found a home in the Christian celebration of the Lord's Supper, which like this psalm is understood to be a thanksgiving, a eucharist, for the marvelous work of God's redemption. In the Christian context Jesus actualizes the psalmist's cry for help as his own, the psalmist's thanksgiving as his own celebration of the resurrection victory over death, and the psalmist's cup as his own offering of the cup of salvation to his followers.

Second Reading

1 CORINTHIANS 11:23-26 (RCL/RC); 11:23-26 (27-32) (BCP)

Interpreting the Text

Like Exodus 12 and Psalm 116, the Epistle links ritual and proclamation as equally important components of the fellowship that bind us to God. Paul passes on to the Corinthians the tradition of Jesus' last meal with his disciples. The ritual of the Supper involves the sharing of ordinary bread and wine. In Jesus, however, the ordinary things of life are transformed into extraordinary rituals that are full of new meanings. The broken bread becomes the symbol of Jesus' body, which will be broken in death. The poured cup becomes the symbol of Jesus' blood, which will be poured out in death. Jesus gives the bread and the cup, blesses them, and invites his disciples to take these extraordinarily ordinary condiments of life as an invitation to share in the "new covenant" that joins them to God's purposes in the world. They are to "do this," that is, to act out this ritual of eating and drinking, "in remembrance" of him. The emphasis on remembrance, which appears with reference to both the bread and the cup, signals that this ritual, like all rituals of faith, is an invitation to theological reflection on *who God is*—broken and poured out for the sake of the world—and *who they are to be.*

Rituals of faith are always more than simply passive exercises in cognitive reflection. Paul teaches the Corinthians that the ritual observance of the Lord's Supper is itself a way to proclaim the gospel. As often as they eat the bread and drink the cup they say something to the world about the God they have seen in

Jesus. The gospel of the Lord's Supper is, however, a peculiar message. It hangs on the word "death," surely an odd proclamation if one wants to attract followers. But like the extraordinarily ordinary elements of bread and wine, Jesus transforms ordinary death into a wondrously new invitation to life. To make this proclamation and to enact its truth is to live in the fraught interim between the "now" of the ritual and the "then" of its anticipated completion. Until Jesus comes again in the final affirmation of God's ultimate triumph over death, the gospel of the Lord's Supper keeps the message of the cross alive and pregnant with new possibilities.

Responding to the Text

Paul's words concerning the "institution" of the Lord's Supper are so familiar that many of us can and do repeat them almost verbatim every time we celebrate communion. Because this text is so familiar, we may be tempted to slide past the context in which they occur. Paul begins by saying that Jesus offered the bread and the cup "on the night he was betrayed" (v. 23). The Gospels introduce the prospect of betrayal in the context of Judas' decision to hand Jesus over to the authorities who seek his life (see the discussion of John 13:21-32 for Wednesday in Holy Week). When Paul addressed the Corinthians, the context in which betrayal arose was different. In the preceding paragraph (11:17-22) Paul admonishes the church at Corinth for allowing the rituals of fellowship to become empty vehicles for furthering their own self-serving ends. It appears that some were serving the choicer foods to their own social peers and the less desirable foods to those whom they deemed beneath their social status. Eating and drinking thus became a means of dividing the community against itself. The objective of their "fellowship" was to exclude some from the very life that the meal offered to all. When they "do this," Paul says, Christians "show contempt for the church of God" (v. 22).

The temptation to betrayal comes in many disguises. It may seduce us by inviting us to think that our notions of how to advance the kingdom of God have more merit than those Jesus modeled for us. Like Judas we may cast our lot with the "authorities" of the world in the expectation that their strategies and calculations will bring a greater return on our investment. Like the Corinthians we may subvert the rituals of faith by co-opting them for ugly "fellowship" in the name of the Lord. Our rites of faith have the capacity to close the doors of the church to the very persons whose brokenness most mirrors the brokenness of him who gave his body and blood that they may be healed. Like the whiskey priest in Graham Greene's novel *The Power and the Glory*, we may be guilty of turning the Lord's Supper into an empty but destructive ritual that means "no more to anyone than a black cat crossing the path." Like him, we may be "risking" all the lives of those who yearn to be at table with the Lord "for the sake of spilt salt or a crossed finger."[13]

Perhaps it is because the temptation to betrayal is always present, and perhaps especially so when we think we are engaged in the most intimate rituals of faith, that Paul ends his instructions concerning the Lord's Supper by admonishing the Corinthians to "examine" their motives carefully before they eat and drink (vv. 27-33). In his words, when we come to the Lord's table we "will be answerable for the body and blood of the Lord" (v. 27). By the way we practice the ritual we may proclaim the gospel of new life in Christ Jesus, or we may "eat and drink judgment" (v. 29) on ourselves and our faith.

The Gospel

JOHN 13:1-17, 31b-35 (RCL); 13:1-15 or LUKE 22:14-30 (BCP); JOHN 13:1-15 (RC)

Interpreting the Text

Matthew, Mark, and Luke each report that Jesus celebrated a last meal with his disciples prior to his departure for the Mount of Olives (Matt. 26:20-30; Mark 14:12-26; Luke 22:14-30; for discussion of the Lukan text, the alternate Episcopal reading, see The Sunday of the Passion [Palm Sunday]). John's Gospel, however, is different, for he moves the eucharist traditions to chapter 6 (cf. 6:25-59), and in the place of the farewell meal he alone gives the account of Jesus washing the disciples' feet. Many Christians will observe the Lord's Supper on Maundy Thursday. John reminds us that as we gather around the table, what we *do* in remembrance of Jesus invites us not only to *communion* but also to *servant ministry*.

Verses 1-3 set the context for Jesus' act. The "hour had come" for Jesus to complete his earthly ministry and return to God. Jesus has loved his disciples from the beginning, and he will love them to the fullest extent even now as the cost for that love begins to crystallize. He knows that betrayal is already in play (vv. 2, 11). He knows that God has entrusted this moment to him. He knows that his obedience manifests the love that will reunite him with God. In the midst of all of the defining elements of this hour—love, betrayal, and obedience—Jesus gets up, removes his robe, girds himself like a servant, takes a basin, washes the disciples' feet, and wipes them dry with a towel (vv. 4-5).

Presumably the disciples would have been familiar with the custom of foot washing, for it was a common gesture of hospitality in both Jewish and Greco-Roman settings. When one's guests arrived for a meal, their sandaled feet dusty from the journey, it was the custom for the host either to provide water for them to wash themselves or to instruct a servant to perform the task for them. On a previous occasion, according to John, the disciples had watched Mary perform a similar act for Jesus himself (12:1-8; for discussion, see Monday in Holy Week). On this occasion, however, Jesus turns a familiar custom upside down. He is their host, yet he assumes the role of their servant. He is their master, yet he acts as if he is their humble slave. The disciples do not understand.

Peter speaks for them all when he protests with a question: "Lord, are *you* going to wash *my* feet?" (v. 6). If Jesus intends to be *his* servant, then Peter objects: "No," said Peter, "you shall never wash my feet" (v. 8 NIV). Jesus knows that Peter cannot understand fully what is happening to him (v. 7), and yet the act is important in its own right. Even without full comprehension, the ritual seeds a sacramental memory of what it means to have a "share" with Jesus in his fellowship with God (v. 8). Peter remains uncertain of Jesus' meaning. If washing his feet is important, then why not his whole body? Peter's response indicates that he understands the ritual of cleansing, but he does not grasp its deeper symbolic reference to fellowship with God. It is his relationship to God through Jesus—not the water in the basin—that makes him clean and fit for the kingdom. In a pregnant reminder of the difference between observing rituals and enacting their truth, Jesus notes that not everyone who is "clean" will share in the fellowship (vv. 10b-11). Even as Jesus washes Judas' feet, Judas is preparing to betray him.

In vv. 5-11 the foot washing is a ritual *to be received*. In vv. 12-17 and 31-35 Jesus explains that it is also an act of ministry *to be imitated*. Just as the ritual subverts the conventional understanding of the function of the host, so the ministry encoded in the ritual subverts the conventional understanding of what it means to follow him who is "Teacher and Lord" (v. 12). If their master becomes their servant by humbling himself to wash their feet, so the disciples must follow his example by becoming the servants of others. They enact Jesus' example not only by observing the rituals he has taught them, but by imitating the love for God he has embodied for them. Just as he has shed the garments of the host to attend to their needs, so they must shed their presumption of authority in order to love others as he has loved them (vv. 34-35). When they *do this* in remembrance of him, they build a community where the commandment to love God is an invitation to serve others, and the service of others is an invitation to give an old and abiding love commandment (Deut. 6:5) a meaning newly informed by the incarnation of discipleship they have witnessed in one who kneels before them on hands and knees.

EACH TIME WE LINGER IN THE TWILIGHT OF THAT LAST MEAL, EACH TIME WE EAT THE BREAD AND THE BITTER HERBS, EACH TIME WE MARK OUR JOURNEY WITH THAT SACRIFICIAL BLOOD, WE ACT AS IF THE SALVATION WE ANTICIPATE IS A PRESENT REALITY.

The commandment to "love one another" as God has loved us is not new. Indeed, during Holy Week, Christians acknowledge this commandment and gladly celebrate its claim on their lives when they partake of the Lord's Supper. The celebration of communion that typically occurs on Maundy Thursday has in fact become so much a part of religious tradition that we have a tendency to settle into a lacquered formality that in reality has little or no claim on us. When the rituals of the bread and the cup are encrusted with tradition and routine, they may be conveniently, even sacramentally, uncoupled from the commandment to enact love in concrete ways beyond the rituals of eating and drinking. Jesus' instruction that we are to "wash one another's feet" is a much more difficult ritual to gloss over or sacramentalize.

While some (e.g., the Benedictines) have found it important to reenact the ritual of foot washing as part of their faith "routines," the majority of Christians find it difficult and awkward to take up the wash basin and the towel. To get up from the table, where we are secure and comfortable, is hard. To take off the clothes that give us identity and status in the community can be embarrassing. To put on a towel, take a basin, kneel, and wash dirty feet requires that we regard humility as a virtue, not a defect. At best, we will want to believe that we can be obedient to the *spirit* of Jesus' example without engaging in the literal act. At worst, we will want to avoid John's account of Jesus' foot washing altogether. In either case, the Gospel for today will likely jar us, for there is no escaping the radical imperative that Jesus gives to his disciples: "If you know these things, you are blessed if you *do* them" (v. 17).

With Jesus' disciples we may grope for understanding when we hear this summons. Like Peter, we may first resist being washed, then misunderstand by wanting to be washed from head to toe, but nothing more. All who share Peter's suspicions and misplaced desires can expect to hear Jesus say, "Unless I wash you, you have no share with me" (v. 8). Like Judas, we may accept Jesus' washing but carry on nonetheless with the plans we have already made, as if the ritual has no bearing on the destinies we construct for ourselves. All who share Judas' understanding of discipleship can expect to hear Jesus say "Not all of you [who have been washed] are clean" (v. 11). Some may want to imitate Jesus as teacher and proclaim his Lordship to the world, but find it difficult to believe that the teaching and proclamation must be done by attending to the dirt and grime that sullies our comfortable notions of discipleship. When we yield to this temptation we can expect to hear Jesus say, "I gave you an example; you are to do exactly as I have done for you" (v. 15).

Given our common frailties and failures, we may take comfort in Jesus' affirmation that in the future, after his earthly ministry is finished and he has returned to God, we will at last comprehend the full meaning of his model for ministry (v. 7). In the meantime Jesus leaves us with a ritual, in the hope and expectation that observance of the symbols will lead us to be obedient to their truth. Such a promise may in turn lead us to reevaluate the importance of communion that is enacted not only as eating and drinking but as washing and drying. We may wonder if perhaps there is in fact something sacramental in this odd and awkward rite of foot washing. Perhaps, as the great Jewish philosopher and theologian Abraham Heschel noted, to be obedient to God's commands requires a "leap of action rather than a leap of thought." That is, we must be willing to do more than we understand in order to understand more than we do.[14]

As we ponder whether we ought to get up from the table and go find a towel, we do well to remember that the future of which Jesus spoke, the time when he expected his disciples to comprehend and act upon what he had shown them, is *now*. As John puts it, "Now the Son of Man has been glorified, and God has been glorified in him" (v. 31). On this side of that celestial glorification, Maundy Thursday offers all those who would be Jesus' disciples an opportunity to enact a ministry that glorifies God on earth as well as in heaven.

GOOD FRIDAY

APRIL 13, 2001

REVISED COMMON	EPISCOPAL (BCP)	ROMAN CATHOLIC
Isa. 52:13—53:12	Isa. 52:13—53:12 or Gen.22:1-18 or Wis. 2:1, 12-24	Isa. 52:13—53:12
Ps. 22	Ps. 22:1-21 or 22:1-11 or 40:1-14 or 69:1-23	Ps. 31:2, 6, 12-13, 15-17, 25
Heb. 10:16-25 or Heb. 4:14-16; 5:7-9	Heb. 10:1-25	Heb. 4:14-16; 5:7-9
John 18:1—19:42	John (18:1-40) 19:1-37	John 18:1—19:42

A SERVANT SUFFERS ON BEHALF OF OTHERS. A psalmist despairs of being utterly and inexplicably abandoned by God. A new covenant is remembered. Jesus is crucified and buried. Such are the themes of the four lessons for Good Friday. With the crowd who looks on Isaiah's servant, we too may wonder, "Who can believe what we have heard?" Who can believe that suffering is redemptive? Who can believe that inexplicable abandonment will yield to inexplicable intimacy? Who can believe crucifixion and death have anything to do with new covenants? Who can believe that anything about this Friday's liturgy is good? The Epistle to the Hebrews gives us three admonitions that are instructive: let us approach, let us hold fast, and let us love and encourage one another.

FIRST READING
ISAIAH 52:13—53:12

Interpreting the Text

The fourth Servant Song is the traditional reading for Good Friday. It has become so familiar and well-rehearsed that it is difficult to hear anything new in its old words. The text is in fact quite difficult; both its historical referents and its theological meaning are open to multiple understandings. Readers will profit from a careful review of the insights the commentaries provide. The comments here are but a first step in the interpretive process. *Before we analyze* the text, we should simply *listen to the text* as if we were hearing its words for the first time. Our first objective should be to catch the echo of the astonishment that it evoked from our ancestors in faith: "Who can believe what we have heard?" (53:1 NJPS).

The text is framed with two pronouncements by God. At the beginning (52:13-15) God announces *in advance* that the servant will prosper, to the astonishment of those who will see something they have never seen and contemplate things that go beyond anything they have heard before. So startling will be the new things embodied by this servant that nations and kings will be reduced to silence. Like Job's friends (Job 2:13), those accustomed to speak forcefully and act decisively must first look and listen to this servant of God before they can speak a word. At the end of this pericope (53:11b-12) God reasserts the promise that the servant will prosper and adds a further promise that he "shall make many righteous."

Inside these divine promises, the body of the song (53:1-11a) proceeds to subvert our conventional expectations of what prosperity and righteousness means. The servant has "no form or majesty" (v. 2) that anyone would associate with success or acclaim. He is "despised and rejected," regarded as "no account" (v. 3), "struck down," "afflicted" (v. 4), "wounded," "crushed" (v. 5), "oppressed" (v. 7), and "cut off from the land of the living" (v. 8). By any conventional assessment the servant is a failure. His entire life span, from birth to death, marks him as one who finds no comfort, no respect, no justice, no place among the righteous who yearn for the divine promise of a just reward for their obedience.

More startling still is the gradual recognition of those who look on in disbelief that God has charted this course for the servant for their sake. "It is the will of the Lord" (v. 10) that the servant should be "wounded for our transgressions" and "crushed for our iniquities" (v. 4). In God's mysterious providence the servant's life is an atonement for sin that he has not committed but bears for the sake of others (vv. 9-10). Though he is buried with contempt, his death is a source for progeny that prolongs his days. Though his days are full of anguish, he has light and satisfaction and knowledge that transcend what the world can fathom (v. 11). Though he can claim no justice in his own life, his life becomes a prayer through which those who are guilty receive a pardon that transforms justice with undeserved mercy (v. 12).

Responding to the Text

The gospel of the fourth Servant Song begins and ends with a promise that is familiar and comforting. The servant will prosper and be exalted and be given a place with the great. We need little encouragement to buy into this gospel, for on its surface it is a divine assurance of victory that squares with conventional calculations of success. Who would not embrace a religious tradition that promises the faithful will win in the end?

The challenge of Good Friday is to live inside this promise, where words like "despised," "rejected," and "afflicted" define victory in ways that evoke silence, questions, and careful contemplation. Until we are astonished by the servant's appearance and silenced by his apparent lack of blessing, we will likely regard him as no more than a disfigurement of faith. Until we understand that his suffering has the capacity to heal our brokenness, we will not have much patience for the vulnerability to pain and despair that the servant offers to us as a gift. Until we have contemplated what it means to believe that a "perversion of justice" (v. 8) can be the path toward righteousness, we will not see the wisdom of following in the footsteps of one who is led to the "slaughter like a lamb."

Inside the promises of the fourth Servant Song, God's estimation of the "prosperity" that awaits all who yearn to be righteous ought to startle and amaze us. Before we claim the promise we must pause before the question that begins Isaiah's gospel: "Who can believe what we have heard?" Until and unless we enter fully into this question, we may find ourselves hiding our faces (cf. 53:3) from the servant who comes to us "wearing the crown of thorns and a purple robe" (John 19:5; see further today's Gospel).

Responsive Reading

PSALM 22 (RCL); 22:1-21 or 22:1-11 or 40: 1-14 or 69:1-23 (BCP); 31:2, 6, 12-13, 15-17, 25 (RC)

Portions of the alternate reading from Psalm 31 have been discussed in the commentary for The Sunday of the Passion. Readers may consult the comments there for reflections on the appropriation of this psalm. The comments here focus on Psalm 22, which will also be appropriated by today's Gospel (cf. John 19:24 and Ps. 22:18).

Psalm 22 comprises two parts, a prayer of lament (vv. 1-21) and a song of thanksgiving (vv. 22-31). The lament weaves together in one arc of faith an individual's complaint about God's inexplicable abandonment (vv. 1-2, 6-8) and the vexed affirmation that God has in times past been more present than now (vv. 3-5, 9-11). Verses 12-21 describe the "trouble that is near" (v. 11) when God is absent. A company of evildoers, symbolized as vicious and ravenous animals (bulls, dogs, lions), stalk the individual as their prey. As they circle and wait for the kill, the individual's body (bones, heart, breast, mouth, tongue) shows that death is imminent. In the midst of this situation the individual's petitions for God to act like God become increasingly urgent and desperate: "be not far from me" (vv. 11, 19), "deliver my soul" (v. 20), "save me" (v. 21).

Verses 22-31 shift from a prayer for help to a prayer of thanksgiving for help that has been received. In the first part (vv. 22-26) the individual who once felt abandoned by God now invites the congregation to share in the joy of experienced salvation. In the place of scorn and humiliation at the hands of others, there is now the comfort of fellowship "in the midst of the congregation" (v. 22). Instead of an absent God who inexplicably hides from the needy, there is now a God who answers the call for help (v. 24). In the place of the lament about imminent death, there is now the hope to live and praise forever (v. 26). Verses 27-31 extend personal thanksgiving to a summons to cosmic praise. "All the ends of the earth" and "all the families of the nations" (v. 27) are called to remember and celebrate the God who delivers the afflicted. Because God's dominion is trustworthy and unending, so too should be the praise that God is due. "Future generations will be told about the Lord" (v. 30), and the praise that begins with one person's deliverance will ripple across time, catching up in its wake those who have already died (v. 29) and those who are yet unborn (v. 31).

Like the fourth Servant Song, Psalm 22 is a traditional reading for Good Friday. Indeed, Christians are so familiar with Jesus' quotation of the psalm's opening verse that it is difficult to hear this psalm without thinking immediately of Jesus' passion. Just as Jesus gives new meaning to this psalm, however, so this psalm provides the context for new understandings of Jesus. By entering fully into Israel's world of lament and praise, Jesus learns from the faith of his forebears that God knows the human experience of suffering and joy from the inside. By stepping into Psalm 22's vexed world of lament and praise, Jesus declares that God

> knows what it is like to hang between these two poles, and to experience joy not as infinite serenity but as a fierce happiness snatched from the jaws of darkness and despair.[15]

Second Reading

HEBREWS 10:16-25 or 4:14-16; 5:7-9 (RCL); 10:1-25 (BCP); 4:14-16; 5:7-9 (RC)

Interpreting the Text

Hebrews 10:16-25 and 4:14-16; 5:7-9 may be treated as alternate readings, for each stands as an independent unit. Readers may find it instructive, however, to take the two lessons as *complementary* rather than *alternative* texts. Together the two texts trace a movement from God's exaltation of Christ (Heb. 4:14-16) to the human travails of Christ (Heb. 5:7-9) that recalls the route of Isaiah's servant in Isaiah 52:13—53:12. Christ's embodiment of the new covenant and its claim on our lives (Heb. 10:16-25) provides in turn a suggestive commentary on the praise of which the psalmist speaks in Psalm 22:27-31.

Hebrews 4:14-16 exalts Christ as the "great high priest" whose relationship with God enables us to "approach the throne of grace with boldness" (vv. 14, 16). Like God's exaltation of Isaiah's servant (Isa. 52:13; 53:12), Christ's exaltation derives not from strength but from blessed weakness. Like Isaiah's servant, Christ's weakness is not a blemish or a failure; it is a testimony to his willingness to participate fully in the human vulnerability to pain and suffering. Christ is able "to sympathize with our weaknesses" (4:15). He knows by experience how to stand naked and needy in the world and pray for God's presence with "loud cries and tears" (5:7). Like Isaiah's servant (Isa. 53:1-11; cf. 50:4-6), Christ knows what it means to endure oppression and affliction with unyielding faith in God's abiding and transforming presence. God exalted Christ not because of his claim to divine power, but "because of his reverent submission" (5:7). Christ learned what it means to be a child of God "through what he suffered" (5:8), not because he avoided suffering. For these reasons the salvation Christ offers to those who image his servanthood is "eternal."

Hebrews 10:16-25 enlarges upon Christ's high priestly exaltation by describing his embodiment of the new covenant promised long ago by Jeremiah to him and his forebears (cf. Jer. 31:31-34). This covenant, no longer external but internal, no longer vulnerable to the perversion of human sin but transformed by the unmerited grace of God's forgiveness, changes the calculus of the divine-human relationship. This covenant bears witness to God's relentless commitment to sustain the partnership with humankind. It also means that the gift God gives summons humankind to a new way of living in the world. The author of Hebrews elaborates with three "therefore" (v. 19) admonitions: (1) "*let us approach*" God with a "true heart," that is, let us stand before God with the "full assurance" that both the evil outside us and the evil within us has been countered by a love greater than anything that seeks to thwart it (v. 22); (2) "*let us hold fast*" to the hope that rests not on the frailty of our faithfulness but on the surety of the unfailing promises of God (v. 23); and (3) "*let us consider*" how to "love" and "encourage one another" through Christian fellowship that embodies God's abiding commitment to "sustain the weary with a word" (Isa. 50:4) of comfort and assurance. If, as the psalmist says, the experience of God's deliverance is cause for praise to redound "to the ends of the earth" (Ps. 22:27), then the community of faith must love the world into the covenant with God that promises "mercy" and "grace" sufficient for every need, every cry, every tear (Heb. 4:16; 5:7).

Responding to the Text

The pericope from Hebrews 10 ends with an admonition for the faith community to be vigilant and steadfast as they see the "Day approaching." This elliptical reference to the "Day" points to the eschatological time of Christ's coming to secure the ultimate victory of God's plans for the world. For first- and twenty-first-century Christians the challenge is to live faithfully in between the first and second (end-time) advents of Jesus. In Jesus, God has assured us that the final victory is secure. Christ *is exalted* at the right hand of God, and in the end we too *will be exalted* with him through faith. The problem is that for us, as for those addressed by the author of Hebrews, the final victory seems so long in arriving that we lose heart and grow discouraged. Given our despondency, our temptation to despair, our haunting fear that we are alone in a journey that asks more of us than we have, the good word is that Christ knows our weaknesses, shares our cries and our tears, and has prepared a way for us to walk *through* it all to the throne of God's mercy.

In *The Cloister Walk*, Kathleen Norris recalls that the poet Emily Dickinson, who was attracted to Paul's confession of "weakness and much fear and trembling" (1 Cor. 2:3), wrote these words in a letter near the end of her life:

> When Jesus tell us about his Father, we distrust him. When he shows us his Home, we turn away, but when he confides to us that he is "acquainted with Grief," we listen, for that is also an Acquaintance of our own.[16]

Christ exercises his priestly ministry as "an Acquaintance of our own." Being acquainted with grief becomes in turn the foundation of our priestly ministry to each other and to the world until that day when Christ comes again. In the interim between now and then, an interim which has stretched longer than the prophets and early Christians expected, we are to live out the gospel of the new covenant with hope, faith, and love.

The Gospel

JOHN 18:1—19:42 (RCL/RC); (18:1-40) 19:1-37 (BCP)

Interpreting the Text

The lengthy reading from John's Gospel comprises five units: (1) Jesus' arrest (18:1-12); (2) the interrogation by Annas (18:13-27); (3) the trial before Pilate (18:28—19:16a); (4) Jesus' crucifixion and death (19:16b-30); (5) the removal and burial of Jesus' body (19:31-42). Clearly the full sweep of this narrative is central to the church's Holy Week proclamation, and ministers will need to immerse themselves in the commentaries in order to keep the whole picture intact. Against the backdrop of the full narrative, it may be useful to isolate a single episode for special attention. One suggestion is to focus on the interrogation of Jesus by Annas (18:13-27), which provides John's distinctive perspective on one of the central events all the Gospels hold in common.

All the Gospels combine Jesus' interrogation by the Jewish authorities with the account of Peter's denials. Luke treats Peter's three denials in a continuous narrative (Luke 22:54-62), which is placed before Jesus' trial before the Sanhedrin (22:66-71). Mark and Matthew also treat the three denials as one unit (Mark 14:66-72; Matt. 26:69-75), but both locate them after Jesus' interrogation by the high priest and the Sanhedrin (Mark 14:53-65; Matt. 26:57-68). John's presentation of these events is different. He introduces the scene of Jesus' interrogation by Annas (18:13-14), interrupts that scene by reporting Peter's first denial of Jesus (18:15-18), resumes the account of the interrogation (18:19-24), then concludes by reporting Peter's second and third denials (18:25-27). With this sequencing of the events, John suggests that Peter's denials of Jesus were simultaneous with Jesus' affirmation of himself. At the very moment when Jesus was boldly confessing himself before the religious authorities, Peter was fearfully denying the one he once promised he would love to his death (cf. John 13:37).

John begins by setting the stage for the interrogation by Annas (18:13-14). Annas was the high priest from 6 to 15 C.E. His son-in-law, Caiaphas, was high priest from 18 to 36 C.E. John suggests that Annas' influence continued after his term as high priest ended. Perhaps we should understand Annas as conducting a preliminary hearing to determine whether Jesus should be held over for trial before the full Sanhedrin, where Caiaphas would preside (cf. v. 24). The mention of Caiaphas reminds us, however, that in an earlier meeting of the Sanhedrin he has already unconsciously set in motion the events that lead to Jesus' death (John 11:46-53).

NOW FELLOWSHIP WITH JESUS MEANS SOMETHING DIFFERENT. NOW WE HAVE BEEN IMPLICATED IN JESUS' PASSION. NOW WE MUST DECIDE WHETHER DISCIPLESHIP IS WHAT WE WANT AFTER ALL.

Before the questioning of Jesus begins, John breaks away from the scene to show us Peter, standing outside the gate (vv. 15-18), where he now becomes the subject of interrogation. A woman asks him, "Are you not also one of this man's disciples?" The wording of the question (introduced with the particle *mē*) normally invites a negative response. It is Peter's first invitation to deny Jesus, and he does not hesitate to give the expected answer. His words, "I am not" (*ouk eimi*; see further 18:25), stand in sharp contrast with Jesus' bold self-assertion, "I am" (*eg¯eimi*), in 18:5, 6, 8. Following this response, John reports that some "slaves" and "police," part of the same detachment that arrested Jesus (vv. 3, 12) were warming themselves by the fire (v. 18). Peter stands among them. John offers no comment on Peter's camaraderie with this group, and none is needed.

As Peter is being questioned outside, Annas begins his questioning of Jesus inside (vv. 19-24). Annas questions Jesus on two general matters: his disciples and his teaching (v.19). As to his teaching, Jesus responds that he has always spoken openly "in the synagogues and in the temple," where both the religious leaders and the general public could judge for themselves the merit of what he said. On the matter of his disciples, Jesus declines to answer directly and instead responds with a question to Annas: "Ask those who heard what I said" (v. 21). The implication is that "disciples" are defined not by what Jesus says about them but by what they say and do with what Jesus has taught them. As the Epistle of James puts it, disciples are those who are not only "hearers" but "doers of the word" (James 1:22). Even as Jesus speaks, one disciple, Peter, is in the process of demonstrating that being "called" as a disciple is not the same thing as "living" as one.

The final scene (vv. 25-27) returns to Peter and his second and third denials of Jesus. One from the crowd asks him the same question he had been asked before (v. 25). Once again the question (with the particle *mē*) assumes and invites a negative response, and for a second time Peter denies that he is one of Jesus' disciples. A third question follows, this time from a relative of the man "whose ear Peter had cut off" (cf. 18:10): "Did I not see you in the garden with him?" This question, unlike the first two, assumes a positive answer. The questioner is an eyewitness to the event and no doubt already knows the truth about the matter. Again, Peter denies his association with Jesus. Without comment, John reports that the "cock crowed."

Responding to the Text

At this juncture in Holy Week, the liturgy brings us all from the table of fellowship to the cross. We have remembered how Jesus washed the disciples' feet, preparing them for the journey that lay ahead (John 13:1-17). We have remembered and reenacted the communion of the bread and the cup (John 13:21-32). We have heard Jesus warn that one of the disciples will betray him, and we have seen Judas leave the table (John 13:30), leaving us behind to continue our fellowship with the one who has promised to love us to the very end (13:1). Now everything has changed. Jesus has been arrested and is being questioned, not only about his teaching but also about his disciples. Now fellowship with Jesus means something different. Now *we* have been implicated by Jesus' passion. Now *we* must decide whether discipleship is what we want after all.

The test of any conviction is how well it holds up under pressure. Standing before the authorities who hold titular power over him, Jesus faces a decision. If he gives the answer they want, perhaps he can avoid the fate they have prepared for him. In John's Gospel, Jesus' confrontation with the authorities is the opportunity to turn conviction into practice. Jesus boldly faces his questioners and declares that he is in their presence the same one who has spoken openly to the world about his commitments and his purpose. When asked if he is who he claims to be, Jesus responds three times by saying, "I am he" (18:5, 6, 8).

Peter now faces his questioners. He is no longer at the table, inside the inner circle, where love is easy and there are few encumbrances to commitment (cf. John 13:37). Now he is outside, among the police who have arrested Jesus, where the price for confession is high indeed. As John describes the scene, Peter is beyond the scrutiny of his peers who have heard him declare his loyalty to Jesus. He is beyond the range of what Jesus can hear or see. He is alone. No one will know what he says but those who stand around him, and even they begin by assuming that he is not under suspicion. In his moment of truth Peter denies in private that he is who he claimed to be in public when he was with Jesus. When asked if he is a disciple of Jesus, Peter responds by saying, "I am not" (18:17, 25; cf. v. 27).

As we gather inside our sanctuaries to celebrate the memory of Holy Week, the pomp and pageantry of the ceremonies will likely make it easy and natural for us to profess our love and commitment to Christ. We may comfortably disassociate ourselves from the memory of Judas, for we know that we are not like him. We may spontaneously join our voices to those of our fellow congregants and sing, "Hallelujah, Christ is risen!" But outside the public liturgy, on the front side of the cross, we may find that the pressure to conform our convictions to the private and pressing realities of our lives is more daunting than we want to admit. Perhaps that is why Peter's presence in our midst is so painful and sobering. Perhaps we would never be guilty of saying out loud "Crucify him!" (19:15). But when we are outside the public eye, when we think no one is listening, we may find it easier to deny our discipleship with the quiet resolve of one of the most haunting confessions of this day's lesson: "I am not." Like Shakespeare's Richard, who seizes Edward IV's throne by public charm and private deceit, we may feign loyalty and practice betrayal. Richard's confession is Peter's, and perhaps ours, in different words:

I clothe my naked villainy
With odd old ends stolen forth of holy writ,
And seem a saint when most I play the devil.
(*Richard III*.I.iii.335)

THE GREAT VIGIL OF EASTER HOLY SATURDAY

April 14, 2001

Revised Common	Episcopal (bcp)	Roman Catholic
	Service of Readings	
Gen. 1:1—2:4a	Gen. 1:1—2:2	Gen. 1:1—2:2
Gen. 7:1-5, 11-18; 8:6-18;	Gen. 7:1-5, 11-18;	Gen. 22:1-18
	8:6-18; 9:8-13	9:8-13
Gen. 22:1-18	Gen. 22:1-18	Exod. 14:15—15:1
Exod. 14:10-31; 15:20-21	Exod. 14:10—15:1	Isa. 54:5-14
Isa. 55:1-11	Isa. 4:2-6	Isa. 55:1-11
Prov. 8:1-8, 19, 21; 9:4b-6	Isa. 55:1-11	Bar. 3:9-15, 3:32—4:4
or Bar. 3:9-15, 3:32—4:4		
Ezek. 36:24-28	Ezek. 36:24-28	Ezek. 36:16-17a, 18-28
Ezek. 37:1-14	Ezek. 37:1-14	
Zeph. 3:14-20	Zeph. 3:12-20	
Lutheran lectionary adds:		
Jonah 3:1-10		
Deut. 31:19-30		
Dan. 3:1-29		
	Second Lesson	
Rom. 6:3-11	Rom. 6:3-11	Rom. 6:3-11
	The Gospel	
Luke 24:1-12	Matt. 28:1-10	Luke 24:1-12

The Easter Vigil brings us from the cross to the empty tomb. The Old Testament readings remind us that the Christian journey through Holy Week is part of the larger journey of the community of faith with the God who creates, sustains, and relentlessly loves the world. Paul reminds us that we are baptized into Christ's death so that we might be alive to the God we have seen in Christ Jesus. Luke invites us inside the tomb and then reminds us that we must look for Jesus and the God who raised him among the living, not the dead. In different ways each of the readings for today keep us mindful that when this day is over, we must be prepared to leave the empty tomb, for Easter is always about beginnings, not endings.

Listening and Responding to the Texts

To this point the Old Testament lessons for Holy Week have invited us to focus on specific texts that recall singularly pregnant moments in Israel's history with God. Today's lessons have a different objective. Typically, the Old Testament lessons for the Easter Vigil are simply read, not preached. Moreover, the large number of readings effectively shifts our focus from looking for a sermon to listening to a story. The story comprises some of the strategic episodes in Israel's long and ongoing journey with God. While any one of these episodes is worthy of isolation, the service of readings invites us to listen to them without interruption or comment. The cumulative effect of moving through the vast span of Israel's story reminds us that Holy Week is more than a single span of days on the calendar. It is the extension of a journey that God embarked upon before the world was created, a journey that gathers in its wake all peoples of the world, a journey that will not be complete until God's hopes and expectations for all the world and all peoples have been realized. On Easter eve, when our journey brings us to the cross and the tomb, we are invited to find our place inside this sacred story, there to be reminded of God's relentless commitment to love us beyond anything a single sermon can ever convey.

The readings generally cluster around two chapters in Israel's journey with God: the journey toward the promised land and the exile, when the promises of God appeared to be lost forever. Both the story and the journey begin with God's creation of a world ordered, blessed, and empowered to be "very good" (Gen. 1:1—2:4a). By God's design the world is vulnerable to sin and grace, to inscrutable divine commands and equally inscrutable divine promises, to oppressive tyranny and redemptive freedom. Human sin has the capacity to undo God's hopes and expectations for the world (Gen. 7:1-5, 11-18), and God's grace has a greater capacity to reclaim and recreate the world in accordance with covenantal commitments that will not be subverted (Gen. 8:16-18; 9:8-13). God's inscrutable expectations require extraordinary faith and obedience (Gen. 22:1-11), and God's inscrutable promises declare that God will provide what is required, if the faithful will but trust the One who has called them (Gen. 22:12-18). Human tyranny may enslave and oppress God's people, but the God who created the world will trump oppression, free the captives, and bring them to a place of new beginnings and new possibilities (Exod. 14:10-31). On the other side of oppression, the cry for help will become a song of praise: "Sing to Lord, for he has triumphed gloriously" (Exod. 15:21).

The exile calls God's promises into question. It portends a dead end to the journey of faith. It turns the song of praise into a cry of lament. The latter half of the readings brings us into this sad world of exile where, as Ezekiel puts it,

"Our bones are dried up, our hope is lost, and we are cut off completely" (Ezek. 37:11). If the journey is to continue, nothing short of a miracle will be required. Israel's prophets announce that a miracle is exactly what God is about. Isaiah declares that God will accomplish that which God intends. Israel must "listen carefully" and "seek the Lord" whose "steadfast love" makes and sustains an "everlasting covenant" (Isa. 55:1-11). Ezekiel prophecies that even dry bones will live. God will create a new spirit and a new life and give new meaning to the old words "you *shall be* my people, and I *will be* your God" (Ezek. 36:24-28; 37:1-14). Zephaniah announces that God will restore the oppressed, the lame, and the outcast. God will "change their shame into praise" that reverberates "among all the peoples of the earth" (Zeph. 3:14-20).

The journey from promises received to promises lost is hard. Miracles may be announced, but in exile, where there is more darkness than light, more death than life, miracles are bewilderingly elusive. Tucked into the middle of today's readings is another memory that offers a paradigm for how Israel finds and sustains faith in the interim between what has been and what will be. The passage from Baruch, set in the context of the exile, but probably written somewhere between 200 and 60 B.C.E., instructs the faithful to "learn where there is wisdom, where there is strength, where there is understanding" (Bar. 3:14). Baruch reminds the fatigued of faith that wisdom is not found among the strong and the powerful. It is not found among the rich and the famous (3:22-28). God alone possesses wisdom, and according to the inviolable purposes of God, God has committed to share that wisdom with the people (3:32-37). God has bequeathed wisdom to Israel in the form of an everlasting Torah (4:1-3). That Torah is more than a list of commandments and promises. It is Israel's story. And that story is the key to life.

During the Great Vigil of Easter, this Torah, this story, this promise of life, is the memory on which we stand when come to the cross and the tomb. With our forebears in faith, we seek wisdom, strength, and understanding for the living of these days. With Israel we are empowered to say "Happy are we . . . for we know what is pleasing to God" (Bar. 4:4).

Second Lesson
ROMANS 6:3-11

Interpreting the Text

We now move from remembering Israel's story to remembering Paul's theology of baptism. In some respects the letter to the Romans is Paul's story. He writes toward the end of his life, probably in the period between 55 and 58 C.E. and thus imparts what he has learned about how believers share in Jesus' death, burial and resurrection. By dying, Christ conquered sin. By rising, Christ conquered death. In baptism, Christians are baptized into Christ's death (v. 5), and thus may regard themselves as dead to the absolute power of sin (v. 7). The ceremony of baptism commemorates this with the descent into the water, which symbolizes entering the grave. As Paul puts it, we are "buried with him by baptism into death" (v. 4). Moreover, "just as Christ was raised from the dead by the glory of the Father," so through baptism Christians "will certainly be united with him in a resurrection like his" (v. 5b).

In Paul's theology, baptism is a sacred ritual with practical, ethical consequences. Christ was raised from the dead in order that he might continue to live as completely obedient to and dependent upon God (v. 10). In baptism, believers commit themselves to live following Christ's example. They must consider themselves as not only dead to the enslaving power of sin; they must also submit themselves fully and completely to live as those who are "alive to God in Christ Jesus" (v. 11). In other words, baptism is a ritual that transforms Christians both spiritually and morally. Once Christians emerge from the waters of death, they are summoned to live in a way that shows the experience with Christ has changed them. On the other side of baptism, Christians are to live as the people they have become. They are to "walk in newness of life" (v. 4). Paul develops this ethical admonition in vv. 12-14 by instructing Christians to manifest the symbolic move from death to life by becoming "instruments of righteousness" (v. 13).

Responding to the Text

On first encounter it may appear that this lesson has little connection with the sacred memory of Israel's story that we have heard in the Service of Readings. Two observations may tune our hearts to a deeper understanding.

First, we may remember that originally the liturgy of the Easter Vigil was the occasion for the baptism of those who by profession of faith were welcomed into Christian fellowship. Typically the ceremony of baptism included a homily addressed to the candidates. Paul's text gives us a link to this ancient practice, thus reminding us that Easter eve is the occasion for the celebration of one of the founding rituals of Christian faith. In this same context, however, it is instructive to note that Paul addresses his words to those who are already Christians. The language throughout is in the form of the first person plural "we." Not only the newly baptized but *we* are celebrating the transforming movement from death to life. We remember on this day that all believers have been freed from enslavement to sin. We remember and pledge ourselves to live anew, flush with the enthusiasm of first day Christians, more fully and completely into the hopes and expectations of the God who created the world and loved it so much "that he gave his only Son" (John 3:16).

Second, Paul teaches that although we have *already shared* in Christ's death through baptism, we have *not yet* participated fully in Christ's resurrection. Our death to sin is described in the past tense—"we *have been* united with him in a death like his" (v. 5a)—but our resurrection is described in the future tense—"we *will be* certainly united with him in a resurrection like his" (v. 5b; cf. v. 8: "we believe that *we will* also live with him"). This does not mean that our life in Christ is postponed until we have our own literal resurrection from the grave: for the Christian, the future in Christ begins now. But it does mean that there is an interim between the initiation of the promise of new life and its completion, when we are raised from death to become fully transformed participants in the kingdom of God (cf. 1 Cor. 15:42-55).

Easter eve brings us to the dark and foreboding interim between the cross and the tomb, between death and resurrection. In this interim we enter into an exile of forsakenness, abandonment, silence, and absence that connects us with the exile of our forebears in Babylon. We have seen what Friday means. When we remembered Jesus' cry, "My God, my God, why have you forsaken me?" (Ps. 22:1; see the Responsive Reading for Good Friday), our story connected with Israel's story of lament. We yearn for Sunday's "Hallelujah," when our song, informed by the promises of Israel's prophets, will change from lament to praise. But today we must be baptized into Christ's death. Today we stay inside in the tomb and wait. As George Steiner has put it, today we remember that our story has brought us to "the long day's journey of the Saturday."[17] Inside the tomb, "Saturday's faith" requires that we, like our forebears in faith, must "learn where there is wisdom, where there is strength, where there is understanding" (Bar. 3:14) sufficient for the living of this day.

The Gospel

LUKE 24:1-12 (RCL/RC); MATTHEW 28:1-10 (BCP)

Interpreting the Text

Both Luke and Matthew report the discovery of the empty tomb, although they do so in different ways. Matthew reports that the women witnessed the miraculous opening of the tomb (28:2) and that subsequently Jesus appeared to the women and instructed them to go and tell the disciples what they have seen (28:9-10). Luke reports that when the women arrived at the tomb the stone was already rolled away (24:2). The women do not see Jesus, but they receive an angelic announcement that summons them to "remember" what they have seen and heard of Jesus' story. This memory in turn compels them to go and share their discovery with the rest of the disciples (24:5-10). Luke adds that Peter went to the tomb to see for himself (24:12). Both Matthew and Luke agree on the central message that the empty tomb conveys: "He is not here, but has risen" (Luke 24:5; Matt. 28:6; cf. Mark 16:6).

Luke's most distinctive contribution to the common proclamation of the empty tomb is his report of the angels' announcement to the women (vv. 5-7). The angels' appearance follows the common pattern of theophanies in the Old Testament; Luke thus presents the women as receiving special revelations from God in a manner that links them and their experience with the Hebrew forebears (cf. Judg. 6:11-24; 13:2-23). The women are terrified and bow their faces to the ground (v. 5). Like Moses before the burning bush (cf. Exod. 3:6), they instinctively discern that they are in the presence of a transforming revelation.

The revelation comprises three components. First, there is a question: "Why do you look for the living among the dead?" The Jesus they knew had been buried in the tomb, thus they had come to the logical place to find him and complete the proper burial the Sabbath day had interrupted (cf. v. 1). But the new revelation confirms that they are looking in the wrong place. Second, there is an affirmation: "He is not here, but has risen." The verb "has risen" (v. 6: *ēgerthē*) is best understood as a passive. It affirms that Jesus has been raised *by God*. That is, Jesus has been the recipient of a divine miracle, and it is this miracle that now becomes the substance of a new revelation: God has accomplished something in raising Jesus from the dead that lays the foundation for what all who hear and respond to the gospel of the empty tomb may receive. Third, there is a summons to "remember" Jesus' story, specifically the previous teaching about his betrayal (cf. Luke 9:44; 18:32), crucifixion (cf. Luke 23:21), and resurrection on the third day. The resurrection on the third day is part of the church's early *kerygma* (cf. 1 Cor. 15:4). But Jesus' "story" affirms that what God did for him on the "third day" is part of the larger story of God's ongoing salvific work in the cosmos: God created the earth on the third day (Gen. 1:9-13); God made a covenant with Israel at Sinai on the third day (Exod. 19:11, 15-16); God delivered Jonah from the belly of the fish on the third day (Jonah 1:17); Hosea prophesied that "on the third day he [God] will raise us up, that we may live before him" (Hos. 6:2). Luke reports that when the women "remembered his [Jesus'] words," they left the tomb to share the good news of what they had seen and discerned (vv. 8-10). They did not have to be instructed to proclaim the memory (cf. Matt. 28:7, 10). The memory, now reclaimed and enlarged by the miracle of what God has done, was itself the catalyst for spreading the gospel.

TODAY WE MUST BE BAPTIZED INTO CHRIST'S DEATH. TODAY WE STAY INSIDE THE TOMB AND WAIT.

Luke concludes this part of his account by reporting that the experience of the empty tomb, for all of its revelatory capacity, meets with mixed response. The women proclaim; they do not analyze or question. The disciples do not proclaim; they evaluate—the words seem to them "an idle tale" (v. 11)—and they search for something more that will move them from amazement to belief (v. 12).

Responding to the Text

Both Luke and Matthew announce the gospel of the empty tomb: "He is not here, but has risen." For all of our preparation for this moment, for all of the sacred rituals and holy lessons that we have reenacted and shared, we now discover that at this penultimate moment in the liturgical drama, we have arrived at an end which is not an ending. We have followed Jesus into Jerusalem, but he is no longer there. We have seen him nailed to a cross, but the cross is now vacant. We have seen him buried in a tomb, but the tomb is now empty.

Inside the empty tomb nothing seems to have been resolved. There has been a death, but there is no body. There has been a funeral, but it has not been completed. There has been a report of something truly remarkable—a resurrection—but there is as yet no consensus on what this means. Some believe without question, some question in search of belief. Those who believe, like the women, carry their message with mixed emotions: they are perplexed and terrified and transformed beyond explanation. Those who question, like Peter, do so eagerly, but with a vexed mixture of settled disbelief and restless amazement. The disbelief inclines them to consider the grave the end of the journey. The amazement inclines them to keep looking for something more. Such are the responses we bring to the empty tomb. Some believe, others doubt. Some are eager to proclaim, others are curious, but unpersuaded. By any rational assessment, the "first day of the week" (v. 1), the day we remember and celebrate as the "first Easter," begins in a most inauspicious way.

Inside the empty tomb, where nothing seems to be resolved, there is a summons to remember. We remember the crucial events that Holy Week commemorates: the betrayal, the crucifixion, the resurrection. We remember the ongoing story of God's relentless commitment to love humankind into covenant partnership that promises life, purpose, and wholeness. From the retrospective of this memory about what God has done in Christ, the empty tomb becomes revelatory. What we hear is the sound of God speaking in silence that has been redeemed. What we see is the witness of God's presence in emptiness that has been transformed. Our proclamation is simple—"He has risen"—and we run to catch up to its full meaning with shifting surges of confidence and bewilderment, belief and amazement.

For all these reasons Easter is not an ending but a beginning. We come to Jerusalem in order to depart into the world. We stand at the cross where Jesus suffered in order to be able to see his hands and feet in the suffering of others. We enter into the empty tomb, but we do not stay there, because we have learned to look for Jesus among the living, not the dead. The journey from the Sunday of the Passion to the Saturday of the Easter Vigil is but six days long. It is a relatively brief period of time, but each step of the journey carries us deeper and deeper into the sacred memory of the God of Jesus. On the seventh day, the Christians' Sabbath day, we will celebrate the Easter message, "Hallelujah, Christ has risen!" But on this Sabbath day, as on that primordial seventh day when God blessed and sanctified creation, we are to know that life in the fullness of God's revelation is about a journey, not a vigil. Seventh days and Easter days are always about beginnings, not endings.

NOTES

1. C. R. North, *The Second Isaiah: Introduction, Translation and Commentary to Chapters XL-LV* (Oxford: Clarendon Press, 1964) 201.

2. Paul Hanson, *Isaiah 40–66,* Interpretation, a Bible Commentary for Teaching and Preaching (Louisville: John Knox, 1995) 42.

3. M. Dorris, "The Myth of Justice," *Outside the Law: Narratives on Justice in America*, ed. S. Shreve and P. Shreve (Boston: Beacon Press, 1997) 77.

4. Ibid.

5. E. Wiesel, *All Rivers Run to the Sea* (New York: Knopf, 1995) 321.

6. M. Tate, *Psalms 51–100,* Word Biblical Commentary (Dallas: Word, 1990) 207.

7. A. Tennyson, "In Memoriam," *Tennyson's Poetry*, ed. R. Hill (New York: Norton, 1971) 147-48.

8. L. Wieseltier, *Kaddish* (New York: Knopf, 1998) 68.

9. Ibid. 75.

10. H. Fielding, *The History of Tom Jones, A Foundling* (New York: Collier, 1917), 1:19.

11. Henry Wadsworth Longfellow, "Evangeline," II.I.60, in *The Cambridge Poets Students' Edition, Longfellow*, ed. H. E. Scudder (New York: Houghton Mifflin, 1922) 85.

12. D. Betts, "All That Glisters Isn't Gold," in *The Astronomer and Other Stories* (Baton Rouge and London: Louisiana State Univ. Press, 1965) 97.

13. G. Green, *The Power and the Glory* (New York: Penguin, 1962) 79-80.

14. S. Dresner, ed., *I Asked for Wonder: A Spiritual Anthology of Abraham Heschel* (New York: Crossroad, 1990) 5.

15. J. Barton, *Love Unknown: Meditations on the Death and Resurrection of Jesus* (Louisville: Westminster/John Knox, 1990) 5.

16. K. Norris, *The Cloister Walk* (New York: Riverhead, 1996) 27.

17. G. Steiner, *Real Presences* (Chicago: Univ. of Chicago Press, 1989) 232.

DECEMBER 2000

Sunday	Monday	Tuesday	Wednesday	Thursday	Friday	Saturday
					1	2
3 1 Advent	4	5	6	7	8	9
10 2 Advent	11	12	13	14	15	16
17 3 Advent	18	19	20	21	22	23
24 4 Advent Christmas Eve	25 Christmas Day	26 Boxing Day *(Canada)*	27	28	29	30
31 1 Christmas New Year's Eve						

JANUARY 2001

Sunday	Monday	Tuesday	Wednesday	Thursday	Friday	Saturday
	1 Name of Jesus New Year's Day	2	3	4	5	6 Epiphany
7 1 Epiphany	8	9	10	11	12	13
14 2 Epiphany	15 Martin Luther King Day *(U.S.A.)*	16	17	18	19	20
21 3 Epiphany	22	23	24	25	26	27
28 4 Epiphany	29	30	31			

FEBRUARY 2001

Sunday	Monday	Tuesday	Wednesday	Thursday	Friday	Saturday
				1	2	3
4 5 Epiphany	5	6	7	8	9	10
11 6 Epiphany	12	13	14	15	16	17
18 7 Epiphany	19 Presidents' Day *(U.S.A.)*	20	21	22	23	24
25 Transfiguration Last Epiphany	26	27	28 Ash Wednesday			

MARCH 2001

Sunday	Monday	Tuesday	Wednesday	Thursday	Friday	Saturday
				1	2	3
4 1 Lent	5	6	7	8	9	10
11 2 Lent	12	13	14	15	16	17
18 3 Lent	19	20	21	22	23	24
25 4 Lent	26	27	28	29	30	31

APRIL 2001

Sunday	Monday	Tuesday	Wednesday	Thursday	Friday	Saturday
1 5 Lent	2	3	4	5	6	7
8 Passion/Palm Sunday	9 Monday in Holy Week	10 Tuesday in Holy Week	11 Wednesday in Holy Week	12 Maundy Thursday	13 Good Friday	14 Vigil of Easter
15 Easter	16	17	18	19	20	21
22	23	24	25	26	27	28
29	30